Cognitive Therapy
Techniques in
Christian Counseling

RESOURCES FOR
CHRISTIAN COUNSELING

RESOURCES FOR CHRISTIAN COUNSELING

(Other volumes forthcoming)

VOLUME TWENTY-SEVEN

Cognitive Therapy Techniques in Christian Counseling

MARK R. McMINN, Ph.D.

RESOURCES FOR CHRISTIAN COUNSELING

General Editor

Gary R. Collins, Ph.D.

WORD PUBLISHING

Dallas · London · Vancouver · Melbourne

To my children:
Danielle, Sarah, and Anna.
You inspire me.

Library of Congress Cataloging-in-Publication Data

McMinn, Mark R.
    Cognitive therapy techniques in Christian counseling / Mark R. McMinn.
       p.   cm.— (Resources in Christian counseling: v. 27)
    Includes bibliographical references and index.
    ISBN 0-8499-0876-0
    1. Pastoral counseling.   2. Cognitive therapy I. Title. II. Series.
BV4012.2.M25   1991
253.5—dc20   91-3071
                                              CIP

Printed in the United States of America

1 2 3 4 9 AGF 9 8 7 6 5 4 3 2 1

ACKNOWLEDGMENTS

Some have jokingly concluded that the best things about college teaching are June, July, and August. I have found the other months enjoyable as well. But a seventh-year sabbatical was a special pleasure and enabled me to write this manuscript. Thus, I am grateful to the George Fox College administration and board of trustees for the time to write this book.

My colleague and good friend, Dr. Rebecca Thomas Ankeny, read and made many helpful suggestions for the manuscript. Dr. Clark Campbell, another good friend and colleague, has helped me understand counseling better through our many conversations. My wife Lisa has helped me expand the boundaries of my psychological training through our discussion of her work in sociology. I am also indebted to several mentors who influenced me during my graduate training, internship, and residency: Drs. Martin Katahn, Kenneth Wallston, and Arthur Wiens. Dr. Gary Collins has been an encourager and supporter of my work, and the editorial staff at Word Publishing has been a pleasure to work with.

CONTENTS

EDITOR'S PREFACE

SOME TIME AGO, I WAS INVITED to appear on a television program with Mark McMinn and his teaching colleague, James Foster. We three were to be pitted against three of the more prominent critics of Christian psychology. The debate, we were told, would be exciting and informative to the thousands who might watch.

Several weeks prior to the proposed program, I watched some previously released segments of the show, talked with former guests, and concluded that our side would not get a fair hearing and that no useful purpose would be served by the debate that was being scheduled. I called Mark, discussed the situation with him at length, and eventually we all withdrew.

This was my first real contact with the author of this book. Since that time we have talked often and I have come to respect Mark McMinn as a Christian brother, a careful thinker, a top-quality therapist, and a very fine writer. I suspect you will agree as you read the following pages.

Books on counseling sometimes sound very theoretical. The reader gets information but wonders how the proposed techniques are applied and whether or not they work. You are unlikely to wonder about these issues after reading this book. Dr. McMinn explains what he is doing, gives numerous examples, anticipates questions or problems that a reader might encounter, and gives us a clear look over his shoulder as he does his own counseling work. This volume presents a theory, but it does more. It demonstrates how cognitive therapy techniques actually work in practice as a method of Christian counseling.

In my work with publishers, I often have heard that most readers skip introductory segments like the one you are reading and go directly to chapter 1. Clearly that is not true of those who are reading these words. If you have also read the forewords to earlier books in this series you will have an understanding about what these volumes seek to accomplish.

Word's Resources for Christian Counseling books have attempted to address those issues that we most often face in our counseling work and to bring practical guidance, especially to those who identify as evangelical Christians.

From the beginning, we have tried to find authors who have a strong Christian commitment, impeccable counseling credentials, and extensive counseling experience. We have attempted to produce books that are useful and helpful examples of accurate psychology and the careful application of Scripture. Each is intended to have a clear evangelical perspective, careful documentation, a strong practical orientation, and freedom from sweeping statements or unsubstantiated conclusions. Our goal has been to provide books that would be clearly written, up-to-date overviews of the issues faced by contemporary Christian counselors—including pastoral counselors. As you doubtless are aware, each of these books has a similar blue and silver cover and together they comprise what we hope is a helpful encyclopedia of Christian counseling.

Most of the earlier books have dealt with problem issues such as depression, marital conflicts, or eating disorders. This book is different. It is technique-oriented rather than problem-centered. Various problems are discussed, but the emphasis is on applying cognitive therapy methods, within a Christian context.

Like perhaps every other field of study, counseling has changed in many ways during this century. At present, cognitive therapy and cognitive-behavioral approaches are popular, widely used, and frequently found to be effective. Unlike some of the earlier approaches to counseling, cognitive therapy is highly consistent with biblical emphases on thinking.

In the pages that follow, Dr. McMinn gives a clear presentation of the complexities and application of this emerging method of helping. Whether or not you agree with the cognitive therapy approach, this book should give some useful tools to make your counseling more effective.

Since he and I withdrew from that television program, I have not had the opportunity to observe Mark McMinn as a debater. In this book, however, we observe him as a cognitive Christian counselor, guiding us into a greater understanding of this effective way to help those who come for counseling. Hopefully you will like what you see.

Gary R. Collins, Ph.D.
Kildeer, Illinois

PART I

CONCEPTS OF COGNITIVE THERAPY

CHOOSING A ROAD MAP

DURING TRAINING, EVERY COUNSELOR GOES shopping for a theoretical persuasion. The shelves of the therapy store are stocked with a variety of techniques and philosophical assumptions. Some brands, like psychodynamic therapy, are promoted as thorough and comprehensive. Other brands, most notably the behavior therapies, are advertised as being cost-effective and scientifically based. Some brands, such as humanistic therapy, are based on assumptions of human goodness; others begin with the premise of human depravity. Some, such as Gestalt therapy, are strangely packaged and are only rarely selected while the more conventional brands sell quite well.

Many counselors find the plethora of attractive brands so compelling that they do not choose a single theoretical persuasion. Instead, they select several and call themselves eclectic counselors. Eclectic counselors enjoy the advantages of flexibility, suiting the techniques to the particular client and the presenting problem. However, it is difficult for eclectic counselors to become highly skilled at the techniques they use because they try to master so many.

Others avoid the choice of a theoretical persuasion because they believe caring deeply for their clients is sufficient to bring about results. After all, they reason, if we care enough for those we are helping, our clients will naturally feel better. These counselors enjoy the benefits of a caring relationship, a necessity for effective counselors. In an early paper on humanistic psychotherapy, psychologist Carl Rogers suggested that a caring relationship was both necessary and sufficient for good results in psychotherapy.[1] But is it *enough*? Now, most psychotherapy researchers agree that being warm, accepting, and genuine is necessary but *not* sufficient for good results in counseling. These effective ways of relating need to be combined with good counseling techniques.

Other counselors identify themselves with a single persuasion and become known as psychoanalytic therapists, biblical therapists, Gestalt therapists, systems therapists, behavioral therapists, primal integration therapists, hypnotherapists, cognitive therapists, rational emotive therapists, or humanistic therapists. Because these counselors have chosen one theoretical persuasion, they can concentrate on developing a specific set of skills. Also, they enjoy the benefits of having a theoretical plan to guide their work with clients. Just as a road map guides travelers through a crowded city, a theoretical plan guides both counselor and client through the complexities of past traumas, present symptoms, and future goals. The benefits of a theoretical road map are explored in detail later in this chapter.

WHAT'S IN A BRAND?

Counselors, like good shoppers, learn to think critically about their options and ask themselves important questions before choosing a specific counseling orientation. Which theoretical orientations are most effective? What are the active ingredients that make the various techniques useful? What advantages will I have if I align myself with a specific theoretical persuasion?

Effectiveness

Diverse opinions have been offered about the effectiveness of counseling. Several decades ago, in 1952, British psychologist Hans Eysenck reviewed twenty-four studies on psychotherapy and concluded that those receiving therapy improved at about the same rate as those receiving no help.[2] Since Eysenck's report, many researchers have disputed his methods and his conclusions.[3] Nonetheless, Christian critics of psychology have used Eysenck's conclusions to support their opposition to psychotherapy and counseling.[4] The reports of these critics have been confusing to many Christian counselors who want to see their work with hurting people as a significant ministry.

Fortunately for those who counsel and those who see counselors, recent studies have cast doubt on Eysenck's conclusions. Whereas Eysenck was able to find only 24 studies to evaluate in 1952, Mary Lee Smith and her colleagues were able to find 375 studies to evaluate in 1977 and 475 in 1980.[5] Smith used a technique called *meta-analysis* to study the effectiveness of psychotherapy and found that while not everyone benefits from counseling, and some even get worse, most do better than those who do not get counseling. In fact, Smith found 80 percent of those receiving counseling do better than the average person receiving no counseling. Smith and her colleagues (1980) conclude, "Psychotherapy benefits people of all ages as reliably as schooling educates them, medicine cures them, or business turns a profit."[6]

In addition to testing the general effectiveness of psychotherapy, in their 1977 research Smith and Glass were able to test how effective the various theoretical approaches are. They evaluated the following approaches to therapy: psychodynamic, Adlerian, transactional analysis, eclectic, rational-emotive, Gestalt, client-centered, systematic desensitization, implosion, and behavior modification. They found only minor differences. Smith and Glass write:

> Despite volumes devoted to the theoretical differences among different schools of psychotherapy, the results of research demonstrate negligible differences in the effects produced by different therapy types. Unconditional judgments of superiority of one type or another of psychotherapy, and all that these claims imply about treatment and training policy, are unjustified.[7]

So it now appears that counseling *is* consistently effective in helping overcome emotional disturbances, but the specific "brand" of therapy is not critical. In other words, those using psychodynamic techniques in counseling are about as effective as those using humanistic or behavioral techniques, and those using long-term counseling approaches are about as effective as those using time-limited methods. Counselors shopping for a theoretical orientation do well to remember that one works about as well as any other.

Active Ingredients

If most or all theoretical techniques have similar effectiveness, what are the "active ingredients" in counseling techniques? Why *do* people get better with counseling? Do counselors even need a theoretical persuasion? Jerome Frank describes several commonalities in all counseling techniques that contribute to clients' improvement. Frank suggests at least six features that all emotional healing techniques include.

First, all counseling techniques involve an intense, emotional, confiding relationship.[8] Counselors are trusted listeners who often hear things that clients have not told anyone before. Psychologist Carl Rogers believed that counselors need to be genuine, empathetic, and have unconditional positive regard for clients in order for a therapeutic relationship to be established.[9] This trusting, confiding relationship is necessary for all effective counseling techniques.

Second, all counseling procedures provide a system of explanation to the client which helps the client understand his or her complaints and guides the direction of counseling.[10] Clients often arrive for counseling confused and unsure about their feelings. They know they feel bad, but they are not sure what went wrong to lead to their feelings. In this sense, all therapies, whether they are Freudian or Skinnerian, change ways of thinking. Psychodynamic (Freudian and neo-Freudian) therapists change clients' understanding of early-life events, allowing them to think in new ways about themselves. Humanistic therapists provide an atmosphere where clients can develop new ways of thinking about themselves, improving self-esteem and self-acceptance. Behavior therapists change rewards and stimuli to alter behaviors; but many of those rewards and stimuli are internal thought processes. Biblical counselors work to enhance clients' views and applications of Scripture by teaching and exhorting, changing their ways of thinking about God or the Bible. Thus *all* therapies change thinking patterns.

The importance of having a theoretical persuasion, even if no one theory is clearly superior to others, was demonstrated by my work with a client named Lori. Angry about her husband's insensitivity and selfishness, Lori came to my office because she said her marriage was falling apart. But as we talked, it became clear that Lori was experiencing symptoms of clinical depression. She awoke early each morning, her appetite had declined, she had difficulty with memory and concentration, and she felt hopeless about the future. By the end of our first session, she understood the cause of her feelings—she was depressed because she had learned early in life that it was her job to keep other people happy. Since it is impossible to keep everyone happy, she felt defeated and worthless. Although therapy required several months of work with Lori and her husband, the helplessness she expressed during the first session never recurred. Having a new way to understand her problem allowed her to experience more joy in her life and her marriage.

My cognitive (focusing on beliefs, thoughts, and expectations) explanation—that Lori told herself she needed to keep others happy—gave her a new way of understanding her problem and helped clear up some of the confusion she was feeling. If I were a psychodynamic therapist, my explanation might have been different, but it still would have changed Lori's thinking, resulting in less confusion about her feelings.

Third, counseling techniques not only allow clients to understand their problems in new ways, they also teach clients new ways of coping with problems.[11] Clients who benefit from counseling learn new skills to deal with the stressors and feelings they face. The skills clients learn reflect the theoretical assumptions of their therapists. Psychodynamic therapists teach their clients skills of insight and interpretation, cognitive therapists teach new ways of thinking, humanistic therapists teach skills of self-acceptance, and so on.

Fourth, counseling methods create expectations in clients that the counseling will be effective.[12] Much has been written about the Pygmalion effect in recent years. This phenomemon, named for a mythical sculptor who fell in love with a statue he created, occurs when expectations create realities. For example, when teachers are told that certain randomly selected students in their classes are very bright, those students actually do better than others by the end of the school year. The teachers may unintentionally give more attention to the students they expect to be bright and their expections become self-fulfilling prophecy.[13] In the same way, when clients expect they will improve, their expectations help create the reality of improvement.

Fifth, counseling provides successful experiences for clients.[14] Many clients come to counselors feeling defeated and worthless. As they succeed in the counseling process, they begin to feel more competent. Instead of thinking, *I'm no good at anything*, they may say to themselves, *I'm making progress and understanding myself better.*

Sixth, counseling creates emotional arousal in clients.[15] This is significant because motivation often walks hand in hand with emotion. Those with emotional arousal are motivated to improve their situation.

Although therapeutic techniques appear very different to counselors and clients, they share these six commonalities. In fact, these commonalities may be the active ingredients that make counseling effective.

Choices, Choices

If all counseling theories have similar effectiveness and the same active ingredients, then why choose? Because having a theoretical perspective, whether cognitive or some other type, is part of what makes counseling effective. As Jerome Frank notes, a framework for explanation and understanding is a necessary part of effective counseling.[16] A theoretical framework guides counselor and client through the maze of counseling as stress, confusion, and past memories are confronted and interpreted in new ways.

A good theory is like a good road map. There may be different maps to get a person from point A to point B, but the person with no map will have problems finding the way. Choosing a theoretical perspective gives a counselor a sense of direction in working with clients and also helps the client understand the counseling goals.

BENEFITS OF A ROAD MAP

Counselors who choose one theoretical persuasion—a clinical road map—enjoy many benefits. A good road map helps a counselor establish expertise, clarifies the goals and process of treatment, allows the client to anticipate the future, and produces a confidence-inspiring atmosphere for the counseling sessions.

It Helps Establish Expertise

Eclectic counselors sometimes report they are able to use a variety of theories and techniques, depending on the needs of their clients. This sounds ideal, but it does not appear to result in more effective counseling. In the Smith and Glass study, the results of eclectic counseling were among the worst. Sixty-eight percent of those receiving help from eclectic counselors did better than the average person not receiving counseling. (The only therapy that showed worse results was Gestalt therapy where 60 percent of those receiving help did better than the average person not receiving help.)[17] Although Smith and Glass use their results to conclude that theoretical orientation has little or no effect on outcome, it is fair to say that eclectic counseling is not superior to other forms. The advantage eclectic counselors have in using a variety of techniques is off-set by limitations of time and expertise. Is it realistic that a counselor could master two or more theoretical perspectives when most of us spend years trying to master one?

One advantage of a single theoretical persuasion is that it helps establish expertise. Counselors read books to improve their skills. How do we choose which books to read? In most states, licensed mental-health professionals are required to participate in continuing education each year. How do we choose which workshops to attend from among the dozens of invitations we receive each month? Counselors often form study groups and supervisory relationships with other counselors. How do we choose our supervisors? Those who have a clearly defined theoretical orientation make these choices more easily and benefit from in-depth study of their chosen theory and related techniques. As the eclectic counselor benefits from breadth of understanding, those with a focused theoretical perspective benefit from depth of understanding.

It Helps Define a Destination

Clients come to counselors looking for hope. Many times they feel desperate, pursuing what seems like their last option. They are looking for someone who is kind and sensitive, but also for someone who knows how to diagnose their problems and help them improve their situation.

Counselors give clients hope by describing the destination of the counseling process. Consider the following statement, similar to what I often use at the end of the first session with depressed clients.

I want to take a minute and describe to you the kind of therapy I do. It's called cognitive therapy—cognitive because it has to do with changing thoughts. My assumption is that feelings are always related to thoughts. For example, several times today I've heard you say that you have nothing to be depressed about, but that you're depressed anyway. It sounds like you're saying to yourself, "I *shouldn't* be depressed"— as though you're doing something wrong by having these feelings. Pretty soon you're depressed about being depressed, and it's partially because your thoughts have created those feelings.

I teach people how to think in slightly different ways and, as a result, experience greater control over their feelings. It may sound too easy because you've probably tried to control those thoughts before. But I will have some different strategies for you to try.

What we will probably find is that underneath the everyday thoughts are some deeper beliefs—I call them core beliefs. For example, some people leave their childhood believing they have to be perfect to be loved, and they can never be perfect, so they get depressed. Others think they have to gain the approval of everyone around, so they get depressed when someone doesn't approve.

There are many other possibilities, but I wanted to mention a couple so you can see where we're headed. Cognitive therapy is a very effective way to treat depression. It takes hard work, like any form of counseling, and our work together may take several months; but I would guess that you will start to notice you're feeling better within a few weeks.

This statement describes the destination of counseling at the same time it introduces the theoretical assumptions of cognitive therapy. Most importantly, it gives the client hope that I have a road map to guide the counseling process.

In addition to helping the client anticipate a destination, a theoretical model helps client and counselor determine when the destination has been reached. If we continued counseling until our clients were constantly happy, we would never reach the end. So we need realistic ways of measuring progress to determine when clients are functioning adequately. As a cognitive therapist, I look for evidence of clear, rational thinking and liberation from the faulty beliefs that resulted from early-life trauma.

It Helps the Process of Counseling

A theoretical model not only helps define the destination of counseling, but also the process. A thorough road map helps break long-term goals into short-term goals.

Counselors deal with their own self-talk during counseling, and a common self-talk question for beginning counselors is, *What do I do now?* (This, of course, is better than the recurrent self-talk used by introductory counseling students, *What should I say next?* which keeps them from hearing what the client is saying.)

Julie, recently divorced after her husband moved in with another woman, had blamed herself for the marriage failure. She called at midnight one night, complaining that her anger toward her ex-husband was so intense she could not sleep. As we discussed her thoughts, I pointed out that she had stopped blaming herself for the marriage failure, and, as a result, her feelings had shifted from guilt to anger. Her anger in this case was a sign of progress because we had worked for several weeks to disrupt her self-blaming style of self-talk. Her self-talk had shifted from, *This is all my fault,* to *This isn't fair.* We still had a lot of work to do in counseling, but that midnight phone call symbolized reaching one of our short-term goals. She hung up, still feeling angry, but encouraged with her progress.

This example demonstrates how reaching short-term goals produces hope in clients, even if they have not yet reached their long-term goal. A theoretical model provides clients and counselors with these short-term, as well as long-term, goals.

It Helps the Client Anticipate the Future

A theoretical model also helps the client understand what is coming next in the counseling process and then anticipate what daily stressors might interfere with his or her progress. For example, with cognitive therapy a client can anticipate two major stages in treatment. First, self-talk will be evaluated carefully for several weeks. During this stage, clients learn how distorted self-talk leads to negative feelings; they also learn how to change the self-talk to be more accurate. Second, they learn to understand and revise the underlying beliefs from which self-talk emanates. Clients can anticipate what is coming next in counseling if the counselor has explained the process carefully.

Especially when dealing with painful memories from the past, clients are often more vulnerable than usual to the effects of routine daily stressors. If they are able to anticipate their heightened vulnerability, they will cope better with stress. The woman who is dealing with past sexual abuse is wise to anticipate that sexual advances by her husband may evoke troubling emotions. The man who uncovers deep fears that he is worthless without the love of a woman is wise to anticipate that he will feel empty and lonely when he spends time alone, but that time alone might be particularly healthy.

Another advantage of clients anticipating the therapy process is seen in greater collaboration between therapist and client. If clients understand the purpose of various homework assignments, they will usually complete the assignment. Sometimes the collaborative arrangement works so well that clients can assign their own homework.

For all of the above reasons, having a theoretical model for counseling provides a confidence-inspiring atmosphere for counselors and clients. Despite the difficulty of choosing, there are advantages to identifying oneself with a specific theoretical orientation.

BENEFITS OF COGNITIVE THERAPY

In addition to the general benefits of a theoretical model, cognitive therapy has several specific benefits. Probably because of these benefits, cognitive therapy, which will be the focus of this book, has been one of the fastest growing forms of counseling in recent years.

It Is Short-Term

Cognitive therapy usually lasts between ten and twenty sessions. Of course, as with any therapy, this varies a great deal depending on the nature of the client's emotional difficulties and resources. Occasionally a client will show significant improvement after two or three sessions, and sometimes cognitive therapy continues for a year or more.

Unlike some other short-term therapies, cognitive therapy focuses on past events as well as present symptoms. In his book, *Cognitive Therapy and the Emotional Disorders,* psychiatrist Aaron Beck describes similarities between cognitive therapy and psychodynamic therapy, a long-term method emphasizing insight into childhood experiences.[18] In both forms of therapy, the client is asked to introspect and develop insight regarding thoughts, feelings, and wishes. Both forms attempt to reorganize personality rather than just remove symptoms. Both forms of therapy also require the client to work through maladaptive beliefs and arrive at more healthy ways of thinking.

However, one of the significant differences between psychodynamic and cognitive therapies is the time required for treatment.

Psychodynamic therapists often work for a year or more with their clients, sometimes meeting two or more times per week. Cognitive therapy is much briefer.

Client and Counselor Work Together

Psychodynamic and cognitive therapies also differ in their assumptions about the counselor's role. Whereas psychodynamic therapists look for disguised or hidden meaning in clients' thoughts, cognitive therapists attempt to understand clients' conscious thoughts without looking for a hidden meaning. This means that clients and counselors can collaborate in finding the aspects of clients' thinking that require change.

For example, if a client reports, "I feel like nothing I do is good enough for my wife," the psychodynamic therapist may look for hidden meaning.

"You are still trying to please your mother," the analyst might say. Because the counselor looks for hidden, unconscious meaning, the client cannot participate in determining its accuracy. This puts the counselor in a position of power over the client. If the client disagrees with the interpretation, it is described as "therapeutic resistance." Looking for hidden meaning precludes collaboration.

A cognitive therapist might reply, "It sounds like you're telling yourself you should always be able to please your wife." Because this is an evaluation of conscious thought, the client can confirm or dispute the interpretation. This collaboration is an essential element of cognitive therapy.

Throughout the counseling process, cognitive therapists attempt to develop a partnership with their clients. They are working together toward a common goal. At the beginning of an appointment, counselor and client establish a mutually acceptable agenda for that session. At the end of the session, they discuss how each felt about the progress made. The therapist keeps no secrets from the client about the progress being made or the upcoming counseling goals. Whenever possible, the counselor and the client work together to determine an effective homework assignment.

It Has Demonstrated Effectiveness

Because cognitive therapy is a relatively new development in counseling practice, it was not one of the forms of therapy tested in the 1977 Smith and Glass study described earlier. (Rational-emotive therapy, which shares many assumptions with cognitive therapy, was evaluated in the Smith and Glass study and was at least as effective as other forms of therapy.) But subsequent studies have confirmed the effectiveness of cognitive therapy for a variety of emotional disorders.

One of the first applications of cognitive therapy was clinical depression. A number of controlled studies have confirmed cognitive therapy's effectiveness for depressed clients.[19]

Since its introduction as a treatment for depression, cognitive therapy has been used effectively for anxiety disorders,[20] hypochondriasis,[21] adjustment reactions,[22] childhood disorders,[23] and marital therapy.[24]

It may be that cognitive therapy is no more effective than the other forms of therapy tested by Smith and her colleagues. Nonetheless, cognitive therapy is both effective and rapid—a combination enjoyed by clients looking for relief from emotional pain.

Counselors Can Learn It Readily

While it might take years to learn the skills necessary for other forms of therapy, counselors can learn cognitive therapy techniques rapidly. Cognitive therapy rests on a few relatively simple concepts. These concepts will be summarized in chapter 2. Some other forms of therapy are based on complex personality theories that require years of training to understand. Psychodynamic therapists, for example, have to understand the subtle interactions of abstract concepts such as id, ego, superego, introjection, transference, resistance, and defense mechanisms. Cognitive therapists need not focus on such abstract concepts. If a client fears snakes, the cognitive therapist interprets it as a fear of snakes rather than an underlying unconscious conflict with sexuality or a parent.

Cognitive therapy is highly structured and goal-directed. Cognitive therapists often use homework assignments, handouts, and worksheets to help keep the goals in focus. They learn systematized ways to assess and confront dysfunctional automatic thoughts and the underlying core beliefs from which the automatic thoughts emanate. The road map for cognitive therapy can be broken down into the following steps:

STEP 1. Identify problem thoughts and feelings
STEP 2. Find dysfunctional automatic thoughts
STEP 3. Help client dispute automatic thoughts
STEP 4. Find underlying core beliefs
STEP 5. Help client dispute core beliefs
STEP 6. Help client maintain gains

Chapters 4–9 of this book examine these six steps and describe specific cognitive therapy techniques to accomplish each step.

It is relatively easy to learn cognitive therapy. But as with any technique, the most effective way to learn this method is through a variety of training activities: reading, attending workshops, and being supervised by an experienced clinician.

Counselors Benefit from the Techniques, Also

The techniques cognitive counselors teach their clients are useful in their own lives as well. As our clients sit in our offices describing thoughts and feelings, we counselors have our own thoughts and feelings. As our clients talk to themselves in destructive, inaccurate ways, we are sometimes guilty of the same thing.

Imagine sitting in a counseling session with Henry, who was making good progress in counseling for depression until two weeks ago. Then, without warning, he became as depressed as he was when he first came for help, and he has remained sad and suicidal ever since. Many counselors in this situation will be struggling with their own destructive self-talk: *If I were a good counselor, I would know what to do to make Henry feel better,* or, *This is my fault and there should be something I can do to improve the situation,* or, *He's just trying to get attention. He doesn't really feel bad.* These forms of self-talk produce feelings of anger or ineffectiveness in counselors. The same procedures cognitive therapists use to correct their clients' self-talk can be used effectively in their own situations like this. A cognitive therapist could recognize the faulty thinking and correct it with, *I feel sad that Henry is depressed again, but it is not my fault. I am helping Henry get better, but I am not personally responsible for his feelings of depression.* The same tools we teach our clients can help us deal with our own feelings both inside and outside the counseling office.

Christians Are Well Suited for Cognitive Therapy

Cognitive therapy techniques are suitable for a variety of people, but Christian clients are particularly well suited for this method. There are at least two reasons for this.

First, cognitive therapy requires clients to compare their thoughts with truth to see if they are understanding reality accurately. This is challenging for agnostics, who have difficulty finding standards for truth. Christians believe truth is revealed in Scripture, giving them a useful way to evaluate their thoughts.

Ted, a twenty-three-year-old depressed youth pastor, knew rationally that God loved him, but he could not feel God's love. What he knew in his head needed to sink twelve inches to his heart. As we explored his thoughts and his early-life experiences, we began comparing his feelings with Scripture. He felt he didn't deserve God's grace, so he memorized Titus 3:4–5a:

> But when the kindness and love of God our Savior appeared, he saved us, not because of righteous things we had done, but because of his mercy.

Ted feared God's rejection, so he memorized Romans 8:38–39:

> For I am convinced that neither death nor life, neither angels nor demons, neither the present nor the future, nor any powers, neither height nor depth, nor anything else in all creation, will be able to separate us from the love of God that is in Christ Jesus our Lord.

Scripture gave Ted access to a source of truth with which he could compare his inaccurate thoughts. The counseling involved many other things, such as dealing with emotional scars from the past; but his belief in the Bible as a source of truth was a valuable aid in helping him correct his thoughts.

The second reason this method is well suited to Christians is that they believe in God's love—the only love that is purely unconditional. Many clients, perhaps most clients, find their deepest fears to be of rejection, abandonment, or lack of love. Flawed human relationships with parents, siblings, or peers may have produced deep insecurities and fears. Treating those fears requires disputing the core beliefs that scream out, "Others are bound to reject me, too." Those beliefs can be more easily disputed by people who acknowledge God's unconditional love. Human relationships occasionally result in rejection, even by those closest to us— parents, children, spouses, and friends. God's love never results in rejection.

Cognitive therapy offers many benefits for counselors and their clients as it provides a road map to emotional healing.

CHAPTER TWO
AN OVERVIEW OF COGNITIVE THERAPY

IT OFTEN SEEMS THAT EXPERIENCES and feelings happen *to* us. Going to the dentist, we believe, makes us feel tense. Our spouse or friend makes us mad. The car makes us frustrated and embarrassed when it breaks down in the middle of the freeway.

But a careful look at these examples shows that events are not entirely responsible for feelings. Two people enduring the same dental procedure may have different reactions. One may be terrified while another feels no anxiety. Likewise, one angry person blames a spouse while another in the same situation feels overwhelmed with guilt and self-blame. Some people handle inconveniences such as broken down cars with only slight discomfort, but it seems like a major crisis to others. Even the same person at different times has different reactions. Although it is tempting to believe that circumstances *require* us to feel certain ways, that idea is not accurate.

Consider the apostle Paul writing to the believers in Philippi. Most biblical scholars believe that when Paul wrote the epistle he was imprisoned in Rome, not knowing whether he would be released or executed. We might assume these circumstances would demand despair, but Paul's letter shows a surprising hopefulness. One scholar concluded about the book of Philippians, "its keynote is joy."[1] Paul's words in Philippians 4:4 do demonstrate joy: "Rejoice in the Lord always. I will say it again: Rejoice!" How could Paul feel joy in the midst of such circumstances? His admonition near the end of the letter gives us a clue:

> Finally, brothers, whatever is true, whatever is noble, whatever is right, whatever is pure, whatever is lovely, whatever is admirable—if anything is excellent or praiseworthy—think about such things. (Phil. 4:8)

Here and elsewhere, Paul endorsed a view of feelings and thoughts that resembles two basic assumptions of cognitive therapy—that bad events do not require us to feel awful and that healthy thinking allows us to control our feelings. Events *contribute* to feelings, but they do not *cause* feelings.

Counselors can see this in the clients they help. One woman I worked with was forced to quit her successful career because of Parkinson's disease. Despite her chronic, disabling illness, she was determined to keep active in her community, with her children and grandchildren, and in her church. Although she experienced episodes of serious depression, partially due to side effects of her medications, she maintained hope and joy in her life despite losing her career and her good health.

Another woman was seriously depressed because her supervisor criticized her work. Although she felt secure in her job, she felt worthless without her supervisor's approval. If events cause feelings, the first woman should have been much more depressed than the second. But she wasn't because of the different way she represented her experiences in her thoughts. Healthy, accurate thinking enables people to cope with life's trials.

HUMANS ARE VULNERABLE TO INACCURATE WAYS OF THINKING

Imagine the following dialogue in counseling:

COUNSELOR: How did your week go?

The thesis that the special meaning of an event determines the emotional response forms the core of the cognitive model of emotions and emotional disorders: The meaning is encased in a cognition—a thought of an image.[2]

Albert Ellis, founder of rational-emotive therapy, uses similar philosophical assumptions when he describes the ABCs of emotional disturbance. A is the activating event, B is the individual's beliefs about the event, and C is the consequent emotions that result from the beliefs.[3] Similarly, David Burns, author of a popular self-help book on cognitive therapy, asserts that events cause thoughts and thoughts cause feelings.[4]

The assumption that thoughts cause feelings provides a simple way to explain cognitive therapy to clients. Since many come for counseling assuming that life events cause their feelings, it gives clients hope to hear that thoughts cause feelings and thoughts can be controlled. Imagine the following interaction in counseling:

Counselor: It sounds like you're feeling helpless—like you don't sense any control over the depression you're feeling.

Client: Exactly. It feels like a dark cloud that I can't get out of. I don't know what to do.

Counselor: And it seems that your cloud has a lot to do with your marriage.

Client: Yeah. I always thought I had a great marriage, and then I found out my husband has been unfaithful. Now he's gone. What's the use?

Counselor: We are going to dismantle this cloud one bit at a time by focusing on your thoughts. Depressed feelings come from depressing thoughts, so we need to work on revising those thoughts. When you ask yourself, "What's the use?" you feel depressed because it is a depressing thought. As we explore and revise your thoughts, you'll have better control over those feelings. How does that sound?

Client: Good. I hope it works. I mean it sounds too easy. I feel bad all the time, not just when I'm thinking about my failed marriage.

In this example, cognitive theory has been quickly explained. Events (the husband's leaving) cause thoughts (*What's the use?*), and thoughts cause feelings (depression). Although this is a simple way to explain cognitive theory to clients who need hope, it may also be simplistic. Sometimes clients object, noting that their feelings can't be reduced to inaccurate thoughts.

Psychologist Robert Zajonc argues that sometimes emotions occur before thoughts. He presents several sources of evidence.[5] First, infants are able to feel before they are able to interpret their experiences. An angry or hungry baby probably lacks the ability to cognitively interpret the events of the world, but he or she experiences the feelings anyway. Second, emotions and thoughts appear to have different neural pathways in the brain. Third, thoughts and feelings are often disjointed. A person may understand rationally that jet travel is relatively safe, but may experience tremendous anxiety nonetheless. Finally, some feelings can be induced without thoughts. For example, if people are asked to make facial expressions of different feelings—anger, sadness, happiness—they begin experiencing those feelings and their bodies show physiological evidence of emotional arousal.[6] These feelings appear to occur without conscious thought.

On the other side of the debate is researcher Richard Lazarus, who agrees with Zajonc that some emotions do not require thoughts. But he asserts that many emotions—anger, happiness, guilt, and love—come from our thoughts.[7]

Interpreting the relationship between thoughts and emotion can lead to some of the logical fallacies discussed earlier. When cognitive theorists insist thoughts precede emotions, they are using *linear thinking*, assuming a sequential process of human experience. And Zajonc's conclusion that some emotions occur without thinking can lead to *categorical thinking* if we assume all emotions occur without thoughts.

The most accurate way to view events, thoughts, and feelings is shown as the third option in Figure 2–1. Some feelings may occur automatically, without thoughts, while others occur because of our thoughts. But even the feelings that occur automatically are interpreted cognitively, resulting in a new set of feelings. When Bob, a fifty-two-year-old man with a phobia, sees a snake, he becomes terrified. After his automatic feeling, Bob interprets his experience by thinking, *That was awful. I must avoid snakes at all costs.* His interpretation adds to his feeling of fear.

Although cognitive therapists have traditionally accepted Option 2, the third option is more consistent with the observations of Zajonc and others. Thoughts and feelings are constantly interacting to produce conscious experience. Counselors who understand this more accurate philosophical base are better able to express the principles of cognitive therapy to their clients without seeming simplistic. Consider these revisions to the previous dialogue.

Counselor: It sounds like you're feeling helpless—like you don't sense any control over the depression you're feeling.

Client: Exactly. It feels like a dark cloud that I can't get out of. I don't know what to do.

Counselor: And it seems that your cloud has a lot to do with your marriage.

Client: Yeah. I always thought I had a great marriage and then I found out my husband has been unfaithful. Now he's gone. What's the use?

Counselor: We are going to dismantle this cloud one bit at a time. And we will focus on your thoughts and feelings. With depression, they are tangled together. You feel hopeless so you say to yourself, "What's the use?" And when you say that to yourself, you feel even more hopeless. So we need to untangle the thoughts and feelings and give you new ways of thinking. With time and practice, those new ways of thinking will give you some control over those feelings. How does that sound?

Client: Good. I know my marriage is over and I think I could deal with that if I could just get out of this cloud.

This dialogue gives the client hope without appearing simplistic.

The goal of cognitive therapy, then, is to help clients break out of their unproductive cycles of thinking and feeling by giving them tools to think in more accurate ways. Cognitive counselors teach their clients to think as detectives, analyzing available evidence to come to precise conclusions. However, as with many detective stories, the plot is more involved than it first appears.

DAILY THOUGHTS ARE ROOTED IN CORE BELIEFS

Clients and counselors using cognitive therapy must first untangle the relationship between thoughts and feelings. As clients learn new self-talk strategies, they begin feeling better, more in control of their emotions.

Unfortunately, counselors with limited exposure to cognitive therapy are tempted to stop counseling at this point, assuming the client is all right since the symptoms have improved. Clients participating in this limited form of cognitive therapy often feel better for a time and then show up again at the counselor's office with similar symptoms.

Inaccurate self-talk comes from the assumptions and beliefs one has about oneself and the world. Unless these underlying assumptions are addressed, they will cause the unhealthy self-talk to return again and again. A patient with a malignancy wants the tumor removed, not just the symptoms treated. Similarly, those with maladaptive beliefs need to change the beliefs .

The relationship between self-talk and core beliefs can be likened to an onion, as shown in Figure 2–2. Automatic thoughts, the outer layers of self-talk, are easily identifiable—the client is consciously aware of them. As the outer layer is peeled away, one finds another layer of self-talk, not quite as easily recognized by the client. Deep in the center of the personality is the core, the fundamental beliefs the client holds that are usually not consciously recognized. The client and counselor must use their detective skills to find the deepest core beliefs.

The Relationship between Self-talk and Core Beliefs

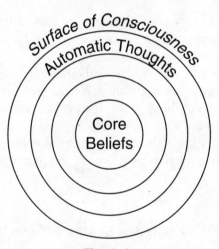

Fig. 2–2

Thoughts are layered, with automatic thoughts at the surface of consciousness and core beliefs embedded in the unconscious.

This layering of beliefs can be seen in Jean, a twenty-four-year-old married woman with three children. She felt guilty for many things, including leaving her children while she worked, eating too much, spending too much, noticing other men, and not reading her Bible each day. Her surface automatic thoughts were easy to find. For several weeks we focused on her "shoulds." *I should be a better mother and not leave my kids with a babysitter. I should lose ten pounds. I should never use a charge card again.* As we explored these shoulds, we traced them to a deeper level of thoughts that focused on her fears: *If I don't lose weight, my husband will leave me. If I keep spending money, we will lose our house.* These fears appeared to be unrealistic, but they were the driving force behind her should statements. What caused Jean's fears? As we peeled off this layer, we found that although she never would have described herself as a perfectionist, she believed she needed to be perfect. Her need for perfection motivated her fears: *If I'm not perfect, awful things will happen, like losing my house and my husband.* After many weeks of counseling we got to her core belief: *I have to be perfect to be loved.* This belief originated in Jean's childhood when her father repeatedly criticized Jean for her weight and her grades. She felt she needed to earn his love by being skinny and perfect. But she never felt successful, so she left her home feeling imperfect and unloved. Her should statements emanated from her deep feelings of inadequacy and her fears of abandonment. Those core beliefs needed to be revised before her conscious self-talk could be effectively changed.

Core beliefs also affect the intimate relationships we experience. It is natural to assume that others think the same way we do, but this assumption often leads to distress. In Jean's case, she believed she had to be perfect to be loved. So she tried to earn approval and love through her hard work, tidy housekeeping, physical attractiveness, and sensitivity to others.

Her husband, Jim, had his own set of core beliefs. As Jim and I talked, we discovered he longed for approval in his own ways. Jim believed that if others weren't warm and loving toward him, they were bound to reject him.

So Jim and Jean's marriage was troubled. Jean was so busy trying to earn Jim's love that she didn't take time to show relaxed affection to him. Jim felt unloved because Jean was usually working on another project rather than spending time with him. So he resented her work. Jean wasn't earning love with her efforts as she intended; she was earning resentment.

Jim and Jean both felt unloved and unwanted. But as we were able to uncover the core beliefs and explore the dynamics of the relationship, each began to feel loved again and their relationship improved.

Jim and Jean's situation demonstrated the importance of understanding how core beliefs affect our interpretation of others and of our own everyday experiences. And just as core beliefs affect our relationships with others, they also affect the ways we view God.

Core Beliefs Affect Our Views of God

As my counseling sessions with Jean continued, I was not surprised that she viewed God as judgmental and distant. "God doesn't want me," she reported one day, "because I am not a good Christian." She assumed God expected perfection before giving her love. But her efforts at perfection had failed, so several years earlier Jean had given up. She stopped going to church and practicing spiritual disciplines, concluding she could never be good enough to earn God's love.

Those like Jean, who believe they need to *earn* love, have difficulty understanding that God's love is available to all. They see God through their distorted core beliefs, and use those beliefs in approaching Scripture. Those who believe they need to earn God's love often cite Ephesians 2:10, "For we are God's workmanship, created in Christ Jesus to do good works, which God prepared in advance for us to do." This provides evidence to them that God loves us according to our works. But they overlook the preceding verses which remind us, "For it is by grace you have been saved, through faith—and this not from yourselves, it is the gift of God—not by works, so that no one can boast." They also remember Romans 3:23, "for all have sinned and fall short of the glory of God," but forget the next verse: "and are justified freely by his grace through the redemption that came by Christ Jesus." They read Titus 3:3, "At one time we too were foolish, disobedient, deceived and enslaved by all kinds of passions and pleasures . . ." and overlook Titus 3:4,5: "But when the kindness and love of God our Savior appeared, he saved us, not because of righteous things we had done, but because of his mercy. . . ."

This is why we need theology and doctrine—to free us from our unhealthy beliefs and allow us to see God more accurately. God's love—perhaps the only truly unconditional love—can meet our deepest emotional needs. I often listen to clients weep as they describe their feelings of distance from God. They know intellectually that God loves them, but they cannot feel his love emotionally. But as they shed their core beliefs, they find a fresh appreciation and understanding of God's love and feel spiritually and emotionally healthy.

CORE BELIEFS CAN BE CHANGED

The apostle Paul instructed Roman Christians not to conform to the ways of the world, but to be "transformed by the renewing of your mind" (Rom. 12:2). The transformation Paul describes allows us to see the world through a different set of eyes—eyes that seek God's truth above personal comfort or pleasure. The goal of cognitive therapy is similar. Cognitive counselors help their clients identify and change core beliefs, to trade in their old set of eyes for a new set that can interpret the world more accurately. In reaching this goal, clients learn to employ skills of insight, inductive reasoning, experimentation, and repetition.

Insight

All forms of counseling require clients to become students of themselves. Those who profit the most from counseling, including cognitive therapy, are those who are able to look accurately at their thoughts, feelings, motives, and wishes. Some have called this ability "psychological mindedness."

Some come for counseling with good insight. They are able to understand and describe their thoughts and feelings with ease. They come from environments where feelings are openly discussed or they have participated in counseling before. These clients are usually able to progress quickly in cognitive therapy. Once they understand the relationships between self-talk and feelings, they learn to monitor their thoughts and find alternative ways of thinking to control their feelings.

Others come for counseling with poorer skills of insight. They know they feel bad, but they don't know how to describe their feelings carefully nor do they understand the relationship between their thoughts and their feelings. This is especially common for male clients who have not been socialized to understand or express their feelings in our current culture. The following dialogue demonstrates the difficulty poor insight can cause in a counseling setting.

COUNSELOR: How are you feeling today?

CLIENT: About the same.

COUNSELOR: You say about the same. Describe those feelings for me.

CLIENT: I don't know. I just wish things were better.

COUNSELOR: You're having a hard time putting a label on those feelings.

CLIENT: [nods]

Counselors are painfully familiar with interactions like this. When clients with poor insight begin cognitive therapy, they need remedial help identifying and articulating their feelings. Strategies for helping clients develop awareness of their feelings are discussed in later chapters.

Inductive Reasoning

Inductive reasoning, the ability to derive general principles from specific events, is another skill necessary for core beliefs to be effectively changed. Clients in cognitive therapy learn to be detectives, tracing their specific thoughts back to general beliefs, often beliefs that originated years earlier during childhood.

Inductive reasoning was learned by Rachel, a twenty-eight-year-old woman recovering from bulimia. Our first sessions were spent getting Rachel in touch with her feelings, which had been covered by her eating for many years. As she began identifying her feelings, she became aware of her guilt, inadequacy, and anger. She felt guilty and inadequate because she couldn't live up to her own high expectations, and she felt angry when other people put demands on her. Rachel learned to identify her feelings, find specific situations that evoked those feelings, and then monitor what her self-talk was during those times. As she mastered this inductive process, she learned that she placed many unnecessary demands on herself, such as, *I should have a spotless house*, or *My children should always be happy*, or *I should meet the expectations my husband has for me*. These self-demands made her feel inadequate and angry. We then used more inductive reasoning as we looked at specific memories from Rachel's childhood and juxtaposed them with her current perfection demands. We eventually discovered her core belief: *If others don't approve of my actions, then they don't love me*. Throughout the process, Rachel used inductive reasoning by piecing together her feelings and thoughts with specific memories and situations to come to general conclusions about herself.

Experimentation

As a tool for learning inductive reasoning, clients in cognitive therapy also learn to use experiments to better understand themselves and others. If a client reports, "No one at work thinks I do a good job," the therapist is left with several options. One option is to simply reflect the client's painful conclusion: "It would be unpleasant to feel that no one appreciates your work." This is a good active-listening skill, but does not promote inductive reasoning in the client. Another possibility would be to actively confront the belief: "It doesn't seem likely that no one thinks you do a good job. It may be that some people don't like your work, but some others surely do." This may be reassuring to the client, but the counselor has reached the conclusion for the client rather than allowing room for inductive reasoning. A third response, one that promotes inductive thinking, would be: "That's a painful conclusion. I wonder if it's accurate. How could we test your conclusion that no one thinks you do a good job?" In this case, the counselor and client collaborate on an experiment that will address the client's fear. Perhaps the client could interview five co-workers or supervisors. The results of the interviews would then provide data to more accurately evaluate the negative self-talk. After reviewing that data, the client might find it more accurate to conclude, "A few people at work do not think I am doing a good job."

Repetition

Clients also learn to use repetition to battle unwanted core beliefs. Dysfunctional thoughts may have been reverberating through their minds for years, resulting in deep-rooted feelings of inadequacy. The rational thoughts they learn in counseling will not easily conquer the deeply ingrained dysfunctional thoughts. Just as actors need to rehearse lines over and over until they become automatic, clients need to repeat their new ways of thinking, too. This can take several weeks or several months, depending on the background and personality of the client.

Homework assignments help clients remember to rehearse their new beliefs on a daily basis. I often send my clients home with several notecards, each with a specific self-statement that contradicts a faulty core belief. Clients who carry the notecards with them can rehearse their revised beliefs whenever they have a few extra minutes—waiting in the grocery-store line or at the gas station, for example. Daily repetition makes the revised self-talk seem more believable. Strategies for disputing core beliefs will be discussed in detail in chapter 8.

With hard work and patience, core beliefs can be changed. Week after week cognitive counselors hear, "I know I'm *thinking* more accurately, but I just don't *feel* like the new thoughts are true." Then, sometimes suddenly and other times gradually, the client feels the stirring of a new set of feelings. The former way of interpreting the world—the old set of eyes—is replaced with new beliefs that empower him or her to live more joyfully. And we remember why we counsel.

(Option 1), described at the beginning of this chapter, is that the events which happen to us cause us to have certain thoughts and feelings. Many clients who come for counseling see life this way, which denies any relationship between thoughts and feelings. If all our thoughts and feelings are determined by life events, then counseling is useless because counselors cannot control the events in their clients' lives.

Three Ways to View the Relationship of Events, Thoughts, and Feelings

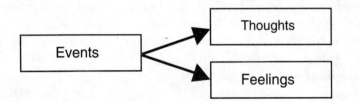

Option 1. Events happen to us, causing both thoughts and feelings.

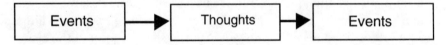

Option 2. Events cause thoughts, and thoughts cause feelings.

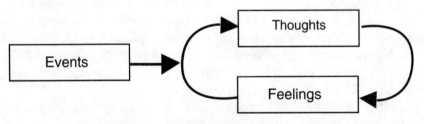

Option 3. Events lead to an extensive interaction between thoughts and feelings.

Fig. 2–1

Option 2 is the assumption usually associated with cognitive therapy. Aaron Beck describes this view in his book, *Cognitive Therapy and the Emotional Disorders*:

husband's insensitivity with the statement, "He didn't do a thing for our last anniversary." As we discussed this, I discovered that her husband had sent flowers and taken her out for dinner, but had not gone out of town with her as she had wished. She filtered out her husband's efforts and focused on her disappointment, resulting in anger toward her husband. A depressed man might be convinced that no one cares if he lives or dies, while overlooking those who love him deeply. By focusing on one or two people who dislike him, he filters out the many who love him.

Self-image is often plagued with negative filtering. One woman described herself as a worthless wretch; but as we explored her life it became clear that she was very competent in her work and was loved by those around her. And she was made in God's image. But by filtering out the things that contradicted her feelings of worthlessness, she had convinced herself she was no good.

When people are first exposed to cognitive therapy, they often note its similarity to positive thinking, which focuses on the positive and ignores the negative. The similarities are only superficial. As a cognitive therapist, I am opposed to positive thinking as well as negative thinking because positive thinking also filters out part of reality. Positive filtering often leads to denial and distortion of reality. One woman I saw in the hospital reported, "I am never depressed." Yet she showed most of the classic symptoms of depression—early-morning awakening, loss of appetite, irritablity, lack of concentration, loss of interest in sex, and fatigue—and she was in the hospital because her husband found her unconscious after she overdosed on her medication. She filtered out the negative and focused on the positive, insisting she didn't need help because her life was "fine." Her positive thinking worked for almost a year before she ended up back in my office with a major depression. Those who filter reality, whether positively or negatively, think inaccurately and end up misinterpreting themselves and others.

Although humans are prone to inaccurate thinking, we can learn skills of rational thinking that allow us to experience control over our feelings. Thus, the task of cognitive therapists is to train people to think in well-reasoned ways. Before clients change their ways of thinking, they need a philosophical understanding of how their feelings relate to their thoughts.

Events, Thoughts, and Feelings

The relationship between thoughts and feelings is not a simple one. Figure 2–1 shows three ways to view thoughts and feelings. One view

The thesis that the special meaning of an event determines the emotional response forms the core of the cognitive model of emotions and emotional disorders: The meaning is encased in a cognition—a thought of an image.[2]

Albert Ellis, founder of rational-emotive therapy, uses similar philosophical assumptions when he describes the ABCs of emotional disturbance. A is the activating event, B is the individual's beliefs about the event, and C is the consequent emotions that result from the beliefs.[3] Similarly, David Burns, author of a popular self-help book on cognitive therapy, asserts that events cause thoughts and thoughts cause feelings.[4]

The assumption that thoughts cause feelings provides a simple way to explain cognitive therapy to clients. Since many come for counseling assuming that life events cause their feelings, it gives clients hope to hear that thoughts cause feelings and thoughts can be controlled. Imagine the following interaction in counseling:

Counselor: It sounds like you're feeling helpless—like you don't sense any control over the depression you're feeling.

Client: Exactly. It feels like a dark cloud that I can't get out of. I don't know what to do.

Counselor: And it seems that your cloud has a lot to do with your marriage.

Client: Yeah. I always thought I had a great marriage, and then I found out my husband has been unfaithful. Now he's gone. What's the use?

Counselor: We are going to dismantle this cloud one bit at a time by focusing on your thoughts. Depressed feelings come from depressing thoughts, so we need to work on revising those thoughts. When you ask yourself, "What's the use?" you feel depressed because it is a depressing thought. As we explore and revise your thoughts, you'll have better control over those feelings. How does that sound?

Client: Good. I hope it works. I mean it sounds too easy. I feel bad all the time, not just when I'm thinking about my failed marriage.

In this example, cognitive theory has been quickly explained. Events (the husband's leaving) cause thoughts (*What's the use?*), and thoughts cause feelings (depression). Although this is a simple way to explain cognitive theory to clients who need hope, it may also be simplistic. Sometimes clients object, noting that their feelings can't be reduced to inaccurate thoughts.

Psychologist Robert Zajonc argues that sometimes emotions occur before thoughts. He presents several sources of evidence.[5] First, infants are able to feel before they are able to interpret their experiences. An angry or hungry baby probably lacks the ability to cognitively interpret the events of the world, but he or she experiences the feelings anyway. Second, emotions and thoughts appear to have different neural pathways in the brain. Third, thoughts and feelings are often disjointed. A person may understand rationally that jet travel is relatively safe, but may experience tremendous anxiety nonetheless. Finally, some feelings can be induced without thoughts. For example, if people are asked to make facial expressions of different feelings—anger, sadness, happiness—they begin experiencing those feelings and their bodies show physiological evidence of emotional arousal.[6] These feelings appear to occur without conscious thought.

On the other side of the debate is researcher Richard Lazarus, who agrees with Zajonc that some emotions do not require thoughts. But he asserts that many emotions—anger, happiness, guilt, and love—come from our thoughts.[7]

Interpreting the relationship between thoughts and emotion can lead to some of the logical fallacies discussed earlier. When cognitive theorists insist thoughts precede emotions, they are using *linear thinking*, assuming a sequential process of human experience. And Zajonc's conclusion that some emotions occur without thinking can lead to *categorical thinking* if we assume all emotions occur without thoughts.

The most accurate way to view events, thoughts, and feelings is shown as the third option in Figure 2–1. Some feelings may occur automatically, without thoughts, while others occur because of our thoughts. But even the feelings that occur automatically are interpreted cognitively, resulting in a new set of feelings. When Bob, a fifty-two-year-old man with a phobia, sees a snake, he becomes terrified. After his automatic feeling, Bob interprets his experience by thinking, *That was awful. I must avoid snakes at all costs.* His interpretation adds to his feeling of fear.

Although cognitive therapists have traditionally accepted Option 2, the third option is more consistent with the observations of Zajonc and others. Thoughts and feelings are constantly interacting to produce conscious experience. Counselors who understand this more accurate philosophical base are better able to express the principles of cognitive therapy to their clients without seeming simplistic. Consider these revisions to the previous dialogue.

Counselor: It sounds like you're feeling helpless—like you don't sense any control over the depression you're feeling.

Client: Exactly. It feels like a dark cloud that I can't get out of. I don't know what to do.

Counselor: And it seems that your cloud has a lot to do with your marriage.

Client: Yeah. I always thought I had a great marriage and then I found out my husband has been unfaithful. Now he's gone. What's the use?

Counselor: We are going to dismantle this cloud one bit at a time. And we will focus on your thoughts and feelings. With depression, they are tangled together. You feel hopeless so you say to yourself, "What's the use?" And when you say that to yourself, you feel even more hopeless. So we need to untangle the thoughts and feelings and give you new ways of thinking. With time and practice, those new ways of thinking will give you some control over those feelings. How does that sound?

Client: Good. I know my marriage is over and I think I could deal with that if I could just get out of this cloud.

This dialogue gives the client hope without appearing simplistic.

The goal of cognitive therapy, then, is to help clients break out of their unproductive cycles of thinking and feeling by giving them tools to think in more accurate ways. Cognitive counselors teach their clients to think as detectives, analyzing available evidence to come to precise conclusions. However, as with many detective stories, the plot is more involved than it first appears.

DAILY THOUGHTS ARE ROOTED IN CORE BELIEFS

Clients and counselors using cognitive therapy must first untangle the relationship between thoughts and feelings. As clients learn new self-talk strategies, they begin feeling better, more in control of their emotions.

Unfortunately, counselors with limited exposure to cognitive therapy are tempted to stop counseling at this point, assuming the client is all right since the symptoms have improved. Clients participating in this limited form of cognitive therapy often feel better for a time and then show up again at the counselor's office with similar symptoms.

Inaccurate self-talk comes from the assumptions and beliefs one has about oneself and the world. Unless these underlying assumptions are addressed, they will cause the unhealthy self-talk to return again and again. A patient with a malignancy wants the tumor removed, not just the symptoms treated. Similarly, those with maladaptive beliefs need to change the beliefs .

The relationship between self-talk and core beliefs can be likened to an onion, as shown in Figure 2–2. Automatic thoughts, the outer layers of self-talk, are easily identifiable—the client is consciously aware of them. As the outer layer is peeled away, one finds another layer of self-talk, not quite as easily recognized by the client. Deep in the center of the personality is the core, the fundamental beliefs the client holds that are usually not consciously recognized. The client and counselor must use their detective skills to find the deepest core beliefs.

The Relationship between Self-talk and Core Beliefs

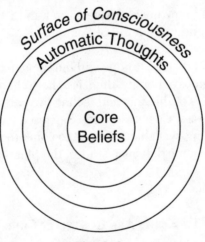

Fig. 2–2

Thoughts are layered, with automatic thoughts at the surface of consciousness and core beliefs embedded in the unconscious.

This layering of beliefs can be seen in Jean, a twenty-four-year-old married woman with three children. She felt guilty for many things, including leaving her children while she worked, eating too much, spending too much, noticing other men, and not reading her Bible each day. Her surface automatic thoughts were easy to find. For several weeks we focused on her "shoulds." *I should be a better mother and not leave my kids with a babysitter. I should lose ten pounds. I should never use a charge card again.* As we explored these shoulds, we traced them to a deeper level of thoughts that focused on her fears: *If I don't lose weight, my husband will leave me. If I keep spending money, we will lose our house.* These fears appeared to be unrealistic, but they were the driving force behind her should statements. What caused Jean's fears? As we peeled off this layer, we found that although she never would have described herself as a perfectionist, she believed she needed to be perfect. Her need for perfection motivated her fears: *If I'm not perfect, awful things will happen, like losing my house and my husband.* After many weeks of counseling we got to her core belief: *I have to be perfect to be loved.* This belief originated in Jean's childhood when her father repeatedly criticized Jean for her weight and her grades. She felt she needed to earn his love by being skinny and perfect. But she never felt successful, so she left her home feeling imperfect and unloved. Her should statements emanated from her deep feelings of inadequacy and her fears of abandonment. Those core beliefs needed to be revised before her conscious self-talk could be effectively changed.

Core beliefs also affect the intimate relationships we experience. It is natural to assume that others think the same way we do, but this assumption often leads to distress. In Jean's case, she believed she had to be perfect to be loved. So she tried to earn approval and love through her hard work, tidy housekeeping, physical attractiveness, and sensitivity to others.

Her husband, Jim, had his own set of core beliefs. As Jim and I talked, we discovered he longed for approval in his own ways. Jim believed that if others weren't warm and loving toward him, they were bound to reject him.

So Jim and Jean's marriage was troubled. Jean was so busy trying to earn Jim's love that she didn't take time to show relaxed affection to him. Jim felt unloved because Jean was usually working on another project rather than spending time with him. So he resented her work. Jean wasn't earning love with her efforts as she intended; she was earning resentment.

Jim and Jean both felt unloved and unwanted. But as we were able to uncover the core beliefs and explore the dynamics of the relationship, each began to feel loved again and their relationship improved.

Jim and Jean's situation demonstrated the importance of understanding how core beliefs affect our interpretation of others and of our own everyday experiences. And just as core beliefs affect our relationships with others, they also affect the ways we view God.

Core Beliefs Affect Our Views of God

As my counseling sessions with Jean continued, I was not surprised that she viewed God as judgmental and distant. "God doesn't want me," she reported one day, "because I am not a good Christian." She assumed God expected perfection before giving her love. But her efforts at perfection had failed, so several years earlier Jean had given up. She stopped going to church and practicing spiritual disciplines, concluding she could never be good enough to earn God's love.

Those like Jean, who believe they need to *earn* love, have difficulty understanding that God's love is available to all. They see God through their distorted core beliefs, and use those beliefs in approaching Scripture. Those who believe they need to earn God's love often cite Ephesians 2:10, "For we are God's workmanship, created in Christ Jesus to do good works, which God prepared in advance for us to do." This provides evidence to them that God loves us according to our works. But they overlook the preceding verses which remind us, "For it is by grace you have been saved, through faith—and this not from yourselves, it is the gift of God—not by works, so that no one can boast." They also remember Romans 3:23, "for all have sinned and fall short of the glory of God," but forget the next verse: "and are justified freely by his grace through the redemption that came by Christ Jesus." They read Titus 3:3, "At one time we too were foolish, disobedient, deceived and enslaved by all kinds of passions and pleasures . . ." and overlook Titus 3:4,5: "But when the kindness and love of God our Savior appeared, he saved us, not because of righteous things we had done, but because of his mercy. . . ."

This is why we need theology and doctrine—to free us from our unhealthy beliefs and allow us to see God more accurately. God's love—perhaps the only truly unconditional love—can meet our deepest emotional needs. I often listen to clients weep as they describe their feelings of distance from God. They know intellectually that God loves them, but they cannot feel his love emotionally. But as they shed their core beliefs, they find a fresh appreciation and understanding of God's love and feel spiritually and emotionally healthy.

CORE BELIEFS CAN BE CHANGED

The apostle Paul instructed Roman Christians not to conform to the ways of the world, but to be "transformed by the renewing of your mind" (Rom. 12:2). The transformation Paul describes allows us to see the world through a different set of eyes—eyes that seek God's truth above personal comfort or pleasure. The goal of cognitive therapy is similar. Cognitive counselors help their clients identify and change core beliefs, to trade in their old set of eyes for a new set that can interpret the world more accurately. In reaching this goal, clients learn to employ skills of insight, inductive reasoning, experimentation, and repetition.

Insight

All forms of counseling require clients to become students of themselves. Those who profit the most from counseling, including cognitive therapy, are those who are able to look accurately at their thoughts, feelings, motives, and wishes. Some have called this ability "psychological mindedness."

Some come for counseling with good insight. They are able to understand and describe their thoughts and feelings with ease. They come from environments where feelings are openly discussed or they have participated in counseling before. These clients are usually able to progress quickly in cognitive therapy. Once they understand the relationships between self-talk and feelings, they learn to monitor their thoughts and find alternative ways of thinking to control their feelings.

Others come for counseling with poorer skills of insight. They know they feel bad, but they don't know how to describe their feelings carefully nor do they understand the relationship between their thoughts and their feelings. This is especially common for male clients who have not been socialized to understand or express their feelings in our current culture. The following dialogue demonstrates the difficulty poor insight can cause in a counseling setting.

COUNSELOR: How are you feeling today?

CLIENT: About the same.

COUNSELOR: You say about the same. Describe those feelings for me.

CLIENT: I don't know. I just wish things were better.

COUNSELOR: You're having a hard time putting a label on those feelings.

CLIENT: [nods]

Counselors are painfully familiar with interactions like this. When clients with poor insight begin cognitive therapy, they need remedial help identifying and articulating their feelings. Strategies for helping clients develop awareness of their feelings are discussed in later chapters.

Inductive Reasoning

Inductive reasoning, the ability to derive general principles from specific events, is another skill necessary for core beliefs to be effectively changed. Clients in cognitive therapy learn to be detectives, tracing their specific thoughts back to general beliefs, often beliefs that originated years earlier during childhood.

Inductive reasoning was learned by Rachel, a twenty-eight-year-old woman recovering from bulimia. Our first sessions were spent getting Rachel in touch with her feelings, which had been covered by her eating for many years. As she began identifying her feelings, she became aware of her guilt, inadequacy, and anger. She felt guilty and inadequate because she couldn't live up to her own high expectations, and she felt angry when other people put demands on her. Rachel learned to identify her feelings, find specific situations that evoked those feelings, and then monitor what her self-talk was during those times. As she mastered this inductive process, she learned that she placed many unnecessary demands on herself, such as, *I should have a spotless house*, or *My children should always be happy*, or *I should meet the expectations my husband has for me*. These self-demands made her feel inadequate and angry. We then used more inductive reasoning as we looked at specific memories from Rachel's childhood and juxtaposed them with her current perfection demands. We eventually discovered her core belief: *If others don't approve of my actions, then they don't love me*. Throughout the process, Rachel used inductive reasoning by piecing together her feelings and thoughts with specific memories and situations to come to general conclusions about herself.

CHAPTER THREE
CHRISTIANITY AND COGNITIVE THERAPY

LEN NERVOUSLY EYED THE DIPLOMAS on the wall, the titles on the bookshelf, and the wilted leaves on the plant I routinely neglect before telling me why he came for help. "I guess I'm here because you're a Christian and I need help dealing with my feelings." Within this first thirty seconds of therapy, Len had revealed some important information about himself. He was nervous. He wanted to talk with a Christian, probably because he was also a Christian. He was troubled with uncomfortable feelings, but wanted to be selective about the help he received. Len, like so many clients, assumed there was a standard set of techniques that make up Christian counseling. Clients often come for "Christian counseling," not knowing there are many different guiding assumptions and techniques used by Christian counselors.

It is easier to define what Christian counseling is not than to define what it is. First, most Christian counselors agree that Christian counseling is not a matter of using Scripture or prayer as a complete answer to emotional problems. Although Scripture and prayer often have a powerful effect within the context of counseling, when they are applied as "Band-Aids," troubled clients often leave feeling misunderstood and patronized.

Second, most Christian counselors assume emotional problems are not necessarily spiritual problems. Their position is supported by many who study the integration of psychology and Christianity.[1] To assume spiritual health must come before emotional health denies that physiological, social, and psychological factors contribute to emotional problems. Furthermore, most Christian counselors do not assume emotional health is always necessary for spiritual health. Some people appear to have vital relationships with God despite their ongoing battles with depression, anxiety, or relationship difficulties.

Although most Christian counselors do not assume spiritual health always leads to emotional health or vice versa, they recognize the overlap between spiritual and emotional health. Indeed, it is our human need for categories that causes us to separate the two concepts in the first place. Christian counselors help their clients experience both emotional and spiritual well-being by using a variety of spiritual disciplines and psychological techniques. Dr. Howard Clinebell, the first president of the American Association of Pastoral Counseling, wrote, "Pastoral care and counseling must be holistic, seeking to enable healing and growth in all dimensions of human wholeness."[2]

Some Christian counselors focus on childhood experiences; others look for present behaviors. Some pray with their clients; others do not. Some assign Scripture verses to be memorized; others believe homework is too invasive or threatening as a therapeutic intervention. But despite the diversity of approaches, there are common emphases on emotional and spiritual wholeness in most forms of Christian counseling. The distinctions of Christian counseling merge well with cognitive therapy techniques, producing the benefits discussed in this chapter.

All counselors view their offices as places for healing and growth, places to pursue truth, and places to be authentic. But Christian counselors can enrich these opportunities by blending excellent counseling with sensitivity to religious values and spiritual awareness.

A PLACE FOR HEALING AND GROWTH

Any form of successful counseling requires a healing atmosphere that generates hope and growth in clients.[3] As L. Rebecca Propst points out in her book, *Psychotherapy in a Religious Framework*, cognitive therapy techniques and Christian ideas can be blended to provide an effective healing environment. Propst notes that cognitive therapy helps in the healing partnership by giving the client a rationale for the treatment procedures, encouraging self-awareness, and teaching new ways of thinking more flexibly and productively.[4] In addition to these benefits, cognitive therapy helps promote a safe, healing environment for Christian clients in several ways.

Healing Factors 1: Individualized Approach

Law-enforcement agencies benefit from human diversity because each person has unique fingerprints. Long-distance telephone companies are now perfecting technology to recognize "voice prints" so that callers can bill their credit card calls just by speaking their name. These are reminders of our individuality.

Just as we have unique fingerprints and voices, our personalities are unique. Each person has his or her own genes, memories, and life situations. Similarly, we are each engaged in our own spiritual pilgrimage and have diverse perspectives of God, the Bible, and theology. The healing counseling environment allows for diversity and individuality.

When my clients ask me if I see a lot of people with similar problems, I respond by reminding them of their individuality. "No two people are alike. That's one of the challenges and the pleasures of my work. Although emotional symptoms and underlying thoughts have similarities, each person is a unique individual made in God's image."

Unlike some forms of counseling based on the medical model of treatment (where standard techniques are applied to all clients with similar problems), cognitive therapy is individualized according to the specific needs of the client. Client and counselor collaborate to understand the client's dysfunctional thinking patterns and to develop treatment strategies. As a result, cognitive therapy is applied differently with different clients. For example, Christian counselors are familiar with the question, "Do you use Scripture and prayer in your counseling?" This question assumes the medical model; if a cognitive therapist uses Scripture and prayer, he or she will vary the use according to the client's needs. Two brief examples demonstrate why an individualized approach provides a healing environment.

Greg brought in, maybe dragged, Cindy for counseling. They had seen three counselors during the two years since Cindy had been involved with another man. Greg was convinced that Cindy had never expressed adequate remorse for her wrongdoing and so he could not forgive her. He selectively pulled Scripture verses out of context to support his rigid views of paternalism and interpersonal behavior. He believed the Bible taught that his wife should not smile at other men. As we tried to explore Scripture together, I quickly realized his views of God and the Bible were not amenable to change. He had his mind made up. Our time was better spent uncovering his fears of abandonment and the feelings of rejection resulting from his wife's extramarital affair. In working with Greg, I did not use Scripture in counseling.

Sandy sought counseling for help with depression. She felt unloved and unlovable. Raised in the church, she had given up her faith because she felt she could never be good enough to meet the church's expectations. She recognized the authority of Scripture, but had built emotional walls to protect herself from the guilt she experienced when she read Scripture. In order to take down her emotional walls, we needed to explore her fear of God and the Bible. She was open to new interpretations of passages she had previously thought pointed to her guilt. Before she had pulled condemning verses out of context, but soon she was able to see themes of grace and forgiveness blanketing isolated verses about sin and inadequacy. Scripture was an important part of working with Sandy.

These cases illustrate the importance of individualizing treatment and counseling techniques. Sometimes Scripture and prayer are important components of Christian counseling, but other times they are not; it depends on the beliefs and environment of the client. A healing atmosphere is enhanced by viewing each client as a unique individual. As clients learn to feel confident and safe in the counseling office, they are better able to learn skills and accept God's love to heal their pain.

Healing Factor 2: Metacognition

Metacognition is the ability to think about thinking—to understand and control one's thought processes. As clients progress in cognitive therapy, they become adept at metacognition, recognizing inflexible and destructive thoughts and replacing them with adaptive ones.

Like cognitive therapy, Christian healing has traditionally required skills of metacognition. Those looking for spiritual help are often directed to passages of Scripture that require metacognition. This common methodology provides a sense of safety for many Christians as they begin cognitive therapy—safety that promotes a healing, therapeutic atmosphere. Consider the following examples of familiar Scripture passages emphasizing metacognition.

Do not conform any longer to the pattern of this world, but be transformed by the renewing of your mind. Then you will be able to test and approve, what God's will is—his good, pleasing and perfect will. (Rom. 12:2)

The idea of renewing our minds requires us to understand our thoughts and feelings and examine them critically in the light of Scripture and Christian theology. The context of this passage (see Romans 12:1) suggests it is our Christian obligation, an act of worship, to renew our minds. As a result, many Christians are experienced introspectors. Some are skilled at analyzing their thoughts and looking for alternative ways of thinking, while others introspect but come to inflexible or unreasonable conclusions.

Finally, brothers, whatever is true, whatever is noble, whatever is right, whatever is pure, whatever is lovely, whatever is admirable—if anything is excellent or praiseworthy—think about such things. (Phil. 4:8)

In the context of describing peace and joy, the apostle Paul clearly emphasizes thinking about thinking. He admonishes his readers to seek pure, correct thoughts. This same connection between thoughts and feelings is suggested by cognitive therapists. Dysfunctional, inflexible thinking leads to negative feelings; accurate, true thinking leads to peace.

Do not think that I have come to abolish the Law or the Prophets; I have not come to abolish them but to fulfill them. I tell you the truth, until heaven and earth disappear, not the smallest letter, not the least stroke of a pen, will by any means disappear from the Law until everything is accomplished. Anyone who breaks one of the least of these commandments and teaches others to do the same will be called least in the kingdom of heaven, but whoever practices and teaches these commands will be called great in the kingdom of heaven. For I tell you that unless your righteousness surpasses that of the Pharisees and the teachers of the law, you will certainly not enter the kingdom of heaven.

·You have heard that it was said to the people long ago, "Do not murder, and anyone who murders will be subject to judgment." But I tell you that anyone who is angry with his brother will be subject to judgment. Again, anyone who says to his brother, "Raca," is answerable to the Sanhedrin. But anyone who says, "You fool!" will be in danger of the fire of hell.

Therefore, if you are offering your gift at the altar and there remember that your brother has something against you, leave your gift there in front of the altar. First go and be reconciled to your brother; then come and offer your gift.

Settle matters quickly with your adversary who is taking you to court. Do it while you are still with him on the way, or he may hand you over to the judge, and the judge may hand you over to the officer, and you may be thrown into prison. I tell you the truth, you will not get out until you have paid the last penny.

You have heard that it was said, "Do not commit adultery." But I tell you that anyone who looks at a woman lustfully has already committed adultery with her in his heart. If your right eye causes you to sin, gouge it out and throw it away. It is better for you to lose one part of your body than for your whole body to be thrown into hell. And if your right hand causes you sin, cut it off and throw it away. It is better for you to lose one part of your body than for your whole body to go into hell. (Matt. 5:17–30)

Jesus came to fulfill the law and in the process, he helped his listeners better understand sin. In his Sermon on the Mount, Jesus taught that murder and adultery result from malignant thoughts. While it may be hyperbole to say that thoughts are as evil as actions, it demonstrates that thoughts are powerful forces that need to be controlled.

These examples demonstrate ways Christians learn about metacognition. When they come for counseling, many of them are already familiar with thinking about thoughts. As a cognitive therapist explains the road map for counseling, Christian clients are put at ease by the emphasis on thoughts— an emphasis with which they are familiar. As their comfort grows into feelings of safety and trust, it enhances the healing environment.

Healing Factor 3: Support for Religious Beliefs

Christian counselors routinely hear horror stories about other therapists who tell their clients they must give up their religious beliefs in order to be well. Psychotherapist Albert Ellis, for example, has suggested the concept of sin causes virtually all psychopathology.[5] And psychologist Gary Walls has implied that religious beliefs are not carefully reasoned and that counselors should help their clients develop better reasoning.[6] However, empirical studies suggest that these claims are inaccurate.[7]

When counselors discredit clients' beliefs, clients often feel unnecessarily threatened and defensive. In study with middle-aged adults, potential clients found religiously sensitive counselors more trustworthy, likable, and approachable than agnostic or atheistic counselors.[8] In one survey, 79 percent of respondents selected from a phone book believed religious values were important to discuss in therapy and over half of the respondents preferred to seek therapy at a pastoral counseling center.[9]

Constructing a healing environment requires the counselor to work sensitively with clients' religious values. Feelings of security are unlikely to develop if the counselor requires clients to give up beliefs they cherish. Cognitive therapy is well suited for working within the client's religious framework, because it involves collaborative experiments rather than direct confrontation.

If a client believes good Christians are not attracted to members of the opposite sex (except the spouse), one approach would be to directly confront the belief. A therapist might say, "Even Christians find others attractive." This might be received well by the client or it might be threatening, depending on the strength of the original belief. Another approach, one cognitive therapists would be likely to try, is to collaborate with the client to evaluate the belief. "You feel it is wrong to find others attractive. Could we set up an experiment to test your belief?" The experiment might include interviewing a pastor or another respected Christian leader. The client becomes responsible for altering religious beliefs and doesn't feel threatened by the counselor's differing beliefs.

As counselor and client work together to establish a safe, trusting environment, a place for healing is created. When Christians are involved, the place of healing can include an open consideration of religious values, Scripture, and prayer. Although I have focused on the benefits of cognitive therapy, many forms of Christian counseling create such a place where healing can occur.

A Place to Pursue Truth above Happiness

The following conversation is familiar to counselors.

COUNSELOR: What would you like to see happen as a result of counseling?

CLIENT: I just want to feel happy.

COUNSELOR: Happy?

CLIENT: Yeah. I just want to be happy like other people are.

Happiness is pleasant but elusive. Often those who vigorously pursue happiness are the ones feeling the most unhappy. Some pursue happiness through extramarital affairs, but they produce an unhappy existence for themselves with broken promises, broken children, and broken dreams. Some pursue happiness through consumerism and materialism. During the past three decades, an increasing number of college freshman report that making a lot of money is an important life goal while a decreasing number see gaining a meaningful philosophy of life as important. However, while personal income has consistently increased, the percentage of Americans who report being very happy hovers around 30 percent.[10] Prosperity doesn't make people happy. After interviewing two hundred Americans, sociologist Robert Bellah and his colleagues concluded, "few have found a life devoted to 'personal ambition and consumerism' satisfactory, and most are seeking in one way or another to transcend the limitations of a self-centered life."[11]

Happiness is slippery. Those who seek it watch it ooze through their fingers as their hands become empty. In contrast, those who seek purpose and meaning and truth often find happiness, too. The apostle Paul does not instruct the Philippians to set their minds on whatever makes them happy, but on whatever is true and right. Then he instructs them to live obediently, concluding, "And the God of peace will be with you" (Phil. 4:9).

In his book, *Effective Biblical Counseling*, Dr. Larry Crabb comes to a similar conclusion. He writes:

Many of us place top priority not on becoming Christ-like in the middle of our problems but on finding happiness. I want to be happy but the paradoxical truth is that I will never be happy if I am concerned primarily with becoming happy. My overriding goal must be in every circumstance to respond biblically, to put the Lord first, to seek to behave as He would want me to. The wonderful truth is that as we devote all our energies to the task of becoming what Christ wants us to be, He fills us with joy unspeakable and a peace far surpassing what the world offers.[12]

Christian counselors help their clients look beyond happiness or symptom relief to seek truth. Cognitive therapy and Christianity blend nicely as counselors seek to move their clients beyond a futile search for happiness.

Truth-Seeking Factor 1: Critical Thinking

Cognitive therapy assumes emotions stem from personal beliefs about events in the world. Thus, accurate, critical, flexible thinking is the key to changing unwanted feelings.[13] The cognitive therapy model works well for counselors who want to emphasize truth-seeking above happiness-seeking, because teaching critical thinking skills is an essential part of treatment. Clients repeatedly confront the truthfulness of their thoughts and beliefs in cognitive therapy. The following conversation reflects this truth-seeking emphasis.

CLIENT: I'm so tired of him [husband] never appreciating me. I do so much for him and he just does whatever he wants. I just don't think I can stand it any more.

COUNSELOR: You're saying to yourself, "I just can't take this anymore." I'm wondering if that's true.

CLIENT: Well, I can take it. I mean I have been for twelve years. But I don't like it and it's driving me crazy!

COUNSELOR: Crazy?

CLIENT: Not literally, but I sure am tired of doing things for him and not getting any appreciation.

COUNSELOR: Does it feel different when you say, as you did a minute ago, "I can't stand this any more," than it does when you say, "I'm getting tired of this."

CLIENT: A little. I suppose I can stand it, but I am tired.

COUNSELOR: That's good. Now let's go back a minute. You also said your husband never appreciates you. Tell me about that.

CLIENT: I see what you're getting at. He has been nice to me lately, but there are so many things he forgets. I have asked him hundreds of times to put his dishes in the dishwasher after breakfast, but he still puts them on the counter.

COUNSELOR: I see. So another way to say it would be that he has some troubling habits and he forgets some things easily, but he shows appreciation sometimes.

CLIENT: Yes. That's what I mean.

This conversation demonstrates the centrality of truth-seeking in cognitive therapy. This client's initial assumptions were based on happiness-seeking: "If I can't be happy in my marriage, then I can't stand it." When she believed her husband was never appreciative and that she could no longer stand her marriage, her only options were to leave her husband or to feel miserable. But as she looked at the situation more accurately, she realized she could survive with her husband, although some of his behavior was disappointing. Once she accepted the option of working on the relationship, she critically examined her confusion between submissiveness and passivity, learned to assertively express her feelings, and convinced her husband to come with her for marital therapy. Seeking short-sighted happiness by leaving the marriage would have resulted in a painful child-custody battle and feelings of loneliness, despair, and guilt.

Truth-Seeking Factor 2: Models in Scripture

Christian counselors attempting to create a truth-seeking atmosphere in therapy can point to examples in Scripture when godly men and women altered their beliefs and obeyed, sometimes sacrificing happiness to do so. Throughout the Bible, God's people stood firm in the midst of tribulation because they were committed to godliness through truthful and productive thinking.

- Abraham chose to believe God's promise of a child though it seemed impossible.

- Job survived crises and resisted his friends' conclusions that his troubles were caused by sin.

- Daniel obediently prayed, though he knew he could be punished with death in the lions' den.

- David thought of God's power rather than Goliath's size.

- Hosea chose to forgive Gomer's unfaithfulness, overcoming his anger.

- The apostle Paul sought obedience above personal safety.

These examples demonstrate independent, critical thinking in the midst of danger or emotional pain. It is useful in cognitive therapy with Christian clients to speculate on the thought processes that were involved. Consider the following example.

COUNSELOR: You're facing a tough situation, feeling committed to your marriage, but finding yourself attracted to your co-worker. And he seems to be interested in you, too. What kind of thoughts are going through your mind as you describe this situation?

CLIENT: I feel helpless. I'm happily married but I don't know how long I can resist this temptation. It's like there's a war going on inside. It seems impossible to resist.

COUNSELOR: You use the word "impossible." And your situation feels impossible to you at times, I'm sure. I was thinking of Job in the Old Testament. What do you suppose went through his mind after he lost his children and his property?

CLIENT: That was even worse. I imagine he thought he could never survive. He did, though. I get it. You think I can survive this, too.

COUNSELOR: Yeah. And when it was all over, Job said to God, "I know that you can do all things." I'm not suggesting this will be easy. I'm just questioning the word "impossible."

CLIENT: I see what you mean.

In this example, Job's story is used to help dispel the belief that the client's temptation is too strong to bear. Although temptations sometimes feel overwhelming, Scripture gives examples of those who have stood firm in the midst of monumental hardships. Because counseling is not a place for preaching, Scripture is best used cautiously in a collaborative way rather than in a prescriptive or condescending way. The story of Job is a better choice in this case than quoting 1 Corinthians 10:13, "No temptation has seized you except what is common to man . . . ," because the Job story allows the client to collaborate in understanding the thought processes involved.

Many other examples in Scripture produce useful discussions of truth-seeking in counseling. Cognitive therapists who weave the examples into discussions of clients' thoughts help produce an environment where truth is valued more than happiness.

A Place to Be Authentic

A Christian counselor's office is also a place for authenticity. Because we show our best selves to one another, church attenders sometimes assume the church is filled with flawless saints, or at least those who see themselves as flawless. As a result, church congregations are not a likely place to admit weaknesses. Those wanting to authentically discuss temptations, fears, or doubts often end up talking with Christian counselors.

In an earlier book, *Your Hidden Half*,[14] I described how authenticity is hindered by two categories of impulse, which I call *dark side* and *glossy side*. The dark side is comprised of our pleasure-seeking impulses and the glossy side is made up of our impulses to appear perfect to others. Glossy side and dark side are synergistic—that is, they are much worse together than either would be alone.

This synergistic effect is shown in Figure 3–1. All Christians experience temptations. Most Christians believe temptation is not sin. Even Jesus experienced temptation. But those same Christians who rationally believe temptation is not sin often feel the emotions of guilt. Their glossy side says, *The best Christians are the ones who aren't tempted*, or, *You are a weak Christian if you have those desires!* It may be that most Christians face the same temptations from time to time, but since we don't talk about our temptations openly, we each feel alone and weak when we are tempted. This is *irrational guilt*, guilt based on faulty thinking rather than violating God's moral law. But once a person already feels guilty for temptation, it is not a big step to go ahead and sin. The dark side reasons, *As long as I'm already feeling guilty, I might as well enjoy myself.* By analogy, once dieters go off their diet, they show less restraint in eating than those who are not dieting.[15] Once sin has occurred, the person feels confirmed guilt as the glossy side reasons, *I knew I was weak; others would never sin like I do.* In looking for ways to prevent future sin, people often resort to self-deprivation. But temptation comes anyway, and the cycle begins again.

The Vicious Cycle of Dark-Side and Glossy-Side Impulses

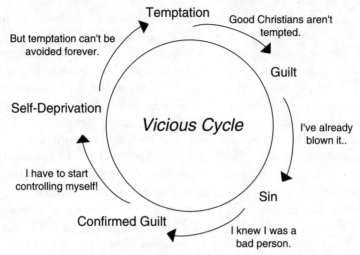

Fig. 3–1

In order to interrupt this vicious cycle, we need to compare our irrational guilt feelings with Scripture. If we have violated a moral law, then guilt can be our friend—guiding us to repentance and correction. But if the guilt is irrational it is our enemy—guiding us to self-condemnation and greater temptation. In cognitive therapy, clients can examine their beliefs with Scripture and come to a rational evaluation of their guilt.

Another way to interrupt the cycle is to authentically discuss temptation with other Christians so the irrational guilt can be managed. Knowing that others face similar temptations and being reminded that temptation is not sin helps break the vicious cycle created by the dark-side and glossy-side impulses, and allows people to live authentic lives before God and others. Cognitive therapy provides benefits for counselors wanting to create this atmosphere of authenticity for their clients.

Authenticity Factor 1: Fighting "Shoulds," "Musts," and "Oughts"

Christians often come for counseling with a rigid set of personal rules. Cognitive therapists help their clients develop a different vocabulary to eliminate the unnecessary pressure of "shoulds," "oughts," and "musts." The client whose self-talk is, *I must be friendly to everyone I know*, finds it freeing to say instead, *It would be nice to be friendly to many different people*. Since glossy-side impulses—shoulds, musts, and oughts—inhibit authenticity, cognitive therapists can free clients from unrealistic

45

expectations by helping them understand and revise unnecessary demands they place on themselves.

I had one Christian client write down the reasons she believed herself to be a bad person. She returned with a detailed list of glossy-side impulses. She was a bad person because she didn't read her Bible or pray as much as she should. She was grumpy with her husband sometimes and didn't always want to have sex when he did. Her house wasn't always clean. She overused her credit card. She sometimes found men other than her husband attractive. Years earlier, when she babysat as a high schooler, she sometimes took food from the families' cupboards without telling anyone about it. These shoulds convinced her of her worthlessness before God and others. Not surprisingly, she did not feel authentic because she felt a continual need to hide her real self from others, even those close to her. She feared their rejection if they knew what she was really like. As she learned to revise her self-talk, her glossy-side impulses lessened and she gained more control over her emotions and behavior.

As Christian counselors, we need to be prudent about taking away shoulds, musts and oughts. Many of these are irrational impulses, but some clients depend on these ineffective impulses for self-control. Taking away ineffective self-control mechanisms does not mean the client will automatically develop effective means of self-control. Psychotherapist S. R. Graham noted the same problem:

> Quite early in the treatment process, the patient begins to use words like good and bad, and it is our tendency as therapists to diminish the intensity of these words since they relate to a value system within the individual which has led to the current state of stress. My own personal view of the last thirty years of psychotherapy is that we have collectively done an excellent job of diminishing the demonstration of good and bad and a very poor job of replacing these concepts with acceptable definitions which allow the individual self-acceptance and peace.[16]

It is not enough to remove "shoulds," "oughts," and "musts." We need to help our clients replace these glossy-side constraints with more effective rational constraints. Otherwise we encourage authenticity at the cost of Christian obedience. Strategies for removing unnecessary self-demands while giving new strategies of self-control will be discussed in later chapters.

Authenticity Factor 2: Psychology and Grace

Christian counselors can also promote authenticity by emphasizing God's grace as they teach clients to think in increasingly flexible ways. When the apostle Paul was struggling with dark-side and glossy-side impulses in Romans 7, he concluded that God's grace addresses the problem: "Therefore, there is now no condemnation for those who are in Christ Jesus, because through Christ Jesus the law of the Spirit of life set me free from the law of sin and death" (Rom. 8:1, 2). And when Paul struggled with his "thorn in the flesh," which many scholars take to mean temptation, he was reminded that God's grace was sufficient for him (see 2 Corinthians 12:7–10).

Grace paves the way for authenticity. The one who reasons, *If people really knew me they would never love me,* develops inauthentic ways of dealing with others for purposes of self-protection. God's message of grace is the opposite: "I love you regardless of your performance."

> But when the kindness and love of God our Savior appeared, he saved us, not because of righteous things we had done, but because of his mercy. He saved us through the washing of rebirth and renewal by the Holy Spirit, whom he poured out on us generously through Jesus Christ our Savior, so that, having been justified by his grace, we might become heirs having the hope of eternal life. (Titus 3:4–7)

Once people feel loved, they are more willing to be authentic because their acceptability is no longer at stake.

Christian counselors are faced with the task of helping their clients feel God's love. Pastor David Seamands, in *Healing for Damaged Emotions*, writes: "We read, we hear, we believe a good theology of grace. But that's not the way we live. We believe grace in our heads but not in our gut-level feelings or in our relationships."[17] Counselors who help others understand God's grace in their "gut-level feelings" and in their relationships unlock their clients from prisons of self-doubt, inadequacy, and shame, freeing them to live authentically.

POTENTIAL OBSTACLES

In addition to these seven benefits of using cognitive therapy techniques in Christian counseling, there are some potential obstacles to combining the two.[18] Christian counselors do well to anticipate these problems and avoid them by using collaboration rather than confrontation.

Albert Ellis, founder of rational-emotive therapy, openly disputes faulty beliefs with his clients.[19] Imagine the following conversation:

CLIENT: I can't believe I yelled at my kids again. I keep thinking a good person—a good Christian—wouldn't lose control like that.

COUNSELOR: You're telling yourself you're no good because you yelled at your kids. What does yelling have to do with your worth?

CLIENT: Because most people don't do that kind of thing—so I feel worthless.

COUNSELOR: You're using *musts* and *shoulds*, like you've done something awful by yelling at your kids and that you're worthless because of it. That doesn't make sense. You're making yourself feel bad by the things you're choosing to believe.

For many clients, this confrontive style is too threatening. Psychiatrist Aaron Beck and psychologist Donald Meichenbaum prefer collaborating with the client to test their faulty beliefs.[20] This is a better alternative in most cases.

CLIENT: I can't believe I yelled at my kids again. I keep thinking a good person—a good Christian—wouldn't lose control like that.

COUNSELOR: You're telling yourself you're no good because you yelled at your kids. What kind of evidence do you have for connecting your worth with your parenting?

CLIENT: Because most people don't do that kind of thing—I feel worthless.

COUNSELOR: I see. You believe most people don't yell at their children from time to time. That belief leads to feelings of worthlessness. I wonder if it's accurate—that most people don't yell at their children. Can you think of any way we could test that idea?

This collaborative approach allows clients to challenge their own beliefs at their own pace and often results in less defensiveness. Collaboration is an effective way to deal with the obstacles described here.

Obstacle 1: Self-Interest and Self-Direction

In an essay entitled, "The Case Against Religion," Albert Ellis asserted that self-interest and self-direction are qualities of emotionally healthy individuals. Because religious clients have neither, according to Ellis, they are not emotionally healthy.[21]

Ellis is correct that Christian clients are concerned about excessive self-interest. The Bible teaches, "Whoever finds his life will lose it, and whoever loses his life for my sake will find it" (Matt. 10:39); and, "But whatever was to my profit I now consider loss for the sake of Christ" (Phil. 3:7). Many Christians see self-sacrifice as a higher calling than self-interest.

Although self-sacrifice is valued among Christians, Ellis's conclusion that religious people are emotionally unhealthy is not justified. Self-interest and self-sacrifice are not mutually exclusive—Ellis is guilty of categorical thinking in assuming they are. Despite the emphasis on self-sacrifice, religious individuals report having at least as much control over their thoughts and behaviors as nonreligious people.[22] Cognitive therapists need not make religious clients more self-interested.

Some Christian clients, however, have misunderstood self-sacrifice. They feel they must meet all the needs of others and ignore their own needs, and they end up resenting the things they do for others. These irrational ideas need to be evaluated in cognitive counseling. Self-interest and self-sacrifice need to be balanced.

Using confrontation to get a Christian client to become more self-interested and self-directed often produces resistance, especially since Christian clients often come to counseling fearing their values will be attacked.[23] Collaboration with clients more effectively helps them balance self-interest with self-sacrifice. In the process of interviewing friends, pastors, and other Christian leaders, reading the Bible, and praying, many Christians are able to distinguish between voluntary self-sacrifice and the acquiescing that leads to resentment.

Obstacle 2: Rigid Thinking

Cognitive therapists try to change clients' inflexible, rigid thinking. To some extent, this is appropriate for Christian clients since those who are depressed often have unrealistic perfection demands and illogical beliefs,[24] and since effective treatment for Christians often requires examination of their perfectionistic tendencies.[25] But cognitive therapists are guilty of categorical thinking if they assume all rigid thinking is inappropriate. Perhaps it is rigid to believe in the authority of Scripture, the virgin birth, the deity of Christ, or the second coming, but these are central aspects of the Christian faith. When cognitive therapists challenge beliefs central to Christianity, they are likely to face resistance from Christian clients.

Which beliefs are central to Christianity and which are not? Some believe that women are to be submissive to men and hold this belief as a central doctrine of their faith. Others disagree, emphasizing the equality of all people before God. Some believe the rapture will occur before the tribulation, while others insist it will be during or after the tribulation. One client told me the Bible taught that men and women should not be friends unless they are married. Another believed depression is a sin. Are these beliefs central to the faith?

Rather than the therapist determining which beliefs are central and which are not, client and therapist can collaborate to evaluate the necessity of various beliefs. For example, one client's depression seemed directly connected to her beliefs that she was an inadequate Christian. Rather than overtly disputing the belief, I encouraged her to keep track of the internal script she used while sitting in church. Her pastor, who was apparently quite negative and critical in most sermons, evoked many self-statements in her. She told herself, *Other Christians are more committed than I*, and *If I were really a Christian I would do more things for the church*, and so on. We then used Scripture to evaluate the beliefs she had during the sermons and found they were unnecessary. In her new internal script, she challenged the words of her pastor rather than automatically feeling guilty for her inadequacy. She learned the healthier script quickly, generalized it to other self-statements, and showed significant gains in therapy. The key was collaborating in evaluating her self-talk rather than immediately confronting it as irrational.

Some rigid thinking needs to be changed and some needs to be respected. Allowing clients to help determine which beliefs need changing is an important strategy for counselors.

Obstacle 3: Need for Philosophical Change

Albert Ellis suggests that cognitive therapies need to help clients with meaningful philosophical changes in their thinking.[26] He advocates atheistic-humanistic values to his clients.[27]

Because the goal is to change underlying beliefs about the world, clients often leave cognitive therapy with a new set of assumptions about themselves, others, and God. If these values are transferred without respect for Christian convictions, clients' values can be undermined. "There has always been a danger that the rational or cognitive therapies have underplayed the role played by values in the urge to stress the importance of rationality and logic." [28]

The goal of cognitive therapy is to implement philosophical changes in the way clients view their world. However, Ellis's assumptions that religious beliefs need to be changed is not consistent with the goals of pastoral or Christian counseling,[29] nor does it seem reasonable when one considers the many emotionally well-adjusted Christians in our world. Again, collaboration is important in establishing with the client which beliefs need to be changed to reach emotional and spiritual health.

These obstacles require Christian counselors to sensitively collaborate with their clients in designing effective treatments. Cognitive therapy has been effective in treating religious clients,[30] and there are many benefits of using cognitive techniques in Christian counseling.

PART II

THE PROCESS OF COGNITIVE THERAPY

CHAPTER FOUR

THE FIRST INTERVIEW

A PARENT PROTECTIVELY CRADLING A NEWBORN infant knows the importance of good beginnings. So does a pitcher facing the batters of the first inning. Beginnings also are important to preachers or authors who work to find an engaging way of introducing their topics. Even how to begin a new day seems important, as illustrated when we accuse someone of "getting up on the wrong side of the bed."

Beginnings are important in counseling, too. After the first interview, clients leave with an impression of their counselor, what will happen in therapy, and whether they made a good decision to seek counseling. They come feeling hopeless and want to leave feeling hope.

OBJECTIVES OF THE FIRST INTERVIEW

An ideal first interview produces necessary information for the counselor, provides a therapeutic atmosphere for the client, and plots a road map for counselor and client to follow in subsequent sessions. These factors combine to give the client hope.

Gathering Information

Collecting *all* relevant information about the client in the first interview is impossible, but it is important to gather enough to understand the client's current situation. By the end of the first interview, a cognitive counselor should know several bits of essential information.

First, the counselor needs to assess the client's definition of the problem. Although this definition may include distorted ideas or faulty assumptions, it is important to listen carefully and actively to understand the stated problem before questioning any dysfunctional thinking.

Second, the counselor needs to know current symptoms to understand the underlying cause. For example, Doug's description of his problems focused on his poor marriage. But as we discussed symptoms, it became clear that he was depressed. He woke early each morning, had a poor appetite, could not concentrate as well as usual, was irritable, and found little hope in the future. My hunch, which was confirmed in subsequent sessions, was that Doug's marriage seemed bad to him because of his depression. Once he felt better himself, his marriage seemed better, too.

Third, the counselor needs to understand the client's present life situation. What physical problems does he or she have? How long has it been since the last physical exam? Is the client married? Have there been previous marriages? Are children living in the home? How are the children doing in school? What kind of job stress does the person have? What are the client's religious values? As the client describes his or her life situation, a cognitive counselor listens for the typical ways of thinking, as well as for pertinent demographic information. The client who reports, "I'm married, but I might as well not be since my husband only lives for himself," has not only revealed her marital status, but also her propensity toward overgeneralizing, a cognitive distortion discussed in chapter 6.

Fourth, the counselor needs to assess the client's attitudes toward and motivation for treatment. "I'm here because my mom said I had to come," demonstrates an indifference toward counseling. "I've heard such good things about you, I know you can help me," shows a more positive attitude toward counseling but also some delusions of omniscience that need to be dispelled. The statement, "You're my last chance," communicates hopelessness and feelings of desperation, as well as motivation.

An Atmosphere of Collaboration

The most efficient way to collect all this information about a new client might be to interrogate him or her. But the question-answer approach creates problems for the cognitive therapist for two reasons. First, many clients feel defensive in response to a series of questions. They may leave the counselor's office feeling they have been cross-examined or treated like a subject in an experiment. Second, the question-answer approach creates a power differential the cognitive therapist does not want. From the beginning session, cognitive counseling is collaborative—client and counselor work together to find new ways of thinking and coping. The client needs to take responsibility for getting better, but if the counselor takes over the session by asking all the questions, the client easily avoids responsibility by assuming the counselor will find and apply the proper treatment.

Counselors can collect necessary information by using open-ended statements instead of questions, enhancing the collaborative atmosphere. Consider the following alternatives to questions.

QUESTION: How long have you felt depressed?
STATEMENT: Tell me about the time these feelings began.

QUESTION: How many children do you have?
STATEMENT: I'd like to know about your family.

QUESTION: What brings on your anger?
STATEMENT: It might be good for us to talk about the triggers—the things that bring on your anger.

Some questions are necessary and refreshingly direct, but too many questions can produce feelings of defensiveness and powerlessness in the client.

Reflection is the least threatening way to gather information; it simply mirrors back to the client what was just said while prompting more information. The following dialogue shows how a counselor can use reflection to gather information.

CLIENT: I felt so tense last night. I couldn't get to sleep for several hours, just worrying about my job. When I mentioned it to my wife, she told me not to worry, that it would all be okay; but it's not that easy.

COUNSELOR: Your job seems to be a source for your anxiety.

CLIENT: Yeah. Things are crazy there. I have a new boss just out of college and I'm not sure I can do all the things she expects from me.

COUNSELOR: You're feeling overwhelmed.

CLIENT: Exactly. She's an excellent supervisor, and she tells me I'm doing great, but she has high expectations for me.

COUNSELOR: I see. A while ago you mentioned your wife.

CLIENT: Yes. I've been married for ten years. Kathy is a big support for me. She's calm when I get uptight.

A good rule of thumb is to use as many reflections and as few questions as possible to create a collaborative atmosphere.

I have found that avoiding titles—"Doctor," "Pastor," "Ms.," or "Mr."—and having clients use my first name helps prevent a power differential that sometimes disrupts the collaborative atmosphere. Occasionally I use titles if the client seems particularly manipulative or behaves in controlling or seductive ways, but first names create a better sense of teamwork between counselor and client.

A Sense of Direction

The first interview helps the counselor understand the client, but also helps the client understand the counselor's work. The counselor's road map, as discussed in chapter 1, gives the client hope. Clients often have tried virtually everything they can think of to feel better before coming to a counselor. They are often skeptics—what can this counselor do for me that I haven't already tried? This question needs to be answered during the first session. The counselor who outlines a plan of treatment instills hope in clients. Specific ways to introduce cognitive therapy will be discussed in more detail later in this chapter.

Counselors also have an opportunity to demonstrate their counseling style in the first session. Clients have questions as they come for the first session: Can I trust this counselor? Will this person be caring and friendly? Will I have to tell this counselor everything about myself? Counselors who promote trust and a sense of safety with careful listening, gentleness, and genuine concern inspire confidence in their clients. When a counselor's listening and caring are combined with insightful understanding of the client's problem and a road map for improvement, the client leaves the first session feeling hope.

Words for the First Interview

The words counselors hear and use in the first interview and in subsequent sessions are their tools for creating a healing environment. So hearing and choosing words carefully is important. But we also are wise to remember that words are imperfect symbols and that human pain or victory can never adequately be reduced to words. Poet Ed Higgins expresses both the necessity and inadequacy of words with this poem:

Logos

> Listen,
> > words are slippery things
> > (ice slippery)
> > and they are never truth;
> > only the cold flecks
> > that cling to numb fingers.
> > We try, but words freeze
> > and fall from the tongue,
> > shattering into
> > near truth only.

> Listen,
> > come behind the words
> > where I crouch like
> > a masked goalie,
> > armed and padded
> > against you.
> > You must here
> > behind the words
> > to catch me off guard—
> > to score any goals.

> Listen,
>> we are going to have
>> to use words
>> to overcome this problem,
>> but we must never
>> mistake the words
>> for the goal.
>
> Listen,
>> come behind the words.[1]

Clients come to a first interview trying to use words to express their feelings of hopelessness, despair, anger, anxiety, or fear. They use words to express their wishes, fantasies, and ideas, and feel frustrated that those words cannot adequately capture the experiences they have. Because words are imperfect, counselors need to use their empathy skills to look beyond their clients' words.

Effective counselors are caring people who have developed good listening and talking skills through reading books and attending lectures on how to use and listen for words to communicate with and understand their clients. But communication skills are not sufficient by themselves, because caring—human compassion—is an essential ingredient in the helping process that cannot be taught in a classroom or from a textbook. Words are important, but they can never replace human compassion.

Despite the inadequacy of words, we are still left with the reality that they are the counselors' tools. Thus, the specific words chosen in the first interview are important.

Opening Statement

The first words between counselor and client begin the cognitive therapy process, so an immediate focus on thoughts and feelings is appropriate.[2] For example, the counselor might begin with, "Tell me how you're feeling about being here today." This statement immediately focuses the session on the client's feelings and helps creates an informal, collaborative environment. If the client describes feelings of anxiety or fear, then the accompanying thoughts can also be explored. The following dialogue illustrates this process.

COUNSELOR: Tell me some of your feelings about being here today.

CLIENT: I'm glad to finally be getting some help, but I feel kind of nervous. I've never done this before.

COUNSELOR: Those feelings of nervousness are pretty common for a first visit. As you were sitting in the waiting room, what kind of thoughts were going through your mind?

CLIENT: I don't know. I was just thinking about how someone I know might walk in and see me at a counselor's office.

COUNSELOR: I see. So you were saying to yourself, "It would be embarrassing if I saw someone I knew here."

CLIENT: Yeah. I know that's stupid, but I feel that way sometimes.

COUNSELOR: Stupid?

CLIENT: Well, you know. Lots of people get counseling. It's not a sign of weakness or anything. At least that's what my wife keeps telling me.

COUNSELOR: I agree with you there. At first you were saying, "I hope no one sees me here because they might think I'm weak," and you felt nervous. Now you're saying, "Lots of people get counseling—it's not a sign of weakness." How do you feel now?

CLIENT: Fine.

COUNSELOR: It's interesting, isn't it? When you tell yourself one thing, you feel nervous. When you tell yourself something else, you feel fine.

This example illustrates how quickly the principles of cognitive therapy can be introduced into the session while establishing a collaborative, informal atmosphere. Even without specifically asking, the therapist has drawn out some information to pursue. The client is married, his wife seems to support his seeking counseling, he may place a lot of importance on others' opinions of him, and it's his first counseling experience. All these leads can be pursued later in the interview.

Other possibilities for beginning a session in a collaborative way are:

- Tell me how you're feeling about being here today.
- How are you feeling about being here today?
- As you see it, what brings you here today?
- Tell me some of the things that have led up to your coming here today.
- Let's begin by discussing how I can be of help.

Reflecting Self-talk

Cognitive counselors use reflections, as all counselors do, but they customize those reflections to emphasize the importance of self-talk. Consider the following two examples, the first common to any counseling style, and the second common to cognitive therapy.

Example 1: Reflection only
CLIENT: I feel so frustrated. No one at work recognizes how many hours I put in. They just think I waste my time or something. If they knew how hard I worked they wouldn't complain about my making a little mistake now and then.

COUNSELOR: You feel misunderstood.

Example 2: Reflection plus emphasis on self-talk
COUNSELOR: You're feeling misunderstood, saying to yourself, "No one understands how hard I work."

While both reflections communicate understanding and empathy, the second emphasizes self-talk, creating opportunity for discussing how thoughts contribute to feelings. In this example, the counselor could next explore with the client the accuracy of the self-talk.

CLIENT: I feel so frustrated. No one at work recognizes how many hours I put in. They just think I waste my time or something. If they knew how hard I worked they wouldn't complain about my making a little mistake now and then.

COUNSELOR: You're feeling misunderstood, saying to yourself, "No one understands how hard I work."

CLIENT: Yeah. Like I'm being judged without a trial.

COUNSELOR: Those are painful feelings you're describing. A few words that you say to yourself stand out to me and I was hoping we could explore them. You said *no one* recognizes how hard you work. I'm wondering if that's what you meant.

CLIENT: Mostly. A few of my colleagues know.

COUNSELOR: I see. So it might be more accurate to say many people don't recognize how hard you work.

By phrasing the reflection as self-talk, the counselor creates an opportunity to evaluate an inaccurate belief while being supportive and empathetic. The client has learned that exaggeration is not necessary to gain the counselor's understanding and that overstatement will be noticed and challenged.

Recalling Past Statements, Predicting Future Words

Empathy can be expressed in reflecting present feelings and self-talk, but it can also be expressed by recalling past statements or predicting words that have not yet been said.

Because cognitive counselors demonstrate the principles of cognitive therapy as they collect information in the first interview, they often need to recall information from an earlier point in the interview. This is an opportunity to communicate sincerity and care as clients realize the counselor has been listening carefully.

COUNSELOR: Tell me some of your feelings about being here today.

CLIENT: I'm glad to finally be getting some help, but I feel kind of nervous. I've never done this before.

(Counseling continues several minutes.)

COUNSELOR: A while ago, as we were discussing your feelings about being here, you said you've never done this before. This must be your first experience with counseling.

CLIENT: Yes, it is. So far, so good.

COUNSELOR: And you mentioned your wife. Tell me about your family.

I find it useful to jot down on a notepad the ideas or words I want to discuss later. This allows me to work with clients on self-talk immediately when they report it and then later return to the other important parts of the response.

Another important form of empathy, called advanced accurate empathy, comes in predicting a client's thoughts or ideas before the client reports them.[3] This helps the counselor be perceived as understanding and experienced, inspiring confidence in the client. Because self-talk points to underlying core beliefs, cognitive counselors are able to use advanced accurate empathy in describing clients' beliefs. This can be seen in the following example:

CLIENT: I feel so frustrated. No one at work recognizes how many hours I put in. They just think I waste my time or something. If they knew how hard I worked they wouldn't complain about my making a little mistake now and then.

COUNSELOR: You're feeling misunderstood, saying to yourself, "No one understands how hard I work."

CLIENT: Yeah. Like I'm being judged without a trial.

COUNSELOR: The opinions others have of you is quite important.

CLIENT: I suppose that's right. I want them to like me.

The final comment the therapist makes in this example illustrates advanced accurate empathy. The self-talk about being misunderstood at work points to a deeper belief that approval from others is essential. In pointing this out, the therapist is being mildly confrontive and empathetic at the same time.

INTRODUCING COGNITIVE THERAPY IN THE FIRST INTERVIEW

As shown by the previous discussion, cognitive therapy principles are woven throughout the first interview. Nonetheless, it is useful to give clients a description of cognitive therapy near the end of the first interview. The following example of describing cognitive therapy, repeated from chapter 1, is brief, specific, focuses on increased control, acknowledges doubt, and gives examples of typical core beliefs.

I want to take a minute and describe to you the kind of therapy I do. It's called cognitive therapy—cognitive because it has to do with changing thoughts. My assumption is that feelings are always related to thoughts. For example, several times today I've heard you say that you have nothing to be depressed about, but that you're depressed anyway. It sounds like you're saying to yourself, "I *shouldn't* be depressed"—like as though you're doing something wrong by having these feelings. Pretty soon you're depressed about being depressed, and it's partially because your thoughts have created those feelings.

I teach people how to think in slightly different ways and, as a result, they experience greater control over their feelings. It may sound too easy because you've probably tried to control those thoughts before. But I will have some different strategies for you to try.

What we will probably find is that underneath the everyday thoughts are some deeper beliefs—I call them core beliefs. For example, some people leave their childhood believing they have to be perfect to be loved, and they can never be perfect, so they get depressed. Others think they have to gain the approval of everyone around, so they get depressed when someone doesn't approve.

There are many other possibilities, but I wanted to mention a couple so you can see where we're headed. Cognitive therapy is a very effective way to treat depression. It takes hard work like any form of counseling, and our work together may take several months; but I would guess that you will start to notice you're feeling better within a few weeks.

Be Brief

Keeping the description brief is important for two reasons. First, clients are focused on their own troubles and will have a hard time concentrating on a long, elaborate discourse. Second, clients do not come for counseling to listen to a counselor describe a therapeutic technique. If the description goes too long, they may feel the time was not well used.

Although it is only a brief part of the first interview, the description of cognitive therapy is important to give clients hope. The description assures the client that the counselor knows what to do and has successfully helped others with similar problems.

Use Specific Examples

Jesus taught in parables because he knew the power of specific examples. Successful public speakers use illustrations and examples to keep their audience's attention. Try looking around at church and notice the increased attentiveness when the pastor begins an illustration or a specific example. The same benefits of specific examples can be seen in counseling—specific examples help clients apply the principles of cognitive therapy to their personal situation.

In describing cognitive therapy, I try to refer to the specific words of my client: "Several times today I've heard you say that you have nothing to be depressed about, but that you're depressed anyway," or, "Last night as you were changing your baby's diaper you were telling yourself your husband was so insensitive that you couldn't stay married to him." By using specific examples, the description of cognitive therapy can be customized to the client's situation.

Counselors easily assume their clients are skilled at generalizing the results of specific discussions in the counseling office to similar situations in life, but most clients are less able to generalize than their counselors assume.[4] Thus, counselors need to discuss a variety of different situations with clients. Perhaps only one or two will be discussed during the first interview, but specific situations fuel cognitive therapy from beginning to end.

Focus on Increased Control

When describing cognitive therapy at the end of the first interview, it is good to emphasize that the client will feel more control over his or her feelings when the counseling is completed. This is more honest than promising happiness, because many people, especially those with significant stress in their lives, function well without being happy. Counselors hope their clients will eventually feel happy, but many times it is an unrealistic goal.

Greater self-control is often what people seek when coming for counseling. They can handle discouragement, but feel it is out of control when they are clinically depressed. They can handle anger, but get concerned when they feel unable to control that anger. They can deal with an imperfect marriage, but seek help once the marriage seems to be uncontrollably crumbling. They are looking for control strategies, which they can learn with cognitive therapy.

Acknowledge Doubts

Because our society is permeated by positive thinking with its simplistic answers and denial, many people feel doubtful about cognitive therapy. They think the counselor is describing a health-and-wealth theology or philosophy that is too simplistic to address the complicated feelings they are experiencing. This superficial understanding of cognitive therapy cannot be dispelled with a few words. Acknowledging the doubt, noting that cognitive therapy requires hard work and persistence, and engaging the client in a trial period of counseling work better than trying to prove the merits of cognitive therapy in the first session.

Experience is the most effective way for clients to deal with their doubts. As the client begins feeling better, he or she will understand cognitive therapy more accurately and begin to distinguish between flexible, accurate thinking and excessively positive or negative thinking.

Describe Typical Core Beliefs

Another way to dispel the belief that cognitive therapy is superficial or simplistic is to mention that the ultimate goal is to find core beliefs that stem from childhood experiences. This helps further distinguish cognitive therapy from positive thinking. Again, be specific. I usually give two or three examples of the beliefs cognitive counselors find in clients with similar symptoms. Because many clients are frustrated in their spiritual lives, it is good to mention that faulty core beliefs disrupt our understanding of God's love. This relieves their guilt feelings for not feeling closer to God. Faulty core beliefs will be discussed in detail in chapters 7 and 8.

A helpful metaphor is describing core beliefs as a small tumor. The tumor forms in childhood and grows throughout life. A superficial counseling approach would be to treat the symptoms, but the tumor would only grow back. In order to completely treat the problem, one must find the tumor and remove it. Instead of a physical tumor, it is an emotional tumor, so it needs to be treated by understanding emotions and thoughts from the present and the past. This metaphor can be referred to throughout the counseling process, especially when the client faces painful memories or monumental challenges. Fighting a tumor is not easy.

Mention Effectiveness

When closing a description of cognitive therapy, a statement of its effectiveness is appropriate. Although it is not necessary to go into detail about psychotherapy-outcome research (as I did in chapter 1), it produces hope to state optimistically that cognitive therapy has demonstrated effectiveness.

In providing an optimistic statement of hope, be prudent. Statements that are overly optimistic or that could be perceived as a promise or guarantee may produce great hope at first but bring disappointment later. Sometimes clients have unrealistic goals of living happily ever after and are disappointed when they find they have greater control over their feelings but are still not always happy. As counselors, we need to be cautious not to promise what we can't deliver. It is equally important not to imply the change will be effortless or extremely quick. Cognitive therapy requires hard work and usually lasts from ten to twenty sessions. This seems brief to counselors who frequently hear of two-year treatments, but it may not seem brief to clients who hoped to be better within two or three sessions. A statement of realistic hope makes a nice closing to an introduction of cognitive therapy.

OVERVIEW OF THE FIRST INTERVIEW

Throughout this chapter, I have discussed important components of the initial interview, but have not yet addressed how the interview can be structured to include these components. Each counselor develops his or her own style of interviewing, and any number of styles can effectively incorporate these ideas. The structure is less important than the content. One possible structure is outlined here, but many others can be used in an effective initial interview.

Before the Session: Gathering Information

Since one objective of the first interview is to gather information, a pre-session information form is often useful in streamlining the process of collecting essential information. These forms are often the client's first impression of the counselor, so they should be easy to follow, concise, and nonthreatening. The form I use is shown in Appendix A. As part of the pre-session information form, ground rules for counseling can be outlined, including session fees, appointment arrangements, and limits of confidentiality. By the time clients meet the counselor, they already have some information about the counseling process, and they have given the counselor information about themselves by reading and completing the forms.

Beginning the Session: Establishing Collaboration

The early part of the interview is the counselor's opportunity to establish an atmosphere of collaboration. It is tempting to think of the first interview as a set of tasks—a time to define the client's problem, determine its severity and generality, and so on. These tasks are important, but it is better to perceive the first interview as relationship-building. There will be more sessions to collect information, but there will never be another opportunity for counselor and client to establish a first impression of one another. Of course, in the process of building a collaborative relationship, some of the necessary information will emerge.

Discussing the client's feelings about being in counseling is one way to build a collaborative relationship. Another way is having the client describe goals for counseling and then working together to refine the goals. Work to establish an informal environment by offering the client coffee or tea, using first names when possible, sitting in similar kinds of chairs without a desk between, and using sensitive humor at times. Although there is a place for silence in counseling, it is good to minimize it in the first session since long periods of silence will be uncomfortable to the client and may heighten the power differential between counselor and client.

Middle of the Session: Giving a Sense of Direction

Although the entire first session is an opportunity to show the client cognitive therapy processes, the middle of the session can be exclusively devoted to this purpose. I distinguish between showing and telling about cognitive therapy. The middle portion of the session is for showing the client how a cognitive therapist works, and the final part of the session includes telling the client a description of cognitive therapy. The description at the end of the session is enriched by the specific examples discussed in the midst of the session.

Showing how cognitive therapy works requires finding a specific incident from the client's life. Imagine the client who is a depressed woman awakening early (as depressed people frequently do) on the day of the first session. She could not go back to sleep, tossing and turning from 3:30 A.M. until she got out of bed at 6:30. This is a specific incident the counselor can use to show cognitive therapy. Asking the client to describe the incident in *slow motion*, focusing on thoughts and feelings, is a useful way to introduce the exercise.

COUNSELOR: Let's go through those three hours in slow motion. I would like to understand your feelings and some of the ideas going through your mind during that time. Let's start right as you awoke at 3:30. Tell me some of the things you were feeling.

CLIENT: Okay. I was frustrated for waking up so early. It happens every night.

COUNSELOR: Frustrated.

CLIENT: Yeah. And I guess kind of nervous. Maybe that wasn't right away. I think I was frustrated at first and then a while later I started thinking about coming here today and got real nervous.

COUNSELOR: I see. At first it was frustration, and later nervousness. Let's look at both of these feelings, starting with frustration. What I would like for you to do is to think about the exact words that went through your head as you awoke. A minute ago you said, "It happens every night." That was one thing going through your mind. What were the others?

CLIENT: Let's see. I thought about how awful it was that I woke up because I knew I could never get back to sleep. And I knew I would be grumpy all day because of being tired.

COUNSELOR: Uh huh. So you told yourself, "I can never get back to sleep," and, "I'll be grumpy all day long." And as you said those things, you felt frustrated. I was just sitting here wondering if the second part of that is true—that you would be grumpy today.

CLIENT: Well, not yet. But give me time.

This specific instance, waking up early in the morning, can be used to show how cognitive therapy works. After exploring her feelings of frustration, the counselor could probe her nervous feelings, still looking for connections between thoughts and feelings.

Ending the Session: Trial Period

After collecting information and showing how cognitive therapy works, I end the first session by describing cognitive therapy and proposing a trial period for counseling. The trial period consists of three sessions plus psychometric testing, including the Beck Depression Inventory and a personality test such as the Minnesota Multiphasic Personality Inventory.[5] There are several advantages of a trial counseling period.

First, the client is not asked to make a long-term commitment to counseling after one interview. Three sessions give the client an opportunity to experience the counselor's style and decide whether it is a safe environment. Asking the client to make an informed decision to commit time to several months of counseling is more reasonable after three sessions than after one.

Second, a trial period gives the counselor an opportunity to assess the client better. Psychometric tests are often helpful in determining personality style and describing current symptoms. During the second session, I have clients describe their early lives so I have an understanding of how their childhood has contributed to their current situation. Based on the three interviews, test results, and an understanding of childhood events, counselors can more accurately predict how long counseling will take. Estimating the duration of counseling also helps clients make an informed choice about participating.

Third, because clients decide whether or not to participate at the end of the third session, they take more ownership of the counseling process. Having them decide helps establish the collaborative relationship a cognitive therapist seeks, and prevents a "doctor-patient" relationship with its imbalance of power and responsibility.

CHAPTER FIVE

FINDING AUTOMATIC THOUGHTS

SOMETIMES THE LITTLE THINGS IN LIFE, like cooking the spaghetti five minutes too long, bring out the strongest feelings. "He shouldn't expect so much from me!" Sheryl sobbed as she angrily described her husband, Bill. After a few seconds of silence, she continued, "He never appreciates what I do. The more I do, the more he expects." By the end of the session, Sheryl realistically admitted that Bill sometimes expressed appreciation, but not as often as she would like. But during those emotional moments in the middle of the session, we had captured her extreme thoughts—just as they had occurred the night before when Bill complained about overcooked spaghetti.

Automatic thoughts are just that—automatic. They are repetitive and seem plausible to the one experiencing them. They visit without invitation

and outstay their welcome. Sheryl's conclusion—that Bill never appreciates her—popped into her mind spontaneously. After she first entertained
the thought, she repeated it to herself many times. *Bill doesn't appreciate me. He has no appreciation for what I do. He never thanks me for my
work. He doesn't appreciate me.* Her thoughts, though extreme, seemed
reasonable as she experienced them. In contrast, more realistic, flexible
thoughts are not automatic or repetitive. And they do not seem plausible
at first, often requiring reflection and hard work to believe. During early
stages of cognitive therapy, counselors help clients find, evaluate, and
revise automatic thoughts, exchanging distorted repetitive thoughts with
those accurate thoughts which require more work to believe.

As a reminder of the cognitive therapy process, the six steps identified in
chapter 1 are repeated below. This chapter suggests techniques for Step 2,
finding automatic thoughts. Chapter 6 gives ideas for Step 3, disputing them.

STEP 1. Identify problem thoughts and feelings
STEP 2. Find dysfunctional automatic thoughts
STEP 3. Help client dispute automatic thoughts
STEP 4. Find underlying core beliefs
STEP 5. Help client dispute core beliefs
STEP 6. Help client maintain gains

Finding and disputing automatic thoughts accomplishes two goals: It
helps generate symptom relief and points the client to deeper core beliefs. Since most clients feel desperate when coming for help, they anxiously
await symptom relief. By identifying and generating alternative automatic
thoughts early in the treatment process, clients feel better within the
first few sessions. As they feel better, they gain confidence in the counseling process and gather momentum to look deep inside themselves for
faulty core beliefs.

Most clients are aware of their automatic thoughts, but their core beliefs lurk beneath the surface of consciousness, requiring detective work
to find. Automatic thoughts provide clues that point to underlying beliefs.
During the first several sessions, Sheryl and I found a pattern of perfectionism in her automatic thoughts. One week she was concerned about
the spaghetti being overcooked, the next week she worried about not
keeping the house clean enough, and the following week, it was having a
relative question her parenting ability. As we pieced together her automatic
thoughts, we gradually understood her deeper beliefs. Her underlying

core belief was that she had to earn love by unusual accomplishment. As a child, she had been repeatedly compared with her older brother: "Why can't you obey like John does?" "You need to keep your room clean like John does!" Approval from others became her way of measuring her lovability, and since no one finds constant approval, she frequently felt unloved and unappreciated. As we revised her beliefs about herself and her lovability before God, Sheryl found peace she had never experienced. When she began counseling she was ready to divorce Bill, but as she understood herself better she was willing to work to make her marriage better. Identifying Sheryl's automatic thoughts provided her with symptom relief and pointed to a faulty core belief which needed to be changed before she experienced lasting change.

Identifying automatic thoughts requires three steps: Identifying specific situations, identifying feelings, and identifying thoughts.

STEP 1: IDENTIFY SPECIFIC SITUATIONS

Before specific thoughts can be elicited, a specific situation must be identified for several reasons. First, general thought patterns cannot be countered or revised as accurately as specific thoughts. Consider the following two examples:

Example 1
COUNSELOR: You mentioned a minute ago that you are anxious all the time. Tell me about the last time you felt anxious.

CLIENT: It's really bad in the mornings. I get up and feel uptight. I can hardly keep my breakfast down.

COUNSELOR: What thoughts run through your mind during your mornings?

CLIENT: I'm not sure. Often I'm rushed to get to work, but I'm also afraid I'm going to get sick and throw up.

Example 2
COUNSELOR: You mentioned a minute ago that you are anxious all the time. Tell me about the last time you felt anxious.

CLIENT: It's really bad in the mornings. I get up and feel uptight. I can hardly keep my breakfast down.

74

COUNSELOR: I see. How about this morning?

CLIENT: Yeah. It was bad again. I felt really tense after I got out of the shower.

COUNSELOR: What time was that?

CLIENT: About 6:30.

COUNSELOR: Okay. So you were just getting out of the shower, about 6:30 this morning, getting dressed I suppose.

CLIENT: Yeah. I was trying to decide what to wear. And as I was looking in the closet I just started feeling sick—like I might throw up or something.

The counselor in the first example does not adequately specify the situation. Thus, the client only gives general feelings and thoughts that occur some mornings. In the second example, the counselor specifies a particular day, time, and activity that allows the client to remember specific feelings and thoughts.

A second reason to identify specific situations is to break categorical thinking. Clients tend to think in dichotomous, all-or-none terms, distracting them from flexible, accurate thinking. If the counselor settles for a general situation, he or she encourages categorical thinking. In example 1, the counselor encourages categorical thinking by accepting the assumption that every morning is filled with anxiety. Actually, many mornings may be fine for this client. In example 2, the counselor focuses on one specific morning, not accepting the client's assertion that every morning is bad. This sends a subtle message to the client that categorical thinking will be challenged by requiring specific information.

A third benefit in specific situations is getting unedited thoughts. In their original form, many automatic thoughts are extremely unreasonable. But clients are not likely to embarrass themselves by reporting their unreasonable thoughts unnecessarily. If counselors settle for general situations, clients will often report their edited thoughts—those they come to after hours or days of reflection. Recognizing that getting upset about overcooked spaghetti is embarrassingly unreasonable, Sheryl would not have reported the incident if I had simply asked, "How did your week go?" But since I asked when she felt the worst in the last twenty-four hours, she honestly reported the incident. While edited thoughts may have some benefit in counseling, they are not as valuable as the unedited automatic thoughts that are associated with specific situations.

Listen for Specific Situations

The biggest tool for finding specific situations is careful listening. Clients often refer obliquely to specific situations—feeling depressed about the boss's disapproval, feeling angry at the five-year-old who won't eat dinner, feeling anxious when hearing about a tax increase. These sketchy comments can be filled in by the counselor who listens carefully and asks for more detail.

CLIENT: I feel like a failure. I know my boss doesn't like me—she makes that clear every day—so I'm constantly wondering how much longer I will have my job. Then what will I do, be homeless?

COUNSELOR: Those are painful conclusions. You mentioned your boss doesn't like you and that she makes that clear every day. Tell me about today.

CLIENT: She walked by me in the hall, and she gave me one of those looks. I knew what she meant.

COUNSELOR: What time was that? What was happening?

CLIENT: About 1:30. She was coming back from lunch and I was going to the copy machine. She was preoccupied with something, but I said hi anyway. I apparently startled her and she looked at me like she was thinking, *Who gave you the right to say hi to me?*

In this example, the counselor identifies a specific situation by focusing on the client's indirect reference to the boss. The client's conclusions about the encounter may be quite inaccurate, but they would go unnoticed by a counselor neglecting to uncover details.

Ask for Details to Reenact the Situation

Although clients refer indirectly to specific situations, getting specific details usually depends on the counselor's efforts, as in the previous example. When the counselor asked, "What time was that?" it was not for chronological accuracy, but to help recreate the memory in the client's mind. By associating the event with a particular time, the client then recalled the circumstances surrounding the encounter.

Several prompts help clients reenact the situation and thereby recall their feelings and thoughts more accurately:

"Let's go through the situation you mentioned in slow motion. I'm interested in hearing each detail—what you felt, thought, and observed as it happened."

"I'm interested in knowing the details of that situation. No detail is too small. What time of day was it? What smells do you remember? What colors were on the walls? How did you feel? I'm interested in anything you can remember."

"Close your eyes for a moment. I'd like you to recall this situation as completely as you can. Just replay it in your mind, as if it were videotaped and is now being played back. I'll be quiet for a moment and just let you remember every detail you can think of."

These and similar prompts help the client specify the situation being discussed.

Homework Ideas

In cognitive therapy clients need to focus on and recall life events specifically—a skill that can be enhanced with strategic homework assignments. A Daily Mood Record has clients keep track of their activities each hour of each day for one week, then rate the intensity of the moods associated with each activity. This assignment requires clients to notice specific events throughout the week and reminds clients of which events to discuss during counseling sessions. This is particularly useful for those clients who forget the details of their week and resort to categorical impressions, such as, "It was a lousy week," or "It was a great week!" A sample form for this assignment is in Appendix B.

The Emotion Report, also found in Appendix B, has clients write a brief report about the event and their reaction whenever they feel the target emotion (the feelings for which they seek counseling—depression, anger, anxiety, and so on). With this assignment, clients practice noticing and analyzing specific situations.

STEP 2: IDENTIFY FEELINGS

Although specifying the situation is necessary, it is not sufficient to accurately identify thoughts. Insightful clients are sometimes able to report

77

thoughts directly after recalling the situation, but most need to first recall their feelings.

Memories void of feelings are often reviewed in sterile narrative. But when feelings are recalled, concurrent thoughts are also recalled. Below are two examples. The first tries to get thoughts without first getting feelings; the second working through the situation ➜ feeling ➜ thought progression. Notice the emotional distance the client keeps in the first example.

Example 1
COUNSELOR: When in the last twenty-four hours have you felt most depressed?

CLIENT: Last night. Barbara and I disagreed about a little thing, then I got depressed.

SPECIFY SITUATION
COUNSELOR: Tell me more about last night.

CLIENT: She wanted to go to bed and I wanted to stay up and watch a movie. She got mad that I wouldn't go to bed with her, but I stayed up anyway.

COUNSELOR: But you didn't enjoy it much.

CLIENT: Exactly.

SPECIFY THOUGHTS
COUNSELOR: As you were sitting in your living room watching that movie last night, what kind of thoughts were going through your mind?

CLIENT: I was just thinking about the marriage, thinking we fight too much about little things. It's okay, though; I suppose every couple fights sometimes.

Example 2
COUNSELOR: When in the last twenty-four hours have you felt most depressed.

CLIENT: Last night. Barbara and I disagreed about a little thing, then I got depressed.

SPECIFY SITUATION
COUNSELOR: Tell me more about last night.

CLIENT: She wanted to go to bed and I wanted to stay up and watch a movie. She got mad that I wouldn't go to bed with her, but I stayed up anyway.

COUNSELOR: But you didn't enjoy it much.

CLIENT: Exactly.

SPECIFY FEELINGS

COUNSELOR: Now as you were sitting there watching that movie last night, what feelings did you have?

CLIENT: I felt sad, really sad.

COUNSELOR: It looks like those feelings are coming back now as you think about the situation.

CLIENT: Yeah. I don't know. It seems like we fight about every little thing.

COUNSELOR: It sounds like it goes beyond sad to hopeless.

CLIENT: Sometimes. Last night I felt hopeless.

SPECIFY THOUGHTS

COUNSELOR: As you were sitting in your living room watching that movie last night, feeling hopeless and sad, what kind of thoughts were going through your mind?

CLIENT: I was thinking there's no use. Nothing I do is good enough. Our marriage is doomed.

The therapist found automatic thoughts in both examples; but in the first the thoughts were diluted, not as emotionally charged as they were the previous night. In the second example, the therapist evoked feelings first and then obtained the thoughts that created or maintained the emotions.

Evoke or Provoke Feelings

These examples demonstrate why the cognitive counselor needs to evoke feelings from the client. Feelings and thoughts are connected in memories, and they are more accurately recalled if they come as a packet rather than an intellectualized narrative. Counselors need to confront explanations that are void of emotion. In example 1, the therapist might redeem the situation by saying, "So last night you were saying to yourself that you and Barbara fight too much, but that's okay because everyone fights a lot in marriage. That doesn't sound like a thought that would lead to depression." This statement confronts the incongruity between the client's reported thoughts and his depressed emotion and evokes actual feelings and thoughts more honestly.

Sometimes clients are unable to recall their thoughts unless they can reexperience their feelings in the counseling session. Cognitive counselors sometimes therapeutically provoke feelings in their clients in order to have access to their thoughts. Consider the following example:

COUNSELOR: So last night you were feeling down, telling yourself your marriage is doomed.

CLIENT: Yeah.

COUNSELOR: And nothing you do is good enough.

CLIENT: Uh huh.

COUNSELOR: (loudly) You're a real loser!

(Silence)

CLIENT: I'm not sure what you mean.

(Silence)

COUNSELOR: The feelings you were having just now, as you were reflecting on me calling you a loser—were those the feelings you had last night?

CLIENT: Yeah. Like I'm no good. Like everyone thinks I'm a loser.

This example shows the therapist *provoking*, not just *evoking*, a feeling. After being called a loser, the client's emotions in the session mirrored the emotions from the night before. This fresh reminder of feelings brings out the automatic thoughts, *I'm no good,* and *Everyone thinks I'm a loser.* Later, the therapist would need to clarify the intent of calling him a loser, assuring the client it was for therapeutic purposes only.

Distinguish Thoughts from Feelings

Feelings cannot be evoked or provoked for therapeutic purposes from those who do not recognize or admit feelings. Some clients first require remedial work to understand what their feelings are.

Many in our society, men particularly, have been socialized to avoid discussing feelings. With years of practice, they have shut off their awareness and expression of feelings, giving themselves emotional lobotomies. These clients need to learn what they are feeling and how to label their feelings.

Carl was a twenty-five-year-old single male coming for help with depression after his fiancée broke off their relationship. His emotional illiteracy became clear within the first several sessions. He knew he felt sad, but he could not label or discuss other feelings. When I asked him to write down his feelings during the week, he returned with a blank piece of paper. Carl was raised in emotional isolation. He felt alienated from others at school and never had a close friend. His family ate no meals together, and feelings were not discussed in his home. When he was able to talk about his feelings, he reported feeling alone and strange throughout childhood.

Our first sessions were devoted to building Carl's repertoire of feelings. Carl understood when I explained that feelings were tools I need for my work, just as he used tools for his work as a diesel mechanic. We started with checklists. I gave Carl a list of many feelings and had him circle the feelings he experienced during the past week. Then Carl took the checklists home and filled one out each day. Before long, he could report five feelings from the past week in a few minutes at the beginning of each session, even without the checklist. Eventually, he kept track of feelings between sessions. Once he learned to label and discuss feelings, he was able to progress in overcoming his depression.

Even those who recognize their feelings sometimes confuse thoughts and feelings. Consider the following dialogue:

COUNSELOR: Tell me some of the feelings you had when you were turned down for a date yesterday.

CLIENT: I felt he didn't think I was attractive enough. Probably if I were a beautiful model he wouldn't have been busy.

In this example, the counselor asks for a feeling and gets a thought. It is good to clarify this, even though the client may be aware of her feelings, so she will learn the connection between thoughts and feelings.

COUNSELOR: You're reporting a thought to me. "He didn't think I am attractive enough." My guess is that those thoughts led to some difficult feelings. What labels would you put on the feelings you had?

CLIENT: I felt rejected, and maybe a little angry.

On the second try, the counselor obtains feelings from the client. By clarifying, the counselor has emphasized that thoughts and feelings are different, yet connected.

Rate Intensity of Feelings

Feelings vary in type and intensity. After obtaining accurate labels for a client's feelings, counselors need to understand how intense the experience was. Of course, all ways of measuring feelings are subjective, but subjective measurements are the most appropriate in this case. Subjectivity need not concern the counselor since clients compare their feelings with their own previous feelings, not with the feelings of others. Indeed, progress in therapy is subjective, and this subjective sense of progress is what counselors work toward.

In cognitive therapy, clients frequently rate the intensity of their feelings on a 100-point scale. They compare their current feelings with previous feelings.

> COUNSELOR: You said you felt rejected and angry. On a scale of 0 to 100, if 100 is the most rejected you have ever felt, how rejected did you feel yesterday when you were turned down for a date?
>
> CLIENT: I suppose about a 70.
>
> COUNSELOR: And how angry did you feel if 100 is the most angry you have ever been?
>
> CLIENT: Only about 40.

Rating feelings helps the counselor better understand the clients experience and also establishes baseline data so the client later recognizes progress.

Homework Ideas

Two homework assignments, both included in Appendix B, help teach clients to identify feelings. One, Identifying Feelings, gives examples of various emotions and room for clients to list their feelings. This helps clients build their repertoire of feeling "labels" so they can better identify their emotions as they occur.

Another assignment, Feelings and Alternatives, encourages labeling of feelings as well as generating behavioral alternatives. Each troubling feeling is considered, and three possible actions are listed. In addition to building awareness of feelings, this breaks clients out of linear thinking: "Since I feel angry, I must yell," for example. Clients learn to think more flexibly: "When I am angry, I could yell, take a walk to calm down, or discuss my feelings with someone not involved in the situation."

STEP 3: IDENTIFY THOUGHTS

Having specified a situation and defined the associated feelings, the cognitive counselor is able to identify automatic thoughts. Automatic thoughts can then be evaluated and disputed by the client. A number of techniques are used to identify automatic thoughts.

Hot Cognitions

Just as fresh salmon is better than frozen, fresh thoughts are better than those recalled later. The best way to understand thoughts is to capture them as they occur. Cognitive therapists refer to fresh thoughts as hot cognitions.

Counselors are sometimes trained to move to a different topic when the client shows painful feelings. In contrast, cognitive therapists focus on the painful feelings in order to understand the thoughts contributing to the feelings. Cognitive therapists frequently ask, "What thoughts went through your mind just then?" The following example shows a therapist using an emotional moment in therapy to get hot cognitions.

COUNSELOR: I was interested a minute ago when you said your father was never around. Tell me more about that.

CLIENT: He was too busy drinking at the bar to know anything about his kids. He never came to any of my basketball games. He was just never around.

COUNSELOR: You're feeling angry.

CLIENT: No . . . Well, maybe I am. I can't believe . . .

(Silence, client cries quietly)

COUNSELOR: What happened just then? What thoughts went through you mind?

CLIENT: That he never cared. I wish so much I had a father who loved me. I could never do enough to make him notice.

COUNSELOR: You were feeling unloved, thinking your father didn't care. And you felt sad and depressed.

CLIENT: Yeah.

By focusing on the present moment, the counselor obtains automatic thoughts that directly point to deeper core beliefs. The client may believe she is unworthy of love or that she was never good enough to earn her father's love.

Questioning

Even when hot cognitions cannot be uncovered, direct questioning is a useful tool for understanding thoughts. If a client is describing an event from the previous day, the counselor can specify the situation, understand the feelings, and then look for automatic thoughts with a specific question: "What thoughts were going through your mind?"

If the client reports the thoughts as an observer, "I was thinking that I'm a real loser," the counselor reflects back the thought as it would actually occur, "I'm a real loser." The latter statement more accurately recreates the thought as it occurred.

> COUNSELOR: Okay. So you were feeling quite rejected, about a 70 on a scale of 100. What thoughts were going through your mind as you were feeling rejected?
>
> CLIENT: I was thinking that I must not be worthwhile to him.
>
> COUNSELOR: So you were saying to yourself, "I'm not worth much."
>
> CLIENT: Kind of. I thought, "I'm not worth his time. No one thinks I'm worth their time."

Direct questioning works well with insightful clients. For those who have difficulty recognizing or recalling their thoughts, other strategies are necessary.

Imagery

Those unable to recall their thoughts with direct questioning often benefit from replaying the situation in their minds. As they reexperience their feelings, their thoughts come back to them. The counselor asks the client to relax, close his or her eyes, and replay the situation as it actually occurred, as if a videotape were being played. As the situation unfolds, the client focuses on the corresponding thoughts and feelings. The following example demonstrates the imagery technique.

> COUNSELOR: Okay. So you were feeling quite rejected, about a 70 on a scale of 100. What thoughts were going through your mind as you were feeling rejected?

CLIENT: I don't know. I just felt bad. I wasn't aware of any thoughts.

COUNSELOR: All right. Well, let's see if we can go back and find some. Lean back in your chair, take a minute to get comfortable, and relax. Close your eyes. Take some deep breaths. Okay, now imagine yourself in the same situation you were in yesterday—as if it had been videotaped and now you are watching the tape. Notice the surroundings. What do you see around you? What can you hear? And take a few minutes and watch the tape in slow motion. But as you do, focus on what you are saying to yourself as you feel rejected.

(Pause while client reviews image and thoughts)

CLIENT: It was something about not being worth his time.

COUNSELOR: "I'm not worthwhile to him."

CLIENT: Yeah. I'm not worthwhile to him or anyone else.

This example shows imagery working where direct questioning does not.

A variant on this, suggested by Aaron Beck and his colleagues, is called *induced imagery*.[1] The counselor first asks the client to imagine an unpleasant scene, perhaps waiting for a late bus in the cold rain without a coat. Then the counselor and the client discuss what feelings the image evoked and the thoughts going through the client's mind during the image. Next, the counselor describes a positive image, such as walking along an ocean beach enjoying the sand between one's toes, the smell of salt water, and the sun warming one's back. After the image, feelings and thoughts are again discussed. This exercise helps clients understand the connection between thoughts and feelings. Pleasant thoughts lead to pleasant feelings.

Role-Playing

Sometimes neither direct questioning nor imagery successfully elicits the client's thoughts. Role-playing is another alternative. The counselor plays the role of the antagonist and the client plays herself or himself, as they collaborate to recreate the situation and accompanying feelings and thoughts.

COUNSELOR: All right. Well let's see if we can go back and find some. Lean back in your chair, take a minute to get comfortable, and relax. Close your eyes. Take some deep breaths. Okay, now imagine yourself in the same situation you were in yesterday . . .

(Pause while client reviews image and thoughts)

CLIENT: I'm sorry. I just can't come up with anything. It's hard for me to remember exactly what happened.

COUNSELOR: Well, let's try something else. I'll be Rick, the man you asked for a date. You be you. We'll try to replay the situation as accurately as we can; as we do, you think about how you feel and what you think.

CLIENT: Okay. Should I start? Rick, I was wondering if you wanted to go to a movie with me this weekend.

COUNSELOR: Well, I'm pretty busy this weekend.

CLIENT: Do you have any time next weekend?

COUNSELOR: I doubt it. Besides I don't like movies much.

(Remainder of role-play follows)

COUNSELOR: What kind of feelings and thoughts were you having as we replayed that?

CLIENT: I felt rejected, like you didn't care at all about me.

COUNSELOR: Like yesterday?

CLIENT: Yeah, I guess. I must have believed that he thought I was unimportant and worthless.

COUNSELOR: "I'm no good. I'm worthless."

CLIENT: Yeah.

In doing the role-play, the counselor tries to be as abrasive and confrontive as the actual antagonist was. This provokes feelings in the clients, allowing them to remember how they felt in the previous situation.

Multiple Choice

For some clients, questioning, imagery, and role-playing will all fail. The last resort is multiple choice—giving the client several possible thoughts and asking which ones were occurring during the situation.

COUNSELOR: Well, let's try something else. I'll be Rick, the man you asked for a date. You be you . . .

(Remainder of role-play follows)

COUNSELOR: What kind of feelings and thoughts were you having as we replayed that?

CLIENT: I don't know. It seemed different talking to you than it did talking to Rick.

COUNSELOR: Okay. Well, let me give you some choices—kind of like a multiple choice question. I imagine others being turned down for a date might have some of the following thoughts: (A) He's making a real mistake because he would have a good time with me. (B) I'm being rejected as a person. He doesn't think I'm worth much. (C) He's seeing someone else. He won't have anything to do with me now because he's involved with another woman. Which of those seems most familiar?

CLIENT: Definitely not A. B seems the most likely.

COUNSELOR: He doesn't think I'm worth much.

CLIENT: Yeah.

After using multiple choice with several different situations, most clients progress in self-understanding and begin responding to questioning or imagery.

Homework Ideas

Once clients become skilled at finding automatic thoughts, they can keep track of thoughts on their own. Aaron Beck and his colleagues teach their clients to use a Daily Record of Dysfunctional Thoughts, sometimes called the triple-column technique. (Historically it had three columns, but now it has four to six, depending on the version.)[2] An example of the record form is shown in Figure 5–1, and a blank form is provided in Appendix B.

Pretend Bob was driving home from work yesterday and found himself in the middle of a traffic jam. While in the car, he filled out a Daily Record of Dysfunctional Thoughts form to help him deal with his feelings. After specifying the situation, he identified his feelings and rated their intensity. He felt frustrated. If 100 is the most frustrated he had ever felt, he rated his frustration yesterday at 75. He felt angry—80 on a scale of 100. And he was worried—60 on a scale of 100. Next, he identified the automatic thoughts contributing to his feelings. He felt frustrated as he said to himself, *This happens every day. It is awful and I hate it*. He felt anger as he thought, *If people knew how to drive, this kind of thing wouldn't happen.* He felt worried as he thought, *I will be late and miss my son's piano recital.* Bob's next task is to challenge his automatic thoughts and make them more reasonable. His revised self-talk, called rational responses, are written in the blank column of Figure 5–1. He might conclude, *Traffic jams occur frequently, but not every day. It seems awful, but there are many worse things in life. Sometimes traffic jams aren't because of bad driving. My son's recital isn't until 7:30 and I'll probably be home before then.* Rational responses will be discussed more in chapter 6.

Daily Record of Dysfunctional Thoughts

Situation	Feelings	Automatic Thoughts	Rational Responses
Caught in traffic jam while driving home from work.	Frustrated 75	This happens every day. It's awful and I hate it.	
	Angry 80	If people knew how to drive, this kind of thing wouldn't happen.	
	Worried 60	I'll be late and will miss my son's recital.	

Fig. 5–1

Cognitive therapists assign thought recording as homework because the more one practices healthy self-talk, the more believable it becomes. Using the triple-column technique is often useful during counseling sessions also, especially when training the client how to keep track of thoughts between sessions.

The most common homework assignment for identifying thoughts is the Daily Record of Dysfunctional Thoughts, discussed above and shown in Appendix B. Two other assignments are the Should Statement Record and the Catastrophizing Record, also shown in Appendix B.

People often use arbitrary and unnecessary *shoulds* when talking with themselves. Examples are "My house should always be spotless," or "I should be friendly with everyone I meet," or "I should always get the highest grade in the class." These *shoulds*, discussed more in chapter 6, create unreasonable demands for perfection. Having clients record their should statements between sessions helps them identify how their self-talk adds unnecessary pressure.

The catastrophizing record helps clients identify when they make unfortunate events into catastrophes. I once received a notice from my home mortgage company that I had failed to provide them insurance information about my homeowner's insurance, and that they would be adding almost two thousand dollars onto my mortgage because of my oversight. I worried most of the night, unable to recall any request for insurance information from the mortgage company. After missing most of my night's sleep, I called first thing the next morning. "I'm sorry; that was sent out in error," said the voice on the phone line. "All we need is your social security number." I had wasted a night's sleep on a mistake because I made an inconvenience into a catastrophe with my self-talk. The catastrophizing record allows clients to keep track of the times they overreact to an inconvenience by making it seem like an awful event. The homework sheet refers to an awfulness scale which will be discussed in the next chapter.

All three of these assignments—the Daily Record of Dysfunctional Thoughts, the Should Statement Record, and the Catastrophizing Record—help clients become more aware of their automatic thoughts and the ways their thoughts influence their feelings.

CHAPTER SIX

DISPUTING AUTOMATIC THOUGHTS

THE DESERT SUN CURSED THE DAY as Elijah sat hopelessly under a tree and asked God to die. "I have had enough, Lord," he said. "Take my life; I am no better than my ancestors," (1 Kings 19:4b). Jezebel had promised to kill him; Elijah felt tired, discouraged, lonely, and defeated. Elijah had a lot to be discouraged about; He felt alone in battling Israel's idolatry, his life had been threatened by a powerful queen, and other prophets had already been killed. And fueling his discouragement was the thought, *There is no point in living.*

God restored Elijah, not by changing his situation, but by changing his ways of thinking. After forty days and forty nights, Elijah was faced with the same trials as before, but was ready to serve God rather than give up and die. Instead of thinking, *I am all alone, and it is best to die,*

Elijah changed his thoughts to, *I am all alone, but I will obey God none-theless*. Elijah went on to serve God in powerful ways, having fought against his desire to die.

Elijah's account demonstrates a central tenet of cognitive therapy: Counselors cannot make bad situations good, but they can help clients use new ways of thinking to overcome feelings of despair, loneliness, depression, and hopelessness. As in Elijah's day, God's words and other words of wisdom can still be used to control unwanted feelings and enable one to live obediently and productively.

As discussed in chapter 5, one goal of identifying automatic thoughts is to provide symptom relief by teaching clients to argue with themselves—to dispute their automatic thoughts with rational responses in order to gain control over their feelings.

Before discussing automatic thoughts and rational responses, one disclaimer is appropriate. Although the distinction between automatic and rational thoughts is clear-cut among cognitive therapy writers, this can easily produce misleading dichotomous thinking, also called categorical thinking. Not all automatic thoughts are distorted or dysfunctional; some are accurate and adaptive. Christian parents often teach their children to obey first and ask questions later because they recognize the value of healthy automatic thinking. The person who reflexively rejects an opportunity to sin has used automatic thinking for good purposes. So automatic thoughts are not all bad. The automatic thoughts to which I refer negatively are *distorted* automatic thoughts—those based on faulty thinking and leading to inappropriate behaviors or unnecessarily negative feelings.

AUTOMATIC THOUGHTS VERSUS RATIONAL RESPONSES

In chapter 5, I introduced the triple-column technique to record specific feelings and thoughts (see Figure 5–1). The final column in that model is for *rational responses*—cognitive responses to distorted automatic thoughts.

Bob, the stressed commuter caught in slow traffic, automatically says to himself, *This happens every day*. But when honestly appraising the situation, Bob realizes traffic jams don't slow him down *every* day. More accurately, he says, *This happens more often than I would like*. Similarly, he realizes it seems awful to be caught in a traffic jam, but there are many worse things that could happen. For example, he might decide that "inconvenient" is a more accurate label than "awful." Each of his automatic thoughts can be countered with a better-reasoned thought.

Rational Responses to Automatic Thoughts

Situation	Feelings	Automatic Thoughts	Rational Responses
Caught in traffic jam while driving home from work.	Frustrated 75	This happens every day. It's awful and I hate it.	It happens a lot, but not every day. It is inconvenient, but not awful.
	Angry 80	If people knew how to drive, this kind of thing wouldn't happen.	Traffic jams result from too much traffic flow, not from incompetence.
	Worried 60	I'll be late and will miss my son's recital.	I have plenty of time. It's unlikely I'll miss the recital. If I do, my son will forgive me.

Fig. 6–1

Automatic and Plausible versus Intentional and Implausible

Automatic thoughts and rational responses differ significantly. The first difference is implied in the names: automatic thoughts occur without effort—and seem immediately plausible. In contrast, rational responses must be intentionally derived and are rarely easy to believe at first.

Bob's idea that traffic jams occur because of poor driving is automatic and seems reasonable to him as he sits in the hot sun without air conditioning. Bob's more reasonable thought—that traffic jams occur because of excessive traffic flow—is not automatic. His rational thought may not occur to him until later when he is recalling the incident to a family member, friend, or counselor.

Imagine Bob's wife, Brenda, sitting with Bob in the traffic jam. Bob speaks aloud his automatic thought, "These things wouldn't happen if those clowns knew how to drive!" Brenda thinks, *That's ridiculous! Traffic jams happen for many reasons.* She may be wise enough not to confront Bob's thoughts at that moment, but she realizes what Bob does not—his automatic thought is unreasonable. If Brenda confronts Bob's unreasonable thought in the hot car, Bob is likely to have more unreasonable thoughts—*She doesn't understand anything*, for example. Several hours later, as Bob reflects on his argument with Brenda, he may recognize his unreasonable thoughts. At the time of the traffic jam, his automatic thoughts seemed plausible, but after rational reflection, they do not.

Like most of us, Bob eventually sees things more accurately. But sometimes it takes many hours or many days before automatic thoughts give way to rational responses. Cognitive therapy speeds up this natural process, allowing people to quickly challenge their automatic thoughts with well-reasoned perspectives. With practice, Bob can challenge his own thoughts. After automatically thinking traffic jams occur because of inept drivers, he can say to himself what Brenda once would have said to him, *That's ridiculous! Traffic jams happen for many reasons.* By learning to argue against his own automatic thoughts, he can make rational responses seem believable more quickly than before.

Easy to Repeat versus Difficult to Repeat

Automatic thoughts reverberate in one's mind. As Elijah sat under a tree in the desert, his thoughts of despair were probably recycled through his mind over and over. *There is no reason to live. There is no reason to live. There is no reason to live.* The more the distorted thoughts reverberated, the more painful Elijah's feelings became.

When a rational response comes to mind in the midst of stress, it is easily trampled by the recurrent automatic thoughts. If Elijah thought, *God has taken care of me before and will again now*, it was quickly drowned out by, *There is no reason to live. There is no reason to live.* Automatic thoughts are naturally repetitive, whereas rational responses are not.

So it is not enough to teach clients to think rationally; they must also learn to think rational thoughts again and again. Eventually, the rational thoughts become automatic.

Contradicted with Evidence versus Supported with Evidence

Distorted automatic thoughts, as believable as they are in moments of stress, are not supported well with evidence. In the midst of the traffic jam, Bob told himself, *This happens every day.* In the midst of a string of bad bridge hands, I sometimes conclude, *I never get good cards.* Neither of these automatic thoughts is supportable with evidence. Bob frequently has traffic jams on the way home, but not every day. The bridge cards are dealt randomly and players have good cards sometimes, mediocre cards most of the time, and bad cards occasionally.

Counselors benefit from this distinction between automatic and rational thoughts. Since rational responses are supported with evidence and distorted automatic thoughts are not, counselors can be data collectors rather than arguers. Just as Brenda probably would have been unsuccessful if she had confronted Bob with his automatic thoughts about traffic jams, counselors who confront their clients argumentatively will find defensiveness and resistance. Cognitive counselors can instead collaborate with clients to see which beliefs are supported by evidence. Since carefully collected evidence supports rational beliefs and not distorted beliefs, clients find their own reasons to abandon faulty, inflexible thinking. Counselors teach clients to change beliefs by working together to evaluate evidence.

Dysfunctional versus Functional

Whereas rational responses are functional, distorted automatic thoughts lead to dysfunctional feelings of powerlessness and frustration, as they did for Elijah in the Old Testament and Bob in the traffic jam. Sometimes automatic thoughts produce irresponsible behaviors as well.

Jane saw a winter coat in a department store and automatically thought she needed to own it. Although she was being treated for compulsive spending and had filled five major credit cards to the spending limit, she opened an account with the department store and bought the coat. Later the same day she realized she didn't need the coat at all. She already had three nice winter coats. Her rational response came too late.

Rational responses lead to functional behaviors. Jane's rational response would have kept her from buying the coat if she had experienced it earlier.

TECHNIQUES FOR DISPUTING AUTOMATIC THOUGHTS

Since repetition is required to make rational responses believable, most cognitive counselors use several techniques with each client.

Ask for Evidence

What does a counselor do if a client reports a distorted automatic thought as truth? On one hand, if the counselor says nothing, it implies tacit agreement with the distorted thought. On the other hand, if the counselor confronts the thought it might evoke defensiveness in the client. The answer to this question is collaboration. The counselor is *working with* the client to find flexible, accurate ways of thinking.

A good way to collaborate with the client while challenging the automatic thought is to directly ask for evidence.

CLIENT: No one appreciates me at home. My wife doesn't know how hard I work. She just expects me to do more cooking and housework, but doesn't appreciate all the things I do already.

COUNSELOR: You're feeling underrated.

CLIENT: Exactly.

COUNSELOR: One of the troubling thoughts, I'm sure, is believing that no one appreciates you. As you think that, you feel unloved and taken for granted.

CLIENT: Yeah. Like she doesn't care about me; she just wants my paycheck.

COUNSELOR: Okay. There are a number of thoughts you're having that I would like to understand better. The first is, "No one appreciates me at home." Let's imagine we are trying to prove that assertion in a court of law. What evidence can we find for that conclusion? We are also interested in any evidence that contradicts your conclusion that no one appreciates you at home.

CLIENT: Well my kids appreciate me, so I guess it's not quite right to say no one appreciates me . . .

Notice the counselor first reflects the feelings the client describes by saying, "You're feeling underrated." The reflection communicates understanding before the automatic thought is evaluated. The counselor then focuses on the automatic thought, "No one appreciates me at home." Rather than critically confronting the thought, the counselor expresses a desire to understand the thought better. By collaborating with the client to find evidence for the thought, the counselor creates a nondefensive atmosphere where distortions can be recognized and discussed. Other distortions such as the categorical thought, "She doesn't care about me; she just wants my paycheck," also need to be evaluated. It is possible, for example, that the client's wife cares both for him and his paycheck, but his categorical thinking excludes this possibility. As each automatic thought is considered, the counselor asks for evidence supporting or disputing the beliefs. Eventually the client realistically refines the thoughts: "I feel unappreciated at home, but I can't read my wife's mind and she says she appreciates me. My wife likes my paycheck, but she values me, too."

Awfulness Scale

Imagine Gene walking in the door after a long day at work (and perhaps a traffic jam on the way home), and finding a pool of water on the hardwood floor in front of the refrigerator. For the third time in the past six months, his refrigerator has broken. What thoughts go through Gene's mind? How frustrated and disappointed is he?

Most of us would feel strong emotions in this situation. We might say to ourselves, *Nothing is going right today,* or *This is awful,* or *Those idiots don't know how to repair refrigerators even though they charge an arm and a leg.* These automatic thoughts are probably inaccurate, and they heighten frustration, anger, and disappointment. Because of automatic thoughts, most of us would react as if we were experiencing a catastrophe. This demonstrates categorical thinking: things either go well, or they are awful.

Inconveniences seem awful when they first occur, but with time we can put them in perspective. The broken refrigerators of life fade into insignificance with enough time. An awfulness scale helps put minor inconveniences into perspective. Gene's counselor would describe the awfulness scale as a 0–100 continuum with 100 being the most awful thing imaginable. Being killed, watching one's family being murdered, or being paralyzed for life are likely candidates for the top of the scale. After deciding what 100 would be, Gene could determine what a 50 would be—perhaps being diagnosed with treatable cancer or losing a job. Then he could put the refrigerator incident on the same scale. What seemed like an 80 as he walked in the door to see a pool of water is only a 20 when considering the true catastrophes of life.

The awfulness scale needs to be presented sensitively, not in a condescending or belittling way. The following two examples demonstrate a confrontive and a collaborative way to present the awfulness scale to clients. The collaborative method fosters cooperation whereas the confrontive method evokes defensiveness.

Example 1: Confrontive Presentation
COUNSELOR: Gene, you said the refrigerator being broken was awful. I can agree that it is inconvenient, but "awful" seems overstated.

Imagine a scale of 0 to 100, with 100 being the worst thing that could possibly happen to you . . .

Example 2: Collaborative Presentation

COUNSELOR: Gene, you said the refrigerator being broken was awful. It sounds like a real frustration after a long day's work. I would like to understand how bad that felt to you then and how bad it feels now. A tool we can use is called the awfulness scale. It goes from 0 to 100, with 100 being the worst thing you could possibly imagine. . . .

Although some cognitive therapists prefer the directness of the confrontive approach, I find it less effective because clients often defend their catastrophizing thoughts. They sometimes feel their problem has been trivialized and they become more convinced than before that a catastrophe has occurred. With collaboration, they remain nondefensive and evaluate their thoughts more accurately.

Cognitive Distortions

Just as labeling feelings (discussed in chapter 5) helps clients better understand emotions, training them to recognize cognitive distortions helps them identify dysfunctional automatic thoughts. With practice, clients recognize when they use *all-or-none thinking* or *jumping to conclusions*, for example, and then self-correct their thoughts to avoid the distortions.

Cognitive therapy authors generally agree on what constitutes a cognitive distortion, but they label the distortions in varying ways. In his book, *Feeling Good*, David Burns identifies ten distortions[1] while Aaron Beck and his colleagues in their book, *Cognitive Therapy of Depression*, identify only six types of cognitive errors. Beck's list begins with *arbitrary inference*, drawing a specific conclusion without supporting evidence. When Bob concludes traffic jams occur because of incompetent drivers, he does so without evidence and uses arbitrary inference. *Selective abstraction*, Beck and his colleagues write, is taking one detail out of context and ignoring other relevant details when conceptualizing a situation. The man who is convinced his wife is having an affair because his wife is receiving home phone calls from a male co-worker is using selective abstraction. *Overgeneralization* is when a general conclusion is drawn from a single experience. It is the basis of many anxiety reactions. An .

example would be *Because I had a panic attack last time I ate Chinese food, I will always have a panic attack in Oriental restaurants. Magnification and minimization* occur when one magnifies errors and minimizes successes. As a college professor, I fight this distortion each semester when reviewing my course evaluations. The many positive comments seem insignificant, and the few negative comments seem ominous. *Personalization* is the tendency to assume fault for bad events without reason. When children assume responsibility for their parents' divorce, they are personalizing. *Dichotomous thinking* is the tendency to think categorically, discussed in chapter 2. A depressed person may think, *I'm either perfect or I'm awful.* An anxious person may think, *Either things go as I have planned or I am completely out of control.*[2]

Burns's list of ten distortions overlaps a great deal with Beck's six distortions. Burns describes dichotomous thinking as *all-or-none thinking* and selective abstraction as *jumping to conclusions*. He adds *disqualifying the positive* and *emotional reasoning*, and expands arbitrary inference by identifying several related distortions: *mental filter, should statements*, and *labeling*.[3] Burns's list of Ten Cognitive Distortions is shown in Appendix B.

Understanding cognitive distortions helps clients recognize when they are making cognitive errors. In my own practice, I view this as a three-step process. First, I explain cognitive distortions to the client, using specific examples from the client's life as much as possible. After this explanation, I send home the list included in Appendix B describing the ten cognitive distortions identified by Burns.

Second, after explaining cognitive distortions, I begin noting distortions in the client's speech.

CLIENT: I was thinking this week how strange it is that I'm depressed. When I think about my life, I really should be happy.

COUNSELOR: I just heard the word "should."

CLIENT: I did it again, didn't I? That's a cognitive distortion.

COUNSELOR: Can you think of another way to say the same thing without using the word "should"?

CLIENT: I have a lot of reasons to feel good about my life.

COUNSELOR: Very nice. That was a good job of revising your thoughts to avoid a distortion.

After a while, the third step spontaneously occurs when the client notices his or her own distortions and self-corrects speech in the session.

CLIENT: I was thinking this week how strange it is that I'm depressed. When I think about my life, I really should be happy. Oops. I used "should."

COUNSELOR: Tell me what you mean without the "should."

CLIENT: I have a lot of reasons to feel good about my life.

COUNSELOR: Good job.

As clients become aware of their cognitive distortions, they are increasingly able to fight back with rational responses.

Conditioning

Behavior therapists use conditioning methods to treat a number of emotional disorders. Some of these techniques can also be used in cognitive therapy. *Systematic desensitization* has been used for many years by behavior therapists to treat anxiety disorders.[4] Clients learn progressive relaxation and then create mental pictures of things that have previously evoked anxiety. The mental pictures are arranged on a hierarchy, beginning with mildly anxiety-provoking images and progressing to more extreme images.

Carol was a snake phobic who came for counseling after spending a full day in bed because she had seen a snake in her garden. After several sessions of relaxation training, we began systematic desensitization, beginning with mildly anxiety-provoking stimuli. Her first image was of ropes hanging from the ceiling of her grandmother's house—ropes that reminded her of snakes. With practice, she could picture the ropes without feeling anxiety. Next, she pictured herself walking on a city sidewalk, noticing a dead snake on the opposite side of the road. Once she could stay relaxed while picturing the dead snake, we progressed to her next image—a live snake on the opposite side of the road. This continued until she remained relaxed while picturing herself handling a living snake.

Adding a cognitive dimension to the desensitization technique helped Carol. As she was picturing ropes hanging from Grandma's ceiling, she was talking to herself. Her automatic thought was, *One of these is really a snake.* While relaxing, she learned new ways of thinking: *These are ropes, not snakes. I can remain calm.* At each step of the hierarchy, she

99

learned new ways of talking to herself: *This is a snake, but it will not hurt me. I can remain calm.* A behavioral conditioning technique combined with cognitive training effectively helped Carol overcome her snake phobia.

Contingency management has also been used effectively by behavior therapists for many years. Those behaviors which are reinforced are likely to be repeated, so behavior therapists establish reinforcements for desired behaviors and, sometimes, punishments for undesired behaviors. Cognitive therapists can use the same behavioral principles in teaching clients to reinforce healthy thinking. When clients question their automatic thoughts and develop rational responses, they need to recognize their progress and reinforce themselves with their thoughts. Cognitive-behavioral therapist Donald Meichenbaum suggests the following self-rewarding thoughts:

> *It wasn't as bad as I expected.*
> *It's getting better each time I use this procedure.*
> *I can be pleased with the progress I'm making.*
> *Wait until I tell the others how it went.*
> *I handled it pretty well.*
> *Good, I did it. Next time I'll do even better.*[5]

A number of other behavioral techniques can be modified for use in cognitive therapy. Rian McMullin, director of the Counseling Research Institute in Colorado, describes many cognitive conditioning strategies in *Handbook of Cognitive Therapy Techniques.*[6]

Countering

Most people enjoy a good debate. Presidential candidates help or hurt their election chances by confronting one another on national television. High-school and college students enthusiastically join debate teams. Informal debates with friends are stimulating and challenging. Debating oneself is also important. When automatic thoughts try to deceive us, we need *countering* skills to argue back.

Christine's husband says, "Are you putting on weight?" Christine immediately feels depressed and guilty. She says to herself, *I look ugly and fat. I've been eating way too much. I'm a lazy slob. I need to stop eating until I lose ten pounds.* Her automatic thoughts will devastate her unless she can debate them effectively.

Teaching clients to counter automatic thoughts is teaching mental flexibility. One method is finding *alternative interpretations* by asking

"What's another way to interpret that?" In Christine's situation, there are several possible interpretations:

My weight is my concern, not his.
I may be slightly overweight, but I'm still attractive.
He's going through a mid-life crisis and wants me to look like a fashion model.

Generating new interpretations will help Christine debate her automatic thoughts and view herself more realistically.

Another method is *logical analysis*, where the counselor points out an illogical connection between automatic thoughts. Christine's counselor could say, "I understand you would like to lose ten pounds. Can you help me see the logical connection between your desire to lose ten pounds and your conclusion that you are fat and ugly?" Christine will realize her thoughts are not reasonable and develop counters in response: "I am ten pounds over my ideal weight, but that doesn't mean I'm fat or ugly."

Logical analysis sometimes requires what Meichenbaum calls the *Columbo technique*. Named after television's detective, Lieutenant Columbo, the technique requires the counselor to play dumb. While explaining what the counselor already understands, the client realizes the faulty logic being used.[7] In the following dialogue, the counselor starts by using this technique.

COUNSELOR: Christine, you were saying a minute ago that you were fat and ugly, a lazy slob. Then I thought you said you needed to lose ten pounds. I was just thinking about how many people out there need to lose ten pounds, and I was trying to figure out how those go together—being ten pounds overweight and those strong words: fat, ugly, lazy, slob.

CLIENT: I suppose a lot of people are fat—well, not obese, just overweight. It could be a lot worse. Ugly is probably not right, either. I would sure like to lose ten pounds, though.

COUNSELOR: I see. So maybe some of those words—fat, ugly, lazy, slob—could be changed to other words.

A third way to encourage countering is by focusing on *word selection*. For example the counselor could say, "Christine, you said you are a lazy slob. Let's look at that word "lazy." What exactly do you mean by that? Are there other words you could have used?" With time,

Christine will recognize that her negative label, "lazy," describes the same qualities as the positive label, "relaxed." She can counter her automatic thoughts by challenging her word selection. Many negative labels describe qualities that also can be viewed positively. "Gullible" can be viewed as "trusting." "Indecisive" can be seen as "careful." "Compulsive" can be changed to "determined."[8]

Paradox

At a conference I attended several years ago, psychiatrist Aaron Beck told of a time he said to his client, "I've been thinking a lot about your situation, how you feel so miserable and how your wife and others around feel miserable because of you, and have decided the only reasonable solution is for you to kill yourself." Beck was not really advocating the client kill himself; he was using a paradoxical suggestion to arouse a rational response in the client. The client immediately thought of the reasons he should *not* kill himself—reasons that had not occurred to him before.

Counselors need to use paradox cautiously, and only after their clients trust them. If a paradoxical strategy is perceived as rejection or agreement with distorted automatic thoughts, clients may worsen. But used appropriately in the right context, paradox can be very useful.

I use paradox by overstating automatic thoughts. The following example shows how I used paradox with Kyle, a young depressed man. Since it was the first time I had used a paradoxical strategy with him, I warned him before overstating his distorted thought.

CLIENT: I feel I should be doing better. I've been meeting with you a long time (it was our thirteenth session), and I'm not that much better.

COUNSELOR: It sounds like you're saying you're not doing a good job as a client.

CLIENT: Well, I'm not.

COUNSELOR: Kyle, let me warn you that I don't mean what I'm about to say. I think you're the worst client I've ever had. If you were any good at all, you would be better by now. How do you respond to that?

CLIENT: That's the way I feel.

COUNSELOR: You're a lousy client, Kyle! If you weren't, you would be better by now.

CLIENT: Well, I am better than I was a month ago. I guess I shouldn't expect to get better all at once.

COUNSELOR: Excellent. Those thoughts make sense—more sense than your earlier thought that you were a bad client. Let me say again that I didn't mean what I just said. I was trying to exaggerate what you were saying to yourself. What thoughts went through your mind when I called you a lousy client?

Paradox paid off in this case as Kyle acknowledged making progress for the first time in thirteen weeks. By exaggerating his automatic thoughts, I aroused Kyle's emotions enough for him to find a rational response. In addition to warning Kyle before using paradox, I debriefed him afterward to relieve any fears that I was rejecting or abandoning him.

Scriptural Analysis

Many automatic thoughts can be disputed with Scripture. Consider some examples.

Automatic Thought	**Scripture**
I can't stand this any longer!	No temptation has seized you except what is common to man. And God is faithful; he will not let you be tempted beyond what you can bear. But when you are tempted, he will also provide a way out so that you can stand up under it. (1 Cor. 10:13)
What I've done makes me unworthy and filthy.	If we confess our sins, he is faithful and just and will forgive us our sins and purify us from all unrighteousness. (1 John 1:9)
I am a wretched sinner.	And that is what some of you were. But you were washed, you were

103

sanctified, you were justified in the name of the Lord Jesus Christ and by the Spirit of our God. (1 Cor. 6:11)

No one loves me.

But God demonstrates his own love for us in this: While we were still sinners, Christ died for us. (Rom. 5:8)

I can't trust anyone.

Give thanks to the Lord, for he is good; his love endures forever. (1 Chron. 16:34)

These few examples demonstrate how Scripture can be used to directly refute distorted automatic thoughts. Counselors with good knowledge of the Bible can point out relevant passages, but it is equally valuable to let the client do the work. Send clients home with an assignment to find Scriptures to confirm or dispute their automatic thoughts. They can use a concordance or a topical Bible to help them find appropriate passages. Scripture verses can be yanked out of context to falsely support almost any perspective, so review clients' homework with them to see that they are not misusing Scripture to support unreasonable conclusions. The depressed client who comes quoting Job 3:3, "May the day of my birth perish . . . ," needs a reminder to look for context and themes in Scripture.

Shoulds and Whys

We Christians often carry excess baggage by taking the distinctives of our faith and exaggerating them to unnecessary *shoulds*. For example, the virtue of selfless hospitality easily ferments into beliefs such as: *I should be warm and friendly to everyone I meet* or *I should always consider others' needs, and never my own.* The doctrine of Christ's sufficiency can be distorted to emphasize personal insufficiency, as if Christ becomes more sufficient when we criticize ourselves: *I should criticize myself every chance I get,* or *I should constantly think of my inadequacies.*

Cognitive therapists have typically responded by removing *should* from their clients' vocabulary. This can be dangerous, though, if it removes the only means of self-control available to clients. As discussed in chapter 3, it is not enough to disrupt our clients' concepts of right and wrong—we need to replace those concepts with ones that are more biblically sound and lead to Christian obedience and victory. Those who use *should* excessively often have more guilt than obedience. But if we take away the *shoulds* and provide no new thinking strategies, they may have even less obedience than before.

Shoulds are not always wrong, but the ones that are right can be backed up with good reasoning. *I should remain faithful to my spouse,* is a correct way of thinking that is supported by the insecurity, jealousy, and destruction occurring among those who are unfaithful. God had good reasons to instruct us, "You shall not commit adultery" (Exodus 20:14). Every necessary *should* can be supported with a *why*.

Lauren attended a church where arbitrary *shoulds* were given each Sunday from the pulpit. She left church each week feeling guilty and defeated, convinced she was a worthless person. Many of her should statements were unnecessary: *I should meet every need I hear about,* or *I should do all the cooking and housework and always submit to my husband's desires* (Lauren also worked full-time as a secretary), or *I should never be angry,* or *I should never be depressed.* With time, Lauren learned to ask herself *why*? *Why should I do all the cooking and housework? Why should I feel personally responsible to meet every need I hear about? Why should I never be angry or depressed?* And she began asking *why*? as she listened to her pastor's sermons. Soon she was able to think critically, distilling the good from the sermons without feeling overwhelmed with guilt. She eventually learned more realistic expectations for herself and became less depressed.

Rather than eliminating all *shoulds,* we can teach clients to let *shoulds* trigger *why*? questions. Whenever we use a *should,* we can stop and ask *why* it is true. The unnecessary *shoulds* will wilt away and the necessary ones will grow roots as they are supported by critical thinking.

CHAPTER SEVEN
FINDING CORE BELIEFS

GARDENERS KNOW TO PULL UP WEEDS by the roots. If they snap off the weed at ground level, it will grow back. Automatic thoughts, like weeds, will grow back unless the roots are removed. When cognitive therapists weed, they look for core beliefs—those fundamental concepts residing beneath consciousness that shape our perceptions of reality and sometimes shape reality itself.

CORE BELIEFS SHAPE REALITY

Jack's core belief was, "If others don't do what I say, then they don't love me." As expected, he became an authoritarian husband, demanding that Nancy stay home with the children though she wanted to pursue her own career. He insisted they have four children, though she wanted only one. Whenever a man telephoned Nancy, Jack needed complete details. "Who was he?" "What did he want?" "How well do you know him?" He wanted control and responded with fear and anger when he saw it slipping through his fingers. Nancy felt smothered. When she assertively asked Jack for more freedom he responded by demanding more control, insisting "Someone is planting these ideas in your head." Jack then prohibited Nancy from seeing her parents, assuming it was their fault she wanted more freedom. But the more control he exerted, the more freedom Nancy desired.

When a tight cork finally pops, it goes a good distance. Nancy finally rebelled, fell in love with another man, and developed a secret relationship. Because of her moral commitments, Nancy was not sexually unfaithful to Jack, but her secret relationship haunted her conscience. She eventually told Jack and they came for counseling.

Nancy was not blameless. She had made a bad decision by pursuing a secret relationship. She lacked assertiveness and self-confidence. But Nancy did not deserve all the blame. Jack's core belief caused him to try to control Nancy as a drill officer controls new recruits. His core beliefs created the reality he feared most—her rebellion.

Those who believe others are bound to reject them show a similar pattern. This was Erica's core belief, and she had evidence to support it. Her life had been a series of lost relationships. Her friends had rejected her again and again. Erica's life was filled with stories of abandonment. Her recent boyfriend had left her after she threatened and attempted suicide repeatedly. But a closer look told a more complicated story. When Erica had gotten close to him, she had feared his rejection, and so she had tested him to see if he would reject her. She made unreasonable demands on his time, but he didn't leave. When he didn't, she reasoned, *He hasn't rejected me yet, but he will someday.* So she pushed some more and got involved with another man. He still didn't reject her, but she was convinced he would eventually. Then she started the suicide talk and wrist-slashing. Finally he left, confirming Erica's core belief, *Others are bound to reject me.* Erica's belief created the painful reality.

These examples illustrate a tenet of cognitive therapy: *When our experiences and our beliefs do not match, our natural tendency is to misinterpret our experiences rather than to change our beliefs.* Jack's and Erica's core beliefs affected their perceptions of reality and ultimately caused the events they feared most. Rather than changing their beliefs to be more accurate, they continued to misperceive their experiences to fit their prior beliefs.

An Example of a Template

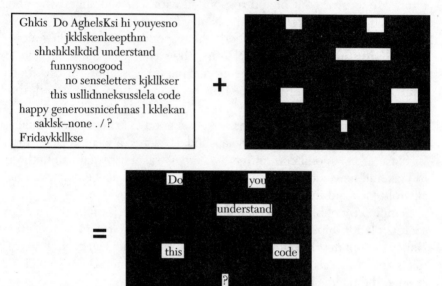

Fig. 7–1

Core beliefs are *cognitive templates*. A template is a pattern or gauge used in constructing or interpreting something. Many of us used templates to interpret simple codes as children, as shown in Figure 7–1. By putting the template over a sheet of scattered words, we decoded the message. We approach our world in a similar way, using our cognitive templates to notice some experiences and block out others. It gives us the impression we understand clearly, but actually we are ignoring everything blocked out by our templates. Cognitive counselors help their clients strip away dysfunctional templates to see reality more accurately and more completely.

CORE BELIEFS AND AUTOMATIC THOUGHTS

Although automatic thoughts point to underlying core beliefs, there are differences between the two. First, automatic thoughts are cognitive responses to specific situations. Core beliefs, in contrast, are general rules that cut across many situations. When Harry burns the lasagna he reasons, *I'm such a bad cook; everything I do fails.* This is an automatic thought in response to a specific situation. His underlying core belief, *I must be competent in everything I do*, is more general. It fuels his automatic thoughts when he burns the lasagna, when he arrives late for work, when he forgets his son's little-league game, and every other time he makes a mistake.

Second, automatic thoughts are conscious and easily accessed by clients. Core beliefs are not. They reside beneath consciousness and must be inferred from conscious thoughts and feelings.

Third, core beliefs are more resistant to change than automatic thoughts. Automatic thoughts can be refuted by evidence, but core beliefs cause people to distort the evidence rather than refute their thoughts.

Automatic thoughts are conscious, situation-specific, and easily refuted with evidence. Core beliefs are unconscious, general, and not easily changed with evidence.

Discussing only automatic thoughts and core beliefs oversimplifies human cognition. Many thoughts are more general than automatic thoughts, but more specific than core beliefs. As described in chapter 2 (see Figure 2–2), thoughts can be compared with layers of an onion. As the outer layer of automatic thoughts is peeled away, another level, more general than the first is uncovered. Each layer becomes more general and more resistant to change.

Imagine Tina walking into her house after a long day at work and finding her husband's socks on the living-room floor. She immediately says to herself, *That's ridiculous! Those socks shouldn't be on the floor. What a slob I married!* Her automatic thoughts reflect some cognitive distortions—an arbitrary *should* statement and a label for her husband. Underlying her automatic thoughts is the more general belief, *My house should always look perfect.* This arbitrary *should* fueled her automatic thoughts when she first saw the socks. More general still is Tina's belief that she must be in control of the things that happen to her: *It is awful when I lose control of my situation.* Her deepest core belief, driving all the others, is her fear that she will not be loved if she loses control of herself or things around her. These various levels of belief are represented in Figure 7–2.

Although there are more layers than automatic thoughts and core beliefs, each layer does not need to be treated with different counseling strategies. Techniques for changing automatic thoughts, as described in

109

Layers of Belief

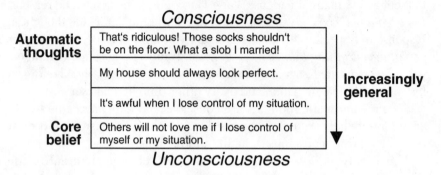

Consciousness

Automatic thoughts	That's ridiculous! Those socks shouldn't be on the floor. What a slob I married!
	My house should always look perfect.
	It's awful when I lose control of my situation.
Core belief	Others will not love me if I lose control of myself or my situation.

Increasingly general

Unconsciousness

Fig. 7–2

chapters 5 and 6, are also useful for changing other conscious cognitions. Techniques for changing core beliefs, described in chapters 7 and 8, also work to change deep intermediate-level beliefs.

Since people have a natural desire to know themselves, they provide their own motivation to peel away the layers of their thoughts. As they understand themselves better, they gain more control over their feelings and desire to look even deeper into their personality and thought processes.

Although core beliefs are unique to individuals, there seems to be a common element: At the deepest level of thoughts is the desire to feel lovable—to be loved and to love. Christian counselors have hope to offer because they point clients to the greatest love of all:

> Who shall separate us from the love of Christ? Shall trouble or hardship or persecution or famine or nakedness or danger or sword? As it is written: "For your sake we face death all day long; we are considered as sheep to be slaughtered." No, in all these things we are more than conquerors through him who loved us. For I am convinced that neither death nor life, neither angels nor demons, neither the present nor the future, nor any powers, neither height nor depth, nor anything else in all creation, will be able to separate us from the love of God that is in Christ Jesus our Lord. (Rom. 8:35–39)

I do not see Christian counseling as a unique set of techniques. Christian counselors often use the same techniques as their secular colleagues, but the process of counseling is enhanced by Christ as his unconditional love becomes known by counselor and client.

CLUSTERS OF CORE BELIEFS

Faulty core beliefs can be grouped into three clusters, all ultimately focused on lovability. The first is *conformity,* beliefs that cause people to seek *approval* in order to attain love. Approval-seeking can become so dominant that personal identity is lost in the search for closeness with others. Some examples of core beliefs of conformity are:

I must be approved of by everyone for the things I do.
If people really knew me, they would think I was a terrible, weak,
  uninteresting person.
I am fully responsible for the feelings of others.
Others will love me more if I am always selfless.
Others are bound to reject me.

Those with conforming templates are cooperative, good team players, and easy to get along with if they feel approval; but when they don't feel approval, they experience depression. They say to themselves: *I'm no good. Others think I'm a loser, so I am a loser. Without love from* _____, *my life isn't worth living. Other people's problems are my fault.* They feel inadequate and guilty, blaming themselves unnecessarily for things beyond their control.

Conformity beliefs are the basis for dependent behaviors. Imagine Paula, a woman who has been repeatedly abused by her husband. She reasons (with help from her controlling husband), *He wouldn't hurt me if I didn't do things wrong.* By blaming herself, she conforms to her husband's excuses and avoids assertive action. Inwardly, she desperately needs her husband's love and is willing to take the abuse to keep being loved.

Conforming beliefs are also the basis of co-dependent behaviors. Co-dependents believe they are responsible for making others happy, so they seek approval above truth. The man who repeatedly tells his wife she is not an alcoholic may be contributing to her denial to gain her approval. The woman who suppresses her desire for a career to please her husband, who believes a woman's place is in the home, is seeking approval above truth-telling. Co-dependents suppress their feelings and true thoughts in order to maintain peace—to keep from driving others away.

The second cluster of beliefs relates to *compulsivity*. These are core beliefs rooted in the assumption that one is loved because of performance. Those with compulsive beliefs confuse who they are with what they do; they confuse lovability with performance. Examples of *compulsive* core beliefs are:

I should be competent at all times.
Love must be earned with unusual accomplishment.
I should be able to satisfy all my own needs.
I should be productive all the time.
Perfection is the only acceptable standard.

Those with compulsive beliefs are responsible and punctual, hard workers who get a lot accomplished. But it goes too far when they attach their personal worth to their performance. Often they come for counseling with anxiety disorders, eating disorders, or other addictive behaviors. They have an impoverished self-image and place unrealistic demands on themselves.

They give to others but don't receive because they want to earn what they get. Since close relationships require both giving and receiving, they often feel isolated from others, alone in their world. They work even harder to earn love, but become so busy they have no time for the love they seek. Eventually they become addicted to achievement, still feeling unloved and pessimistic about the future.

Those with compulsive beliefs have difficulty accepting God's love, because God's love cannot be earned. This may be particularly difficult in a society where earning and individualism are valued. In Matthew 20:1–16, Jesus told a parable emphasizing the inadequacy of our earning mentality. The parable was about a landowner who went to the village to find workers for his vineyard. He wanted an early start, so he recruited workers at 6 A.M. "I will pay you one denarius," he said, promising them a normal day's wages for their labor. At 9 A.M., he returned to the village to recruit more workers, saying only, "I will pay you what is right." He returned again at noon for more workers, and again at 5 P.M. When the workday was done, the landowner called in his temporary help and payed them all one denarius—whether they had been there all day or only an hour. When the ones who had worked twelve hours grumbled, the owner responded, "I have the right to do what I want with my money. I can be generous with whomever I desire." Jesus' point is clear: Our earning mentality does not help us understand a gracious God. We can never earn God's love. Those with compulsive core beliefs have difficulty accepting God's unconditional love.

The third cluster of beliefs relate to *control* of oneself and/or others. Some examples of control beliefs include:

If things do not go as I have planned, I am out of control.
(self-control)
If others don't do as I wish, they do not care about me.
(control of others)
I must be strong because only the strong are loved.
(self-control and control of others)
If anything goes wrong it is my fault.
(self-control)
There are evil people who must be punished.
(control of others)

Control beliefs can focus on self or others. Those focusing on self-control are often disciplined, predictable people as long as they maintain control. But when they lose control, they are unpredictable and impulsive. They often seek counseling for impulse-control problems, relationship problems, and anger management. Those invested in controlling others are often respected for their firm convictions. But they are hard to get along with. They usually don't come for counseling, but their spouses or employees do.

Those with control beliefs sometimes feel like time bombs on the inside because they have so much anger and frustration. Those intent on controlling themselves rarely express these negative feelings because they want to master their own emotions. Those intent on controlling others routinely express their feelings, sometimes aggressively.

The main advantage in identifying belief clusters is that counselors can quickly form hypotheses about their clients' core beliefs. There are many exceptions; but depressed clients often have *conforming* beliefs, anxious and eating-disordered clients often have *compulsive* beliefs, and angry clients often have *controlling* beliefs. Not everyone fits neatly into one core belief cluster, but many people have a primary cluster. That is, they tend to use one cluster in viewing most situations, even if they don't use the same beliefs all the time.

To summarize, cognitive therapy can be viewed as a six-step procedure, shown in Figure 7–3. The first three steps have been described in previous chapters. Step 4, finding underlying core beliefs, requires detective work that is the focus of this chapter. Cognitive detectives look for clues from several sources: automatic thoughts, childhood experiences, and views of God. The core beliefs can only be treated after they are accurately identified.

The Steps of Cognitive Therapy
Presenting Symptoms

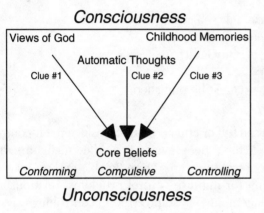

Consciousness

Views of God	Childhood Memories

Automatic Thoughts

Clue #1   Clue #2   Clue #3

▶◀▼▶

Core Beliefs

Conforming   Compulsive   Controlling

Unconsciousness

Step 1
Understand problem thoughts and feelings.

Step 2
Find automatic thoughts.

Step 3
Dispute automatic thoughts.

Step 4
Find core beliefs.

Step 5
Dispute core beliefs.

Step 6
Maintain gains.

Fig. 7–3

CLUE SOURCE 1: AUTOMATIC THOUGHTS

As mentioned in chapter 5, the two reasons for evaluating automatic thoughts are symptom relief and finding core beliefs. Since automatic thoughts flow from underlying assumptions, they can provide clues as counselor and client work to find core beliefs.

Look for Themes

Judy, a young depressed woman, came each week with a new set of automatic thoughts. One week she was discouraged about her marriage because her husband had yelled at her. The next session she was upset with her boss who had expressed disapproval regarding Judy's work. The following session she was worried about an upcoming vacation with her in-laws, whom Judy was convinced had never liked her. Each week, her automatic thoughts were different; but they converged on the common theme, "without the approval of others, I am unworthy of love."

Consistent themes in automatic thoughts point to specific core beliefs. Those who, like Judy, believe they must have approval from others (conforming cluster) struggle with automatic thoughts of rejection or abandonment. Those who believe they must earn love with unusual effort and flawless performance (compulsivity cluster) confront automatic thoughts of inadequacy or impending doom. Those who believe they must control themselves or others to be loved (controlling cluster) confront thoughts of powerlessness and helplessness. The following examples demonstrate how automatic thoughts reflect core beliefs.

Helplessness and Powerlessness. Vic came for marital counseling because he wanted a quick fix for his wife, Chris. She had been sexually unfaithful, and Vic believed she had never adequately repented. Although they had seen several counselors, Vic had not found any way to make Chris repent.

For twenty years, Vic had controlled the marriage. He had determined how the kids were disciplined, whether or not Chris worked outside the home, how the money was spent, and what leisure activities the family pursued. Chris finally rebelled, had an affair with her pastor, and then told Vic she wanted more control over her life. The more Chris asserted herself, the more convinced Vic became that she was rebelling.

Vic and I met separately to discuss his thoughts and feelings. His automatic thoughts centered on helplessness and powerlessness. When Chris spent some money without asking him, he told himself, *She is rebelling against my leadership.* When his kids starting having problems in school, he thought, *they are troubled because their mother is rebellious.* His automatic thoughts were varied, but they centered around control issues. Vic's core belief had to do with controlling others: "Others must do what I say, or they don't love me."

I Must Be Perfect. The theme of Joan's self-talk was, *I am a bad person*. She found weak evidence to support her conclusions. One session it was, "I am a bad person because I can't keep up with my work and give my children as much time as I want." The next it was, "If I weren't a bad person I would have more friends." Later she had told herself, "I'm a bad person because I use my credit card too much."

Joan's abusive self-talk intensified her bulimia. When she felt bad, she ate. She ate lots. Then she felt she was a bad person for eating so much; so she vomited and felt she was a bad person for vomiting. Her automatic thoughts pointed to a compulsive core belief. Joan believed, *I must be perfect in order to earn love.* Since she was not perfect, she felt unloved and inadaquate—she saw herself as a bad person.

Fear of Rejection. Holly smashed her true feelings down inside herself to avoid conflict. Sexually abused as a child, she learned to turn off feelings of pain. Now, as an adult, she still ran away from feelings. Did she ever feel angry? Holly smiled and said, "Not much." Did she ever feel happy? Her silent stare gave the answer.

Before we could discuss automatic thoughts, we did remedial work to get Holly in touch with her feelings. She completed the homework assignments described in chapter 6, identifying and labeling her feelings. Once she understood her feelings of fear and anger, she could describe automatic thoughts accurately. Her thoughts centered around peacekeeping: *I must not show my anger, or my family will fall apart,* and *My feelings aren't important—no one needs to know them.* They pointed to her fear of rejection. Deep down Holly believed, *If I show my feelings, others will reject me.* She had stuffed her feelings inside to cope with her fears of abandonment and rejection.

Look for Hot Cognitions

In addition to looking for common themes, look for hot cognitions, those thoughts that evoke powerful emotions during a session. The thoughts with roots tapping into core beliefs have the strongest emotional impact. This is demonstrated in the following dialogue.

> CLIENT: My kids are sick again. Whenever they're sick, I feel so awful going to work. But what else can I do?
>
> COUNSELOR: You feel trapped.
>
> CLIENT: I want so much for them to know I love them. But we can't afford for me not to work.
>
> COUNSELOR: I'm hearing a connection in your mind between your working and your kids feeling loved. "They won't know I love them if I work all the time."
>
> CLIENT: (*tears come to eyes; long pause*)
>
> COUNSELOR: What went through your mind just then?
>
> CLIENT: I felt like such an awful person.

Cognitive therapists often ask, "What went through your mind just then?" By focusing on the emotion-provoking thoughts, the counselor better understands the core beliefs that drive automatic thinking. In this situation, the counselor may suspect a compulsivity core belief: "I must earn love by meeting the needs of everyone I know."

CLUE SOURCE 2: CHILDHOOD EXPERIENCES

Childhood memories are another important source of information in the search for core beliefs. Several techniques can be used in the counseling office and as homework to bring out relevant memories.

Life Story

Although cognitive therapy does not focus primarily on childhood issues, some understanding of early experiences helps the counselor make sense of current symptoms and recognize core beliefs. I usually introduce the need for childhood information by asking for a life story:

> We've been talking about the feelings and thoughts you currently experience. Even though I won't be talking with you as much about childhood as some counselors do, I can understand your present symptoms better if I know some things about your past. It would be helpful to hear your life story. Tell me some about your parents, your family, your schooling, and so on. I'll interrupt and ask questions as we go.

This open-ended introduction gives clients freedom to describe their early years as they wish, sometimes providing additional data for the counselor. For example, if a client describes childhood without ever referring to a father, it may indicate a desire to avoid feelings associated with the father. Look for expressions of feelings during the life story. Does the client seem depressed when talking about moving a lot as a child, angry when talking of parents divorcing, lost in thought when describing feelings of loneliness in high school? Observing emotions gives counselors leads to important areas of inquiry.

While listening to the life story, look for self-talk the client may have used as a child. A child who believed, *Nothing I do is good enough,* may grow up desperately seeking approval. The child believing, *I can get love with hard work and success,* may unrealistically face perfection demands as an adult.

Sometimes clients will have few childhood memories. In these cases, I have them remember as much as possible during the session, then assign homework to help them recall more. I instruct them to sit quietly five minutes each day, with pen and paper handy, to think about their childhood. Any memory they have, no matter how small, is to be recorded. Most people are able to recall more than they thought possible after just a few days.

Snapshots

Lori's earliest memory was listening to her mother scream, "I hate you, and I wish you were never born!" She felt sad and lonely as she recalled the memory, thinking: *Mother was right—I'm no good at all.* Not surprisingly, Lori was addicted to approval as an adult.

Did Lori's mother cause her to crave approval because of this one burst of anger? Probably not. But for some reason Lori remembered that incident as a symbol of her childhood. Her hunger for approval may have been in place before her mother screamed those words. Maybe her memory was distorted, and her mother's words were much more benign than she remembered. Whatever the case, her memory maintained her faulty beliefs.

Lori's memory is what I call a "snapshot"—a memory of a specific event that is recalled with its associated thoughts and feelings. Snapshots don't give counselors comprehensive views of their clients' childhoods, but they do reflect the beliefs and assumptions of the one who is remembering.

Getting snapshots from clients gives additional direction in the search for core beliefs. They can be asked for snapshots during a counseling session or given a homework assignment such as the Snapshots form in Appendix B. Look for themes in their memories.

Snapshot Categories

	Positive Memories	*Negative Memories*
Conforming Beliefs	Memories of warmth and acceptance.	Memories of blame, teasing, or rejection.
Compulsive Beliefs	Memories of achievement and success.	Memories of inadequacy or pressure to do more.
Controlling Beliefs	Memories of independence and freedom.	Memories of discipline or lack of freedom.

Of course there will be many variations in snapshot memories and exceptions to the categories proposed here; but the themes of the memories provide another clue in the search for core beliefs.

Scrapbooks

Family albums or scrapbooks can also be useful tools in bringing back childhood memories and feelings. Have a client bring a scrapbook or family photo album to the session, look at the pictures together, and ask the client:

1. How is this child feeling?
2. Why does he/she have those feelings?
3. What is this child's image of himself/herself?
4. What fears or worries does this child have?
5. What kind of future does this child dream about having?

Then look for themes in the client's childhood feelings. Did inadequacy, dread, fear, guilt, or loneliness come up again and again as you looked at the pictures? Were there repetitive thoughts of looking foolish or feeling hopeless about the future? Did the client feel pressured to perform as a child? Were memories of power struggles with parents or others recalled while viewing the pictures? These feelings provide additional clues to the client's core belief.

Alternatively, the counselor can assign the scrapbook viewing as homework. Be sure to give specific guidelines so the client knows what to look for in each picture. Scrapbooks and photo albums are also used in *historical analysis*, a technique used to revise core beliefs that is described in chapter 8.

To summarize, those with conforming core beliefs are likely to remember feelings or fears of rejection and abandonment when recalling childhood memories. Those with compulsive core beliefs often felt pressured to be perfect, successful, and attractive. Those with controlling beliefs remember feeling alone, isolated from others, and over- or under-disciplined. Because there are many exceptions and variations to these patterns, childhood memories are best viewed as one source of evidence, not conclusive by themselves.

CLUE SOURCE 3: VIEWS OF GOD

Scott's childhood memories put him on the streets of San Francisco, fistfighting his way to respect. He recalled fighting every week of his life to gain respect. If he lost a fight, his older brothers would beat him up again when he got home. He grew up in a tough world, feeling alone and isolated, and he learned that only the strong survived. His core belief was control-focused: "I must be in control for others to love me."

Not surprisingly, Scott had difficulty believing in God. How can one control an omnipotent God? Scott's faith was strongest when he and others prayed for his wife to be healed from cancer and she was. He had controlled God, getting his way through prayer. But after his wife's healing he drifted away, again feeling distant from God. Scott described a God whose love depended on good deeds. *If I read my Bible and am nice to those around me,* Scott reasoned, *then God may save me.* Whenever I mentioned grace, he dismissed it, insisting he believed differently.

Scott's belief that he had to control every part of his life was projected onto God. He needed a faith that he could control, salvation that he could earn by good works. Any other image of God was not acceptable.

As with Scott, many clients project their core beliefs onto their religious views—providing another clue for understanding core beliefs. Several exercises can be used to assess views of God.

Exercise 1: Adjectives Describing God

I have clients report the first few words or ideas that come to mind when they think of God. They often reveal self-image as they discuss their image of God. One who views God as distant, aloof, and disappointed may be projecting conforming beliefs, assuming God's approval is as hard to obtain as human approval. One who views God as a taskmaster—a heavenly supervisor—may be projecting compulsive beliefs, assuming God's love can be earned with exceptional performance and commitment. One who sees God as judging, harsh, and punitive may be projecting control beliefs such as, "Only the strong survive." Others have emotionally embraced God's grace, recognizing they can never earn God's love. They enjoy resting in God's promises and the assurance of their own lovability.

Exercise 2: Images of God

Clients who have difficulty giving adjectives to describe God often respond to a visual imagery exercise which can be assigned as homework or done in the counseling office. Have the client relax with deep breathing and/or progressive muscle relaxation; then have him or her form a mental picture of standing in God's presence. Be specific when giving instructions:

Notice everything you possibly can as you form this picture in your mind. Look to see God's facial features, posture, and stature. Look around, notice the things around you, the way you feel, and your response to God. Let your imagination take over and see what happens. Feel free to talk with and listen to God. After you are done, think for a few moments about your thoughts and feelings as you stood before God. What do those thoughts and feelings suggest about your views of God?

After the imagery exercise, the client's thoughts and feelings are discussed. The counselor asks, How did you feel about yourself as you were standing before God?" or "What expressions were on God's face?" or "What thoughts went through your mind as you were facing God?"

Critics of visual imagery have correctly noted that we cannot control God with our imagination. The point of this exercise is not to control God, but to understand how one views God and how those views reveal self-image and core beliefs.

Exercise 3: Progress Report from God

Another homework assignment to assess views of God is the Progress Report shown in Appendix B. Have clients complete the form, evaluating themselves as they imagine God would. Most people are familiar with progress reports from work—appraisals that review strengths and weaknesses, focus on goals for the future, and sometimes determine promotions and salary. What if God wrote progress reports for each human? What would he say about each of us? Of course, none of us knows how God views us, so this assignment assesses one's perception of God rather than vice versa.

Interpreting Views of God

After these exercises have been completed, the counselor interprets the results. The perceptions of God I often find with various belief clusters are summarized below.

Image-of-God Categories

	Positive Memories	*Negative Memories*
Conforming Beliefs	God as warm, approving, loving.	God as distant, inaccessible, disapproving.
Compulsive Beliefs	God satisfied or impressed with one's Christian behavior.	God disappointed—expecting more.
Controlling Beliefs	God as powerful and almighty.	God as angry and judgmental.

As with other exercises in this chapter, there are many exceptions to the categories I suggest. These categories can, however, provide one more source of evidence to help find a client's core beliefs. Evidence from several sources usually point to a single core belief or cluster of beliefs.

Once a core belief is identified, the counselor and client go on to the next step—disputing the core belief.

FACT OR FICTION?

Throughout this chapter, I have referred to core beliefs as absolute fixtures of human personality. I have been especially restrictive by implying each person has one and only one maladaptive core belief. These assumptions are debated by cognitive therapists.

One founder of cognitive therapy, Aaron Beck, writes as if cognitive schema (his term for core beliefs) are actual parts of human personality.[1] Another, Donald Meichenbaum, sees cognitive schema as metaphors or fictions that help clients simplify their thinking and identify goals for change.[2] Are templates fact or fiction?

It is both impossible and unnecessary to answer this question. We cannot capture the complexity of core beliefs with simple research designs and can probably never know with certainty whether or not people are always guided by core beliefs. Core beliefs guide perceptions and behaviors, but cognitive therapists simplify and fictionalize the role of core beliefs by suggesting each client has only one faulty belief. We further simplify by assuming we can always accurately identify and change the belief.

The distinction of core beliefs as fact, fiction, or fictionally simplified, is unnecessary. Whatever the case, clients in cognitive therapy believe they are changing their personality by changing their beliefs. As a result, they gain confidence, begin believing they can understand and control their feelings, and develop more flexible thinking. They feel lovable, live more consistently, and enjoy authenticity. Even if the concepts of cognitive therapy are oversimplifications, they are therapeutically oversimplified. And it is good to remember that all human categories and theories are oversimplifications that we gladly accept in order to cope with our world better.

CHAPTER EIGHT

CHANGING CORE BELIEFS

REAL ESTATE COSTS HAVE FORCED many hopeful homeowners to invest sweat as equity. They buy a run-down property and renovate. Some can renew their houses with relatively minor cosmetic changes—stripping old wallpaper, installing new carpet, putting in a new bathroom vanity. Other houses require much more work—removing old walls and building new ones, reinforcing the faulty foundation, removing dry rot, rebuilding floors, and so on. Just as renewing houses can be a lot of work, renewing minds, as Paul instructed Roman Christians to do (Rom. 12:2), often requires hard work also.

C. S. Lewis credits George MacDonald with a similar parable. Lewis writes:

> Imagine yourself as a living house. God comes in to rebuild that house. At first, perhaps, you can understand what He is doing. He

is getting the drains right and stopping the leaks in the roof and so on: you knew that those jobs needed doing and so you are not surprised. But presently he starts knocking the house about in a way that hurts abominably and does not seem to make sense. What on earth is He up to? The explanation is that He is building quite a different house from the one you thought of—throwing out a new wing here, putting on an extra floor there, running up towers, making courtyards. You thought you were going to be made into a decent little cottage: but He is building a palace. He intends to come and live in it Himself.[1]

Although renewing our minds involves much more than cognitive therapy, Christian counselors can help others renew their minds, leading them to God's transforming presence rather than the vapid earning-and-approval mentality so prevalent in our world. As Christian counselors, we draw on greater resources than our secular colleagues. Any cognitive therapist can help free others from faulty core beliefs—beliefs requiring them to earn love or have approval at all times—but only Christian counselors can direct others to God's deep reservoir of unconditional love. God's loving presence can renew minds and transform lives.

Not all Christians have transformed their lives by renewing their minds. Many feel unlovable, unworthy, or unwanted. Christian conversion may have been a powerful experience in their lives, but they feel trapped in their imperfect personalities, caged by painful memories and failure experiences. They see a foggy image of God's love, but do not experience God's clear and freeing presence in their lives.

As I see it, the ultimate goal of Christian cognitive therapy is to free people from core beliefs that keep them from fully experiencing God's grace. By combining spiritual disciplines with techniques from cognitive therapy, we can help others see God and themselves more accurately and know God's transforming love more fully. This chapter includes twelve techniques to change core beliefs. Some of these techniques come from cognitive therapy authors and others from Christian traditions.

STRATEGIES FOR RENEWING MINDS

Before describing techniques to change core beliefs, I restate two general principles of cognitive therapy. First, collaborate rather than confront. Core beliefs, unlike automatic thoughts, are resistant to change and will not be abandoned just because the counselor disagrees. The client who believes, *I must be approved of for everything I do*, will learn to *suppress* the belief when the counselor confronts him or her with, "That's nonsense!" The client wants approval from the counselor and may even feign progress to gain that approval; but *suppressing* a belief is not the same as *changing* a belief. Instead, the counselor could respond, "Your belief—that you must have approval from others—is one we could work together to change." Collaborating with the client leads to *changed* beliefs rather than *suppressed* beliefs.

Second, expect gradual change. Core beliefs have often shaped a person's perception of the world for dozens of years. Changing those beliefs, renewing the person's mind, cannot be done in one session. Typically, the first six to ten sessions of cognitive therapy are spent revising automatic thoughts and finding core beliefs, and the last six to ten focus on changing core beliefs. Repetition is the counselor's friend. Each time a technique is repeated, another fragment is chipped away from the old belief and another brick laid in building a new belief.

The following techniques are listed alphabetically. The order does not imply any system of priority or preference. Counselors need to use clinical judgment in deciding which techniques to use and in which order to use them.

Technique 1: Advantages and Disadvantages

Counselors are mistaken if they assume core beliefs have only bad consequences; most core beliefs have advantages and disadvantages. Asking others to identify advantages and disadvantages of their beliefs helps them see the consequences of the assumptions they make. Once advantages and disadvantages are listed, the original belief can be revised so that most advantages are retained and disadvantages eliminated.

Mindy, a depressed woman whose core belief was, *Without the approval of others, my life is worthless*, recognized several advantages to this way of thinking. First, she always kept her house clean because she feared someone might stop by unexpectedly and judge her negatively if her house were untidy. Since she valued cleanliness, this was one advantage of her belief. Second, she was an outstanding employee because of her belief. She felt she needed to impress her boss, so she went beyond the call of duty. She had received promotions and raises very rapidly. Third, she was a sensitive mother. She wanted her children to like her, so she listened carefully to their words and tried to meet their needs and desires.

Mindy's belief also had disadvantages. One was her depression. Because she felt she needed *everyone's* approval, she usually focused on the one or two people who weren't approving or appreciating her. Her marriage was highly dysfunctional because she tried to get her husband's approval and became depressed and angry when he forgot to express appreciation. He began to resent her need for approval, withdrew more, and the vicious cycle began. The more he withdrew, the more she demanded approval. The more she demanded approval, the more he withdrew. Another disadvantage of her belief was the frantic pace she maintained. Because she tried to earn the approval of all people, she rarely had time to relax or contemplate life. She was burning out.

In contemplating the advantages and disadvantages of her beliefs, it became clear that the belief could be revised slightly to maintain the advantages and lose the disadvantages. Her revised belief, *Approval is nice, but I will not get everyone's approval—I need not base my value on others' opinions,* still motivated her to keep her house tidy, work hard, and attend to her children. But she didn't have to have her house spotless (tidy was adequate). She did not always have to have her husband's approval or to work fanatically. Her new belief granted her time to relax, appreciate God's love, and find meaning in her life. It required time, the use of other techniques described in this chapter, and practice before her new belief was convincing to her; but she eventually learned to live peacefully, even without the approval of others.

Technique 2: Contemplative Worship

Imagine entering the throne room of God. You are stunned with the majesty of the room, but the room pales in comparison to God's own glory. As Isaiah did when he saw the Lord (Isa. 6:1–8), you feel overwhelmed at the greatness of God and inadequacy of humankind. Now imagine God getting up from the throne, approaching you with arms outstretched, embracing you, and saying, "I love you." As God's arms surround you, you feel loved, safe, and welcome.

This imagery exercise is consistent with what the Bible teaches about God's majesty and mercy—God is both powerful and loving. Yet when I have clients imagine God, they often view God as angry and harsh, because they see themselves as unlovable. God gets angry (Jer. 10:10; Rom. 1:18; Heb. 3:11), but the greater theme of Scripture is God's compassion, love, and forgiveness (Ps. 103:13; John 3:16, Rom. 5:8; and Eph. 2:4, 5). Those trying to change core beliefs can use imagery exercises to see God more accurately.

In the last chapter, I described how imagining God can help diagnostically: clients often project their feelings of inadequacy and unworthiness onto God, seeing God as disappointed or angry. In this chapter, images of God are a treatment tool. Client and counselor together define an accurate image of God, then the client uses that image to subvert old ways of thinking and foster more accurate perceptions. Religious imagery is an effective tool in cognitive therapy with religious clients.[2]

When I asked Greg to imagine God, he saw God pushing him aside. A depressed pastor, Greg felt distant from God, alone in his ministry. When we discovered his core belief, *Others are bound to reject me*, we understood that his image of God was a projection of his own core beliefs. God pushed him aside because Greg was convinced that everyone, including God, would eventually reject him. When Greg and I decided a more realistic belief was, *I am loved by God and many others,* he adjusted his image of God accordingly. He pictured himself sitting on God's lap, feeling loved and accepted. Forming this image was difficult for Greg at first, but as he became more skilled at the image, he felt more of God's love and acceptance.

Technique 3: Continuum Technique

After the Oakland A's lost the first two games of the 1990 World Series, a relief pitcher on the team said, "People say we're good. Now we find out. If we don't win the series, we're not good." Two years earlier, after the A's lost the series to the Los Angeles Dodgers, the same pitcher concluded, "I guess you can't say we're a great team. You have to do it all to be a great team." The dichotomous thinking is obvious: if we're not the best in the world, we're not good at all.

Faulty core beliefs are often based on similar dichotomous thinking: *Either I'm perfectly competent or I'm no good at all,* or *If everyone doesn't approve of me, my life is awful,* or *Others must do everything I think they should do.*

The continuum technique allows counselors to challenge the dichotomous thinking in a collaborative way. Rather than using all-or-none thinking, the counselor establishes a scale with the client. The scale forces clients away from dichotomous thinking, as demonstrated in the following dialogue.

COUNSELOR: It sounds like you're telling yourself you are no good.

CLIENT: I'm not. A good person would never do the things I do.

COUNSELOR: You mean, "A good person would never yell at her children as I did this morning."

CLIENT: Yes.

COUNSELOR: Let's make a scale. Zero is the worst we can imagine. Ten is a perfectly good person. Let's start with a mass murderer. Someone who breaks out of prison, walks into a department store and murders fifteen people. Where might that person belong on our scale?

CLIENT: Zero is the worst?

COUNSELOR: Yes.

CLIENT: I'd say zero!

COUNSELOR: Okay. How about the man who has a fight with his wife and in a moment of impulse opens the dresser drawer, pulls out a gun, and shoots her dead.

CLIENT: That's not quite as bad, maybe a two.

COUNSELOR: All right. Where would you put the person who cheats on taxes each year?

CLIENT: That's hard. A four.

COUNSELOR: How about the woman who yells at her children every few weeks and then feels terribly guilty?

CLIENT: I get it.

COUNSELOR: Where would you put yourself on our scale?

CLIENT: About a six.

COUNSELOR: Now let's go back to your original thought, "I'm no good." How can that be revised?

CLIENT: I'm not as good as I would like to be.

COUNSELOR: You're not perfect. And no one else is either.

This client labeled herself, "no good." The continuum technique helped her see the dichotomous thinking and come to a more rational belief, *I'm not as good as I would like to be*. With some more work, she might eventually conclude, *There are things about me I like and things I don't like.* With enough practice and repetition, she can change her destructive beliefs to more adaptive ones.

Technique 4: Probability Estimates and Consequences

Those with anxiety disorders often dread the future, though the things they fear are unlikely to occur. The woman with the core belief, *I am bound to be rejected,* may expect her husband to be unfaithful, even without evidence to support her suspicions. The man who believes, *I must be in control of every situation,* may fear flying despite the relative safety of air travel. A collaborative way to discredit these irrational ideas is to ask how probable events are and what the consequences of the events would be.[3]

Kevin feared flying and his upcoming business trip to New York was evoking anxiety. His automatic thoughts were focused on the flight itself, but his core belief was that he needed to be in control of himself and everything around him. Our interaction went like this:

COUNSELOR: You've discussed feeling fearful. What is worst thing that could happen?

CLIENT: Well the worst thing is a crash.

COUNSELOR: How likely would that be? One chance in ten? One chance in a hundred?

CLIENT: Probably less than that. Maybe one chance in ten thousand.

COUNSELOR: Okay. So the worst thing would be a fatal crash and the chances of that are very remote. What else might happen?

CLIENT: I could have a panic attack on the plane and have nowhere to go.

COUNSELOR: How likely is that?

CLIENT: It feels likely. Maybe fifty-fifty.

COUNSELOR: Okay, one chance in two. Is that consistent with previous flights? About every other flight you have a panic attack?

CLIENT: No.

COUNSELOR: How often have you had them in the past?

CLIENT: Well I only fly a couple times a year, but I've never had a panic attack.

COUNSELOR: I'm a little confused here. You said the chances were fifty-fifty, but you've never had a panic attack on a flight.

CLIENT: Well, the chances feel more likely than they are. Maybe they're one in ten.

COUNSELOR: Okay. Well, let's assume the worst happens and you have a panic attack. What will be the worst thing about that?

CLIENT: I would be miserable and have nowhere to go.

COUNSELOR: I see. And then what would happen?

CLIENT: Well, I'd eventually get over it, but it would be like hell.

COUNSELOR: So the worst thing would be a miserable few minutes. And there's about one chance in ten that that will happen.

Although the focus of this dialogue was automatic thoughts, I was chipping away at Kevin's core belief. "What would be the worst thing . . . ?" challenged his assumption that he must be in control. Although panic attacks are unpleasant, he could live through one on a plane, and it wasn't very likely to occur in the first place. Kevin took the flight, felt nervous, but had no panic attack. It was a success experience, demonstrating he could survive even when he lacked control over his circumstances.

Technique 5: Historical Analysis

Using scrapbooks to diagnose core beliefs was discussed in the last chapter. The same materials can be used in historical analysis, a technique to revise core beliefs. First, have clients bring photographs, scrapbooks, and other memorabilia to a session. This will seem like a strange request, so an advance explanation of historical analysis is helpful.

Second, construct a timeline on a large sheet of paper. The timeline is a worksheet to trace the core belief throughout the client's life. An example for Katie, a young woman convinced her husband would eventually be unfaithful, is shown in Figure 8–1. On the top part of the worksheet is the core belief to be evaluated: "Others are bound to reject me." At the bottom, the client's age is charted by years. As the client goes through various pictures and memorabilia, ask for feelings and thoughts that are associated with the memories. The events and associated feelings are then recorded on the worksheet. The example in Figure 8–1 is abbreviated, having only four memories recorded. A complete historical analysis will have dozens of memories and feelings scattered along the timeline. Also have clients estimate, on a scale of 1–100, how much they believed their core belief at various points in life. Katie's belief, that she is destined for rejection, grew gradually stronger through childhood.

Third, after the timeline worksheet is completed, look for patterns with the client. Was there a sudden change in feelings or memories at a certain point of life? What experiences led to the core belief? For Katie, going to school and experiencing loneliness and rejection from peers was a turning point in her life.

A Sample Timeline

Historical Analysis				
Core belief being evaluated: *Others are bound to reject me.*				
Strength of Core Belief	10	50	75	100
Feelings	Happy	Isolated	Lonely, dumb	Rejected
Memory	Parents' affection	No school friends	Teased at school	Lost relationship
Age	5	10	15	20	25, etc.

Fig. 8–1

Historical analysis helps combat core beliefs because it helps clients answer the question, "Why do I have this belief?" As they associate their beliefs with a certain event or set of events, they realize their belief is optional, created by unpleasant circumstances that may no longer exist.

Technique 6: Logical Analysis

Logical analysis was briefly discussed in chapter 6 as a technique to counter automatic thoughts. It can also be used to change core beliefs. McMullin suggests clients work through the following set of questions:

1. What belief bothers me?
2. Can I logically support this belief? Do I have evidence it is false?
3. Do I have evidence my belief is true?
4. Realistically and objectively, what will happen if I continue to believe this way?[4]

This set of questions breaks clients out of the circular thinking characterizing core beliefs. "It's true because it's true" is the normal way of evaluating core beliefs. By forcing logic into the evaluation process, people learn their beliefs are less inevitable than they originally thought.

Joanna's belief was circular: *Men only love me because I have sex with them.* Her belief created her reality. Whenever she became interested in a man, she had sex with him because she wanted to be loved and she thought she was only loved because of sex. But after having sex, her belief was stronger than ever: *He only cares for me because I'm good in bed.* Her belief pushed her to irresponsible sex and kept her from believing men loved her for nonsexual reasons. Her circular reasoning, stemming from her sexual abuse as a child, kept her from challenging her belief.

Logical analysis was one tool Joanna and I used as we evaluated her belief. Realistically, she had no evidence her belief was true because she had never refused sex with a caring, consenting man. Evidence for the falseness of her belief came from observing other relationships. Many people have good, caring friendships without sex. She also knew her belief was self-destructive: it led to irresponsible behavior and broken relationships. Previously, she wanted to change to avoid guilt feelings. After logical analysis, she wanted to change because she understood where her self-destructive patterns were leading. Although it was not a cure-all, logical analysis helped Joanna break out of her circular thinking and critically examine her core belief.

Technique 7: Overact

Just as paradox can be used to evoke rational responses to automatic thoughts (discussed in chapter 6), people can recognize their faulty beliefs by overacting them. Counselors can emphasize the faulty nature of core beliefs by instructing clients to exaggerate their beliefs and act accordingly for several hours.

Of course, this needs to be done with moral and ethical sensitivity. I would not have asked Joanna to exaggerate her belief that men love her for sex because it might have evoked more irresponsible behavior. But the technique works well for many clients. For example, Lois is a middle-aged accountant who believes she must be perfect to avoid rejection. Her counselor makes the following assignment:

Between the hours of 3 and 5 P.M. today, overact your belief. Pretend that absolutely everything you do has to be perfect or everyone will reject you. Your work must be flawless, your appearance immaculate, your manners perfect. Try doing your work and watch what happens. You'll need to double and triple check all your figures because a mistake would be devastating to your reputation. Remember, if you make even a little mistake, everyone in the world will reject you. Your marriage and all your friendships are at stake.

As Lois overacts her belief, she will probably be overwhelmed with the oppression of such a belief. She will feel tense, vulnerable, inadequate, and hurried. These feelings can be discussed in the next session, helping Lois recognize that her belief, even in its milder form, leads to unnecessary feelings. Paradoxically, by overacting her belief she learns she can control her feelings with her thoughts. Thus, she thinks critically about her unnecessary perfection demands.

Technique 8: Prayer

Christians often use prayer in counseling sessions. Changing core beliefs can be a specific topic of prayer. Counselor and client can pray together for release from unnecessary perfection demands or approval addictions, for example.

Many Christians seek new feelings. They may know rationally God loves them, but they don't feel loved. They may hold to a sterile belief that they don't need everyone's approval, but even minor disapproval starts an avalanche of painful feelings. They need to pray for a new set of feelings that correspond with their rational beliefs.

Because feelings are often viewed skeptically among evangelicals, many are hesitant to pray for feelings. We read and hear that our faith is not feeling-based. Many Christians have seen a train diagram with FACTS pulling FAITH and FAITH pulling FEELINGS. We are told to base our faith on the facts, and the feelings will follow. The principle is good since feelings usually flow from beliefs, but many Christians know the facts, have the faith, and still lack the feelings. As they rid themselves of faulty core beliefs, I encourage clients to pray for feelings consistent with their new beliefs. Sometimes they need permission to pray for feelings because they have learned to undervalue the importance of feelings.

Technique 9: Pretend

When Robert passed gas once as a child, his alcoholic father became angry and made him sit outside in the snow for thirty minutes, wearing only pajamas. He felt powerless and angry and was unable to express his anger because he feared his father. Robert learned that only the strong survive and he developed this controlling core belief: *Others show their love by doing what I say.* But when he controlled others, they became resentful and Robert had to deal with their disapproval. We eventually found another core belief: *It is awful if others don't approve of everything I do.* One core belief caused Robert to control others and evoke their disapproval; the other caused him to feel angry and powerless when others disapproved. The more disapproval he felt, the more controlling he became. The more controlling he became, the more disapproval he experienced. After going through several marriages, Robert came for counseling. Once we found his core beliefs, I made the following assignment:

COUNSELOR: You've been talking today about your relationship with your boss. This relates to your core belief that insists you have everyone's approval.

CLIENT: Yeah. I was thinking that, too. I don't know why it matters so much that he likes me. It doesn't seem to matter, though, because we fight all the time anyway.

COUNSELOR: Well, you two have different managing styles.

CLIENT: We sure do!

COUNSELOR: Here's an assignment for the coming week. I'd like you to find two hours, maybe today, when you go back to work, or tomorrow. During that time, pretend your boss's approval doesn't matter. I know it does matter, but during that two hours, pretend it doesn't. And we can talk about what you find out next week. Which two hours would work the best?

CLIENT: Today would be fine.

COUNSELOR: Okay. From 3 to 5 P.M. today?

Robert came back the following week and reported that those two hours had gone very smoothly. In fact, they had gone so well that he had continued the exercise all week. He and his boss had not fought about any of the usual trivial issues. By pretending he didn't have his core belief, he experienced the benefits of healthy thinking.

Pretending can be used with a variety of beliefs. It allows clients to experience how new beliefs will help them and gives them hope for a brighter future. Brief pretending periods are best. Pretending a novel belief more than a few hours requires more insight, motivation, and adherence than most are able to give.

Pretending need not be seen as pretense or phoniness. Christian psychologists Frederic Craigie and Siang-Yang Tan call the technique, "Doing the truth."[5] Many Christian clients will find an assignment in doing the truth more palatable than an assignment called pretending, though both names refer to the same exercise.

Technique 10: Rehearsal

Rehearsal is the bread-and-butter technique for changing core beliefs. Whereas many of the techniques described here are used occasionally and selectively, rehearsal is used repeatedly with every cognitive therapy client. The basis of rehearsal is a fundamental principle of cognitive therapy: *Old beliefs give way to new beliefs with enough repetition.*

Just as actors have to rehearse lines over and over until they become automatic, those trying to change faulty thinking patterns need to rehearse new beliefs repeatedly. Each time the new ways of thinking are repeated, another fragment is chipped away from the old belief.

Work with clients to list alternatives to their core beliefs. Some examples are:

Core Belief: *I must have the approval of everyone I know.*
Alternative 1: *Approval is nice, but not essential.*
Alternative 2: *Some people love me even when they don't approve.*
Alternative 3: *It is unrealistic to expect everyone's approval.*
Alternative 4: *God's love is forever—whether or not I have approval from others.*

Core Belief: *I must be perfect in everything I do.*
Alternative 1: *I will do the best I can, but perfection is unrealistic.*
Alternative 2: *God's love doesn't depend on my performance.*
Alternative 3: *I have limits of time and energy.*
Alternative 4: *People care for me even when I'm not perfect.*

Core Belief: *If others don't do what I say, they do not love me.*
Alternative 1: *Other people have minds of their own and still care for me.*
Alternative 2: *Others don't need to please me.*

Alternative 3: *Others have different values and perspectives than I.*
Alternative 4: *I will live obediently before God and allow others to make their own choices.*

Have clients write the revised beliefs on notecards or on the Rehearsal handout included in Appendix B. Although this can be assigned as homework, most clients need help writing alternatives to their core beliefs and prefer to complete their notecards during a counseling session. They then carry the cards in their shirt pockets, purses, or wallets to rehearse their revised beliefs during spare time—in the grocery store checkout line, at the gas station, during television commercials, and so on.

Some people need reminders to rehearse their new beliefs. I keep a supply of bright orange stickers in my office and give clients several stickers to place in strategic spots. Whenever they see a sticker—on the car dashboard, a bedroom dresser, or a bathroom mirror, for example—they remind themselves to rehearse their new beliefs. At this point in cognitive therapy, the counselor sounds like a football coach: "Practice, practice, practice!" The practice pays off as clients peel away old beliefs and renew their minds with healthy, liberating ways of thinking.

Technique 11: Scripture Memory

A psalmist wrote to God, "With my lips I recount all the laws that come from your mouth" (Ps. 119:13). Recounting God's words can help Christians renew their minds and transform their thoughts. The one who anticipates rejection from others receives comfort from God's words:

Who shall separate us from the love of Christ? Shall trouble or hardship or persecution or famine or nakedness or danger or sword? As it is written: "For your sake we face death all day long; we are considered as sheep to be slaughtered." No, in all these things we are more than conquerors through him who loved us. For I am convinced that neither death nor life, neither angels nor demons, neither the present nor the future, nor any powers, neither height nor depth, nor anything else in all creation, will be able to separate us from the love of God that is in Christ Jesus our Lord. (Rom. 8:35–39)

And the anxiety-prone victim of perfectionism does well to remember:

So do not worry, saying, "What shall we eat?" or "What shall we drink?" or "What shall we wear?" For the pagans run after all these things, and your heavenly Father knows that you need them. But seek first his kingdom and his righteousness, and all these things will be given to you as well. Therefore do not worry about tomorrow, for tomorrow will worry about itself. Each day has enough trouble of its own. (Matt. 6:31–34)

When used sensitively and appropriately, Scripture challenges faulty core beliefs and helps establish new beliefs. Clients can be assigned Scripture memory as homework. However, two warnings are appropriate.

First, troubled clients resent Scripture being used as a Band-Aid™. Ask any grieving person how many times he or she has been reminded of Romans 8:28, "And we know that in all things God works for the good of those who love him. . . ." Those in grief come to resent this passage because well-meaning friends use it as though the passage should magically remove grief.

So counselors need to carefully explain the therapeutic purpose of using Scripture memory: Scripture can be used as a tool to replace old beliefs with new ones. If a Scripture memory assignment is not well explained, clients might perceive it as another *should*: "You *shouldn't* have these old thoughts and you *should* always think in these biblical ways." In response to *shoulds,* the client feels more guilty and therapeutic progress slows.

Second, be sure to check the context of the Scripture passage before assigning it to a client. If a verse is pulled out of context, the client will often notice and question the counselor's credibility. Matthew 18:20 is a wonderful verse to emphasize God's continual presence, "For where two or three come together in my name, there am I with them"; but the context of the passage is church discipline. The verse refers to a team of two or three confronting one who is living in sin, but we often use it to emphasize God's presence in small group worship or fellowship. Isn't God with us even when we aren't with two or three? Clients with good knowledge of Scripture will view a counselor skeptically if verses are carelessly used to support the counselor's prior conclusions. Conversely, clients sometimes use Scripture out of context to support faulty beliefs, providing the counselor opportunity to correct faulty perceptions and demonstrate the theme of healing grace that pervades Scripture.

Here are a few passages that can be assigned to confront typical core beliefs:

1 Chronicles 16:34	Psalm 25:6	Psalm 30:5
Psalm 32:1, 2	Psalm 42:8	Psalm 46:1
Psalm 103:1–5	Psalm 103:13	Isaiah 40:31
Isaiah 43:2	Isaiah 54:10	Jeremiah 31:2
Matthew 20:1–16	Luke 1:50	Luke 14:16–24
Luke 14:20–24	John 3:16,17	Romans 3:23, 24
Romans 4:4, 5	Romans 4:16	Romans 5:2
Romans 5:8	Romans 8:31, 32	Romans 11:5, 6
1 Corinthians 2:9	1 Corinthians 6:11	1 Corinthians 15:10
2 Corinthians 12:9	Ephesians 2:8, 9	2 Timothy 1:9
Titus 3:5	Hebrews 4:16	James 5:11
1 John 1:9	1 John 3:1	

The context of some of these passages requires explanation to clients. For example, "When you pass through the waters, I will be with you. . . ." (Isa. 43:2), is a promise to Israel. Although this is a historical promise, it seems consistent with the biblical theme that God provides for devoted followers. Although the context is specific, the principle of the passage is as relevant to a client trying to overcome faulty core beliefs as it was to the nation of Israel.

Technique 12: Support Groups

Christians are called to God, but also to one another. Fellowship and community are among the chief benefits of a Christian lifestyle. Those trying to change core beliefs can often draw support, encouragement, and insight from friends and family.

Christian support groups vary in structure. Some are formalized as Bible study or shepherding groups. Once trust develops in the group, which sometimes takes a year or more, members can share intimate personal concerns. Some clients find it useful to share their faulty core beliefs with a support group, allowing the group to help replace the beliefs with more accurate and healthy thoughts. For others, support groups are less formal. Some have close Christian friends they meet with regularly for lunch, racquetball, card games, coffee, and so on. These friendships can often provide support for people as they replace core beliefs. Others live near family and have confiding relationships with siblings, parents, or children. These can also be supportive relationships.

Making a core belief known to at least one trustworthy person other than the counselor provides clients with emotional support to replace old beliefs.

Medical researchers have made tremendous gains in transplants during recent decades. Heart, kidney, and bone-marrow transplants are now common occurrences. The techniques described in this chapter allow counselors to do emotional transplants. Faulty core beliefs that have threatened people's dignity and self-perceptions for years can be replaced with new beliefs, resulting in obedience and a new awareness of God's love.

CHAPTER NINE

MAINTENANCE

MOST GOOD THINGS IN LIFE require maintenance. Our commitment to Christ requires ongoing effort and commitment. The enthusiasm of new love carries marriage along for several weeks or months, but eventually every couple realizes their marriage requires ongoing work. Even possessions—the backyard swingset, automatic dishwasher, stereo, and car—require maintenance.

Those who learn to cope with negative feelings in cognitive therapy also require maintenance. In counseling, there are two sorts of maintenance: regularly scheduled maintenance appointments and appointments clients schedule because of unexpected recurring problems. Regularly scheduled maintenance is part of almost every counseling relationship.

When clients are most distressed, cognitive counselors usually schedule appointments once or twice weekly. But after clients successfully identify and begin revising core beliefs, biweekly appointments are usually adequate. After several biweekly appointments, monthly appointments are set. Sometimes bimonthly or semiannual appointments are useful before termination. This weaning process allows clients to feel confident in their improvements and trust their emotional functioning before counseling is finished.

Because cognitive therapy is short-term and most clients make rapid progress, it is possible to terminate clients prematurely. *When in doubt, schedule another maintenance session.* This is especially important for timid, approval-seeking clients who may resist calling for another appointment because they fear disappointing the counselor, telling themselves, *If I were a good client, I wouldn't have to call for another appointment.*

After several maintenance sessions, I present clients with an option of moving to on-call status. Although we do not schedule another appointment time, I invite them to call whenever necessary for another appointment. This second kind of maintenance—needed because of unexpected recurring problems—is never used by most clients. Nonetheless, it is good to discuss on-call status; just knowing a counselor is available adds security as the counseling comes to an end.

Although most clients do not call, some call several months or years later with further counseling needs. When clients call for another appointment because of recurring symptoms or problems, counselors have to deal with their own self-talk: *If I were a good counselor, my clients would never have to return,* or, *This represents failure in my work.* This is unnecessarily abusive self-talk. There are many reasons clients may return for more help. They are confronting new challenges; they contact their former counselor because they trust him or her to help them cope with life's difficulties.

Although clients appreciate having a counselor available, most do not want to depend on a counselor for years to come. So both forms of maintenance—scheduled follow-up sessions and on-call sessions because of recurring problems—focus on the same goal: teaching clients to be their own counselor. Clients who successfully learn to counsel themselves learn to anticipate and cope with the obstacles they face.

OBSTACLE 1: EMOTIONAL GRAVITY

Just as physical gravity pulls us back to earth, emotional gravity pulls us back to our core beliefs, especially in times of stress. When faced with new or unexpected pressures, we revert to former ways of thinking and coping.

Keith struggled with feelings of depression when he first came for counseling. His job injury had forced him out of his career and into the jaws of a merciless workers' compensation situation. He had lost his work, and his integrity was being questioned by an insurance company that wanted him off the payroll. As we explored his feelings, we discovered a core belief requiring him to have continual approval from others. His job had given him approval, but without it he felt abandoned and rejected. As we changed his belief, he began feeling better and pursued education for a new career in engineering. He graduated with honors and landed an excellent job.

Several years later, Keith returned, again feeling depressed. His job was going well, but his marriage was not. Although there were many marital issues to consider, most of Keith's discussion focused on the division of household labor. When his wife asked for more help around the house, he felt unappreciated. As his marriage had become more stressful, his old template, with its incessant approval demands, had battled its way back.

Keith's situation illustrates how stress, like gravity, pulls people back to earlier beliefs and coping mechanisms. Clients experiencing these reversals benefit from the same techniques discussed in past chapters. They need maintenance in order to return to their higher level of functioning.

Counselors are wise to warn their clients of emotional gravity. In the last scheduled appointment, I try to make a statement like this:

My guess is that strong forces will work against the good progress you make. I think of it as gravity. Just as gravity pulls you back to earth, you'll find it's tempting to start believing those old thoughts— to be pulled back to your core beliefs. This tendency is especially true in times of stress. So watch for the gravity and keep fighting against it. And I want to add that the emotional gravity won't always be as strong as it is the first few months. With enough time and practice, your new ways of thinking will be almost as automatic as your old ones used to be. But it takes practice and perseverance!

Teaching clients to be their own therapist requires showing them a road map—an understanding of what has led to their problems, what changes have been made during counseling, and what will come after counseling is over. Warning them of emotional gravity helps them prepare for the future.

OBSTACLE 2: FAILURE TO GENERALIZE

I was a quarterback for one day of eighth-grade football. The coach saw me passing before practice and was impressed with my abilities, so he had me play quarterback instead of my usual position on the offensive line. But throwing a few spirals before practice does not make a quarterback. Once we started scrimmaging, I lost composure. I threw interceptions, couldn't find open receivers, and generally did a lousy job of quarterbacking. By the end of practice, I was permanently back to my offensive line position.

Like my pre-practice warmup, a counseling office is an artificially protected environment. Like the scrimmage, things are more difficult outside the counseling office. Techniques that work well in a counselor's office may be difficult to apply in other situations.

Some have recurring symptoms because they do not generalize what they learn in counseling to new situations. The previous example of Keith demonstrates this tendency. He learned to cope with his job-related loss but did not apply the same principles when his marriage began to falter.

Teaching others to generalize appropriately is a problem faced by all counselors that cannot be completely eliminated. But two tools help control the problem.

First, counselors can use hypothetical examples to teach generalization skills. These hypothetical or role-play situations work well during the last few counseling sessions, as the following dialogue demonstrates:

COUNSELOR: You've made a lot of progress in the past few months. Summarize for me what you have learned.

CLIENT: I've learned I don't have to be perfect in order to earn love. Lots of people love me—my husband loves me, my kids love me, my friends love me, and God loves me—even when I mess up.

COUNSELOR: That's a wonderful summary. And those changed beliefs have affected the way you feel. You felt very depressed at first,
and now, though you still have times of discouragement, you are in
control of your feelings.

CLIENT: Yeah. It feels so much better.

COUNSELOR: Now, let's look to the future. Let's pretend a year from
now you get a call from the police and find your son is in trouble
with the law. It's a different situation than the depression we've
talked about. How might you apply the same principles to deal with
your feelings then?

CLIENT: That's tough! (pause) I guess my first feelings would be
anger and embarrassment.

COUNSELOR: Embarrassed because of what others might think.

CLIENT: Yeah. So I could tell myself it doesn't matter very much
what others think. Even if they don't think I'm a perfect mother, it
doesn't have to ruin the way I view myself.

The counselor could go on to discuss other hypothetical situations, each
time focusing on how the principles discussed in counseling could be
used to control negative feelings.

Second, homework assignments also help clients generalize principles
discussed in the counselor office to real-life situations. All the homework
assignments discussed in this book and listed in Appendix B require the
client to apply cognitive therapy principles in the absence of the counselor.
As clients successfully complete homework assignments, they gain confidence in their ability to think more flexibly and feel better. They learn
to help themselves in stressful situations before they have opportunity to
discuss the situations with their counselor. They learn to generalize.

Nonetheless, some clients return for more counseling because of a related
problem. Rather than seeing it as a failure of either the client or the counselor, it is best viewed as another opportunity to correct maladaptive core
beliefs. Core beliefs, like malignant tumors, sometimes grow back.

OBSTACLE 3: FAULTY SELF-TALK

Another obstacle to recovery is faulty self-talk when symptoms recur.
All of us, including those recovering from depression, are bound to feel

discouragement at times. Those recovering from anxiety disorders will still struggle with stress and worry at times. Those counseled for anger management will occasionally feel angry after treatment. When the symptoms recur, they interpret their symptoms with self-talk. Their self-talk, in turn, affects the severity of their symptoms.

Let's say Mr. Y has successfully completed cognitive therapy for depression. Several weeks later, his house is burglarized and he feels discouraged and angry. He reasons, *I'm as bad as ever—my counseling was a waste*. This self-talk leads to more discouragement and before long he is clinically depressed again.

Compare this with Ms. X who has also completed cognitive therapy for depression and has also had her house burglarized. She feels discouraged and angry, as Mr. Y did. But her self-talk is different: *This is a difficult time. Most people would feel discouraged about this. I'm sure glad I've learned tools to cope with the discouragement*. Within a few days, she is feeling less discouraged and more hopeful.

Mr. Y interpreted his discouragement differently than Ms. X, leading to feelings of hopelessness and depression. He might have done better if his counselor had reminded him that feelings of discouragement are normal and warned him about unhealthy self-talk he might anticipate during times of discouragement. It is good to prepare clients for three self-statements that are common and likely during times of sadness or anger.

Many conclude, *I'm as bad as ever*, when confronted with negative feelings. They sometimes believe their counseling was worthless. As with Mr. Y, this reasoning often leads them to deeper despair and frustration. Those who anticipate this self-talk can counter with, *I'm experiencing negative feelings, as everyone does from time to time, but I am not as bad as ever*.

The belief, *I'm as bad as ever*, often occurs during counseling as well as after counseling is over. Clients often show dramatic improvement after several counseling sessions, and assume they are "fixed" forever. A week or two later, they arrive for counseling with a downcast face, feeling sure they are as miserable as ever. Counselors can help them interpret their feelings differently: *I've made great progress the last few weeks, but I still get depressed sometimes*. This prepares clients to deal with their feelings of failure when their sadness returns after counseling is over.

Another technique is to spend part of the final counseling session preparing self-statements the client can use when negative feelings recur.

145

The statements are collaboratively derived, written on notecards, and sent home with the client. Anticipating recurring symptoms helps one cope when they arrive.

A second form of self-talk is, *I'll never get better*. This goes beyond, *I'm as bad as ever,* and assumes hopelessness. Clients warned of this self-talk can develop coping self-statements in advance, as demonstrated in the following collaborative interaction:

COUNSELOR: Since this is our last session for now, I thought it would be good to anticipate what might go wrong to sabotage the good progress you have made. Do you remember a few weeks ago when you came to my office saying, "It's hopeless—I'll never get better."

CLIENT: Yeah. That was when my boss had reprimanded me. That was a lousy day.

COUNSELOR: Yes it was. And we talked about your conclusion, "I'll never get better." What do think about that conclusion now?

CLIENT: Well, it was wrong. I am better. I've been getting better all along.

COUNSELOR: Even when you believed you weren't.

CLIENT: Yes.

COUNSELOR: I see. You know, my guess is that you will have that thought again someday: "I'm as bad as ever and I'll never get better." Tell me how you might respond when that happens.

CLIENT: What I'd like to do is argue with myself.

COUNSELOR: Good. How?

CLIENT: By saying, "I've felt this way before and it's not true. I am already better and I will continue to get better."

COUNSELOR: Good. Let me write that down.

At this point, the therapist writes the coping statement, "I'm already better and I will continue to get better," on a notecard and helps the client derive two or three more coping self-statements. The notecards provide the client with tools to fight the rigid, unrealistic thoughts of never improving.

A third form of hindering self-talk is, *I'm still not happy*. This self-statement hints at an underlying belief, *I should always be happy*. Again, warning the client that these thoughts may come is helpful. Coping self-statements can be developed in advance. For example:

Happiness is nice, but I won't always feel happy.

Many people find meaning and purpose in their life with or without happiness.

The most likely path to happiness is obedience and consistency. But there are no guarantees I will find happiness.

Clients who successfully become their own counselors learn to anticipate future stressors and prepare coping strategies in advance. This advance preparation is first modeled in the counseling office as counselor and client work together to anticipate potential problems and their solutions. Those who prepare for the nagging self-doubts and unrealistic expectations that come after counseling are more likely to maintain their progress than those who are surprised by continued feelings of discouragement, sadness, or anger.

OBSTACLE 4: LACK OF SOCIAL SUPPORT

Glenda works to overcome irrational guilt each week with her counselor, then goes home to a husband who uses guilt as a motivator. Because she depends on her husband for financial, spiritual, and emotional security, she accepts the guilt he gives and comes back to counseling each week feeling depressed and worthless. It is simplistic to view Glenda's problem individualistically. She is part of an unhealthy marriage. Her social support system is lacking.

When patients who have no place to live are discharged from mental hospitals, they often end up homeless. Should we be surprised when they again become mentally ill? This is an extreme example of naively releasing someone without regard for his or her social context. Although the case is less extreme, it shows equal ignorance when we terminate clients without understanding the social system to which they are returning. Since we all are social beings, it is unrealistic to expect clients to maintain gains while living in an unsupportive environment. Conversely, those with supportive family and friends are better able to maintain the progress made in counseling.

Counselors can work to enhance social support in several ways. First, *understand*. From the first counseling session to the last maintenance session the counselor works to understand the client's support system. How does the client describe his or her spouse? What role do the children or parents play in the client's life? How important are various friendships? What about church-related involvements and relationships? What cultural or subcultural values affect the client? Systems theorists have had a positive influence on counselors and psychologists, reminding us that individuals come from social systems.

Kathleen's hysterectomy left her believing she wasn't a complete woman. As her cognitive counselor, I tried to change those thoughts, which I called irrational, to more realistic ones. For example, *Even without a uterus, I am still a complete woman.* Despite my efforts, she clung to her belief that she was not a complete woman. After several months of slow progress I discovered her thoughts were shared by others in her ethnic subculture. Her social system was different from mine. Once I understood the differences in our social systems, we collaborated on more effective self-talk, such as, *Even if others think I'm less of a woman, I can still like who I am and who I am becoming.*

Collaboration also enhances social support for clients. Counselor and client work together, deciding what does and does not need changing.

Earl, a Christian counselor who promotes a partnership model for Christian marriage, believes neither husband nor wife needs to take a dominant role: They negotiate the tough decisions and give each other freedom to make personal choices. Sarah, his depressed client, views marriage differently. She believes her husband is the head of the home and is responsible for shepherding the family spiritually and emotionally. Earl may be tempted to destroy Sarah's system by pointing out that it contributes to her depression. Imagine he succeeds, and Sarah begins viewing her marriage differently. But her husband hasn't changed his views of marriage. And Sarah's parents express their concern, pointing out their view that the Bible teaches male headship. Earl has convinced Sarah to give up an old way of thinking but has created more problems than he has solved.

Earl would do better to collaborate with Sarah on which beliefs she needs to change. The headship-submission model may work acceptably for Sarah and her husband; it may not need to be changed. For example, Sarah might decide to work on assertively expressing her opinions and feelings, while still seeking to submit to her husband's final decision. This would not be Earl's ideal solution, but it fits within Sarah's social system.

Third, counselors enhance social support by *getting family members involved* in counseling sessions. Near the end of individual counseling, it is often wise to invite the client's spouse or family to come to some of the maintenance sessions. This needs to be done with the client's permission. Having the spouse and/or family involved in some of the maintenance sessions allows for a more comprehensive discussion of the client's progress and the potential setbacks the client will face in the near future. These sessions often elicit support from family members and help them see the important role counseling has played in their loved one's life.

OBSTACLE 5: UNREALISTIC EXPECTATIONS

A great myth of humanity is that we can somehow avoid pain if we make the right choices, eat the right foods, avoid the wrong activities, or have faith in the right god. But pain comes anyway. Pain is a thread in the fabric of life.

The myth that pain can be avoided crumbles in young or mid adulthood when people realize they are vulnerable to the same losses and pressures as others. Some assume the pain means something is wrong, so they come for counseling, learn to better understand themselves, and feel some pain reduction. But if they leave counseling with the same myth they had years before—that pain can be avoided—they will be disappointed with the future.

In the final stages of counseling, clients need to understand and sometimes revise their expectations for the future. I often begin this discussion by asking clients to complete the sentence, "Life should be _____." The responses I hear often point to unrealistic expectations. Many assert *life should be fair,* but a quick look around shows it isn't. Americans feast on the profits of our information age while children around the world starve from malnutrition. Children die from leukemia. Drunk drivers steal the lives of their innocent victims. Clients who leave counseling expecting fairness are bound for disappointment. Others suggest *life should be happy.* And they feel happy as they finish counseling, liberated from depression or anxiety or relationship troubles. But troubles are bound to come. Parents die. Children rebel. Houses burn. Stocks crash. Many are able to feel God's joy in the midst of these crises, but happiness is too much to ask.

As clients discuss and dismiss unrealistic expectations for the future, Christian counselors can help them find more realistic hopes. Here are a few of my favorites.

Realistic Goal 1: Authenticity

Jesus criticized the religious leaders of his day for their hypocrisy. They taught one life and lived another. Jesus' life and words called his followers to be authentic people, honest and growing in integrity. Authenticity is a noble and realistic goal for clients to pursue as they finish cognitive therapy.

The core beliefs discussed in chapter 7 are obstacles to authenticity. Those who believe they must be perfect to earn love will naturally hide their imperfections. Those who believe approval is essential will hide their flaws to gain approval.

Realistic Goal 2: Obedience

"Blessed are they who keep his statutes and seek him with all their heart" (Ps. 119:2). Those who seek obedience find joy. Those who seek happiness above all else often sacrifice obedience and never find happiness. Joy flows from obedience.

Consider the obedience and joy mingled in the words of the apostle Paul, imprisoned and facing possible execution, as he wrote to the Christians at Philippi:

> Yes, and I will continue to rejoice, for I know that through your prayers and the help given by the Spirit of Jesus Christ, what has happened to me will turn out for my deliverance. I eagerly expect and hope that I will in no way be ashamed, but will have sufficient courage so that now as always Christ will be exalted in my body, whether by life or by death. For to me, to live is Christ and to die is gain. (Phil. 1:18b–21)

> Rejoice in the Lord always. I will say it again: Rejoice! Let your gentleness be evident to all. The Lord is near. Do not be anxious about anything, but in everything, by prayer and petition, with thanksgiving, present your requests to God. And the peace of God, which transcends all understanding, will guard your hearts and your minds in Christ Jesus. (Phil. 4:4–7)

This kind of obedience that leads to joy is a natural response to God's grace and love. Another form of obedience is more oppressive: obedience resulting from a neurotic need to earn God's love. The apostle Paul knew God's grace could never be earned. He wrote to Titus: "But when the kindness and love of God our Savior appeared, he saved us, *not because of righteous things we had done,* but because of his mercy" (Titus 3:4, 5, emphasis added).

Obedience that leads to joy comes from *responding* to God's grace rather than an attempt to *earn* God's grace. Obedience is a reasonable response to God's love.

Realistic Goal 3: Self-Forgetfulness

Christians hear many opinions about self-esteem. Some say we have to love ourselves before fulfilling God's commandment to love others. Some say we need to despise ourselves to properly understand God's sacrifice for humankind. In the process of debating self-esteem, we may miss an important point: *The goal is to be comfortable enough with who we are that we can forget ourselves and begin considering others.*

Some think too highly of themselves and become self-focused or conceited (see Romans 12:3). Others think they are worthless and end up basting in their self-doubt and worthlessness. Both extremes prevent self-forgetfulness. Christian counselors help their clients find self-understanding and self-acceptance so they can become self-forgetful.

Those leaving cognitive therapy cannot realistically expect to continually be authentic, obedient, or self-forgetful; but Christian counselors can emphasize how reasonable these things are for emotional health. As clients and former clients strive toward authenticity, obedience, and self-forgetfulness, they press on in their quest to eliminate approval addictions and perfectionism.

PART III

APPLYING COGNITIVE THERAPY

CHAPTER TEN
DEPRESSION

BRETT STUDIES A SMALL CREVICE on the darkened ceiling as he lies awake in the early-morning hours of a new day. He has become accustomed to waking around 3 A.M. to lie restlessly in bed while contemplating his worthlessness and the pain of his life. He rises at 6:30, cloaked in sadness, to shower and pick at his unappealing breakfast. He drives through heavy traffic to work (where his performance has been suffering in recent months), puts in his eight hours, drives home, eats a few bites of dinner, watches television, and goes to bed. The next morning he starts the same routine again.

Brett is not alone in his depression. Because it is so common, depression has been called the "common cold" of psychiatry. From 25 to 30 percent of college students and 50 to 80 percent of women after giving

─────────────

birth have symptoms of mild depression.[1] Eight to 10 percent of Americans experience severe depression during their lifetime.[2]

TYPES OF DEPRESSION

Counselors frequently see those with *"normal" depression*. While the boundary between normal and abnormal is not precisely defined, mood disturbances resulting from common human experiences are considered normal depression. Those in grief typically feel sad and show symptoms of depression. Grief reactions can result from death, divorce or separation, financial loss, the ending of a friendship, or many other losses. Grieving usually takes longer than friends and family expect it should, but once it is completed, the person returns to a nondepressed state.

College students often have times of normal depression resulting from time demands, broken relationships, uncertainty about the future, or self-criticism. Many students feel pressure to get outstanding grades, please their parents, fit into a group of friends, plan for the future, and develop an intimate relationship. These pressures come in a relatively short period of time, making depression common and understandable.

Counselors also see those with mild or moderate depression that is not considered normal. For those with *adjustment disorders,* a specific stressor triggers a stronger reaction than is typical, leading to depression. Virtually everyone feels discouraged when losing a job, but if a job loss leads to depression for several months, it is considered an adjustment disorder. Others have *dysthymia,* a moderate form of depression that has lasted for at least two years (one year for children and adolescents). Those with *cyclothymia* have alternating mood swings, feeling moderately depressed at times and feeling unrealistically elated at other times.

Major depression, the most severe form, is distinguished from dysthymia by the intensity and breadth of the symptoms. Major depression almost always requires medication and/or hospitalization in conjunction with psychotherapy or counseling. Counselors need to carefully assess suicide risk in those with major depression. Those who have considered or attempted suicide and have a specific plan for killing themselves are at highest risk.

Those with *bipolar disorder*, formerly called manic-depressive disorder, have more intense mood swings than those with cyclothymia. Their periods of severe depression are interspersed with times of extreme hyperactivity, euphoria, restlessness, and rapid speech.

Symptoms

The symptoms of depression can be remembered as A, B, and C. A stands for *affect*, or emotion. Those with depression feel sad, "blue," hopeless, discouraged, demoralized. Sometimes they also feel anxious, especially when their symptoms are first starting.[3]

B stands for *behavior*. With depression, a person's eating behavior changes. Usually depressed people lose their appetite and have weight loss. Occasionally, though, depressed people have excessive appetite and gain weight. Sleeping behaviors also change, causing early-morning awakening in most cases. Depressed people usually lack energy. They feel overwhelmed with all the responsibilities in their lives and have little motivation to complete even small tasks. Those with depression have little interest in sex. And muscular movement changes. Some report *psychomotor retardation*, where their movements slow down and any movement seems like a major effort. Others experience *psychomotor agitation*, where they feel restless, "on edge," and unable to sit still.

The C stands for *cognitive* symptoms. Depressed people think differently than others. They often have concentration and memory deficits, and they think in distorted ways. Aaron Beck describes a *cognitive triad*, a set of negative thoughts characterizing those with depression. First, depressed individuals think negatively about themselves: *I'm no good. I'm a loser. God could never love me.* Second, they interpret their experiences negatively: *Bad things always happen to me. This proves no one likes me.* Third, they view their future negatively: *This will never get better. My life is destined for misery.*[4]

Causes

Many explanations have been offered for the cause of depression. Psychodynamic therapists see depression as a response to loss. When we lose someone, according to Freud, we feel sad; but we also are angry with the person we lost. Because we deal with the loss by seeing the lost person as part of ourselves, we turn our anger inward and feel depression. Thus, depression is seen by some as anger turned inward.

157

Others suggest chronic stress leads to depression. Those living in poverty or facing chronic pain, for example, appear to be more vulnerable to depression.[5] Our fast-paced society makes its members vulnerable to stress and, thus, to depression.

Body chemicals almost certainly play a role in depression. Certain neurotransmitters (chemicals that transmit a nerve signal from one nerve cell to the next) called catecholamines appear to be lacking in some people with depression. Medications that increase catecholamines reduce depression. Conversely, medications that decrease catecholamines help calm those with mania (a hyperactive state of euphoria and impulsive behavior) due to bipolar disorder.[6] However, brain chemistry is much more complex than any current theory of depression, and it is clear that more than catecholamines affect mood. Brain scientists continue to look for biochemical explanations of depression.

Although most cognitive therapists agree that depression results from loss, stress, and brain chemicals, they look primarily for self-talk contributing to depression. Aaron Beck identified several core beliefs that cause depression:

1. In order to be happy, I have to be successful in whatever I undertake.

2. To be happy, I must be accepted (liked, admired) by all people at all times.

3. If I'm not on top, I'm a flop.

4. It's wonderful to be popular, famous, wealthy; it's terrible to be unpopular, mediocre.

5. If I make a mistake, it means I'm inept.

6. My value as a person depends on what others think of me.

7. I can't live without love. If my spouse (sweetheart, parent, child) doesn't love me, I'm worthless.

8. If somebody disagrees with me, it means he [or she] doesn't like me.

9. If I don't take advantage of every opportunity to advance myself, I will regret it later.[7]

If Brett, the depressed man described earlier, believes he must be on top or else he is a flop, then he is prone to depression whenever he feels second best. Since his job performance is faltering, his belief leads him to conclude he is worthless. Brett's beliefs contribute to his depression.

Others believe depression is sociologically based. We live in a society where success, wealth, fame, and prestige are excessively valued. Many people feel demoralized, empty, and directionless. Many dehumanized people believe no one cares about them, but only about what they can produce or provide for others. How could we not expect these and other social conditions to produce depression? And what about attitudes toward God? Could it be that depression results from lack of spiritual rootedness?

Notice that these different causes of depression are not mutually exclusive—all could be true at the same time. Society and religion both shape and reflect individual values, traditions, and emotional health.

COGNITIVE THERAPY FOR DEPRESSION

Although many factors may cause depression, some lend themselves to intervention better than others. Those who focus their treatment on cognitive explanations of depression have reason to be optimistic about the outcome of their work.

Effectiveness

As cognitive therapy gained momentum in the 1970s and 1980s, a number of researchers reported the effectiveness of individual cognitive therapy with depressed clients. The following studies demonstrate the effectiveness of cognitive therapy in treating depression:

Beck, Hollon, Young, Bedrosian, and Budenz, 1985
Blackburn, Bishop, Glenn, Whalley, and Christie, 1982
Collet, Cottraux, and Ladouceur, 1987
Dobson and Shaw, 1986
Kovacs, Rush, Beck, and Hollon, 1981
McLean and Hakstian, 1979
McNamara and Horan, 1986
Miller, Norman, Keitner, Bishop, and Dow, 1989
Murphy, Simons, Wetzel, and Lustman, 1984

Reynolds and Coats, 1986
Rush, Beck, Kovacs, and Hollon, 1977
Shaw, 1977
Simons, Lustman, Wetzel, and Murphy, 1985
Simons, Murphy, Levine, and Wetzel, 1986
Taylor and Marshall, 1977
Teasdale, Fennell, Hibbert, and Amies, 1984
Thomas, Petry, and Goldman, 1987
(*Complete references are provided in the Bibliography at the end of the book.*)

Beck, Rush, Shaw, and Emery cite several more studies, unpublished papers and dissertations, supporting the effectiveness of cognitive therapy.[8] Although many studies support the effectiveness of cognitive therapy for depression, it is important to remember that no one therapy has been proven more effective than others, as discussed in chapter 1. Some of the studies listed previously show cognitive therapy to be as effective as other forms of therapy and some show better results with cognitive therapy. Because of research design problems, it is premature to conclude cognitive therapy is better than other forms of therapy for treating depression.[9] Moreover, it is not clear that cognitive therapy is enough for all forms of depression. Some of the studies indicate cognitive therapy is more effective than anti-depressant medication, while others suggest combining both gives the best result. Medication is usually necessary to effectively treat those with suicidal thoughts, major depression, or bipolar disorder. Despite my warnings in interpreting these studies, *it is clear that cognitive therapy is one effective way to treat depression*. Participants in one study showed marked improvement within two weeks of beginning cognitive therapy.[10]

More recently, several researchers have reported that *cognitive group therapy* is also an effective way to treat depression.[11] The principles of cognitive therapy were applied in small therapy groups, and depressed participants improved.

To date, most researchers have focused on the overall effects of cognitive therapy without looking specifically at the counselor-client relationship. Since cognitive counselors are more than technicians, their relationships with their clients must certainly play some role in the outcome of counseling. Persons and Burns found clients' relationship with their therapist to be an important factor in the outcome of cognitive therapy.[12] Although only a few authors have discussed client-counselor relationships in cognitive therapy, it is an important area of future research.[13]

Special Treatment Considerations

In general, cognitive therapy for depression requires counselors to use the techniques described in previous chapters. But since depressed clients need to overcome their self-defeating ways of talking to themselves before core beliefs can be uncovered, some special considerations need to be mentioned.

Depressed clients often resist talking because it requires more energy than they want to expend. They tell themselves, *I'm too depressed to do anything, including talking*. To overcome this self-defeating talk, they need to observe themselves talking successfully with their counselor. Inexperienced counselors sometimes talk excessively to make up for their silent clients; but this backfires as the client reasons, *See, I knew I was too depressed to talk*. Counselors need to listen, even when their clients don't want to talk. Use reflections and allow reasonable silence. Clients learn they are not too depressed to talk, and they experience victory over their self-defeating thoughts.

Guideline 1. Use Reflections. Reflections demonstrate that the counselor has heard the client without capturing control of the conversation. Consider the following examples:

Example 1
CLIENT: I've been feeling lousy lately.
COUNSELOR: Whenever I feel lousy I go running. It helps a lot.

Example 2
CLIENT: I've been feeling lousy lately.
COUNSELOR: Has this feeling been going on for a long time?

Example 3
CLIENT: I've been feeling lousy lately.
COUNSELOR: When did you start feeling lousy?

Example 4
CLIENT: I've been feeling lousy lately.
COUNSELOR: Tell me more about that.

Example 5
CLIENT: I've been feeling lousy lately.
COUNSELOR: You said lately?

These examples are progressively better examples of what a therapist might say to a depressed client. In the first example, the counselor takes over the flow of the conversation by giving advice. The client will quietly listen and will probably not follow the advice. In the second example, the counselor asks a closed question (one that can be answered "yes" or "no"). Depressed clients will often give short, poorly explained answers to closed questions. By using an open-ended question, the counselor in the third example does not steal control of the conversation. The client can continue by explaining when the lousy feelings began. However, questions evoke defensive reactions in some depressed clients. They may feel it is too much work to answer lots of questions. The fourth example uses a statement rather than a question, thereby avoiding threat to the client. But some are uncomfortable with the direct command, "Tell me. . . ." The fifth example uses reflection in an open-ended way to get the same information. It allows the client to keep control of the conversation and prevents defensive reactions.

Guideline 2. Allow Reasonable Silence. Prolonged periods of silence may make a depressed client uncomfortable; but ten- or fifteen-second silences help the client formulate important thoughts. Again, the following examples illustrate this:

Example 1
COUNSELOR: You mentioned earlier that you are not sleeping well.
CLIENT: Yeah. My sleep is terrible.
COUNSELOR: Do you wake up early?

Example 2
COUNSELOR: You mentioned earlier that you are not sleeping well.
CLIENT: Yeah. My sleep is terrible.
COUNSELOR: Tell me more.

Example 3
COUNSELOR: You mentioned earlier that you are not sleeping well.
CLIENT: Yeah. My sleep is terrible.
COUNSELOR: (silent)
CLIENT: I wake up every morning and can't go back to sleep.

The therapist in the first example uses a closed question which could be answered "yes" or "no." In the second example, the therapist probes with a good open-ended statement. In the third example, silence accomplishes the same purpose. But the depressed client will feel most successful in the third example because he or she is giving information without it being specifically requested. The former self-defeating thoughts, *I'm too depressed to talk*, may give way to self-rewarding thoughts of success, such as, *I'm doing better than I thought I would*.

Other self-defeating thoughts depressed people commonly have are, *I can't do anything*, and, *Nothing in my life is good*. These depressing thoughts need to be changed before core beliefs can be challenged. Cognitive therapists assign progressively more difficult tasks and daily activity records to confront these self-defeating thoughts.

Guideline 3: Assign Easy Tasks First. Those who believe, *I can't do anything*, are unable to break down their goal into manageable chunks. A depressed man may complain, *I have to clean my house, but I just can't*. Cleaning the house seems overwhelming to him, but he might be able to manage smaller behaviors.

COUNSELOR: So you're telling yourself you can't do it—you can't clean your house.

CLIENT: It's too much work. I just don't have enough energy.

COUNSELOR: Tell me the things you have to do to clean your house.

CLIENT: Well, I have to vacuum and clean the kitchen and do the bathrooms. Then I really need to clean my garage. I have tools everywhere. There are cobwebs on the ceiling and the front porch needs to be scrubbed.

COUNSELOR: That *does* sound like a lot of work. Which would be the easiest chore of those you listed?

CLIENT: Vacuuming.

COUNSELOR: Which room in your house is the easiest to vacuum?

CLIENT: The living room. It's right by the closet where I keep the vacuum.

COUNSELOR: You're saying to yourself, "I can't clean my house. It's too much work and I don't have enough energy." Do you think you could vacuum your living room carpet before we meet again on Friday?

CLIENT: Probably.

This example demonstrates how a large task can be broken down to a much smaller one. During the next session, the counselor and client will collaborate on another task, slightly more difficult than vacuuming the living room. With each successful experience, the client feels better about himself and learns to argue against his belief that he lacks energy to do anything.

Guideline 4: Assign a Daily Activity Record. Those who tell themselves they have no pleasure in life are usually incorrect. They selectively forget pleasurable events and remember the rest. Cognitive therapists have clients record their activities for several days and rate each activity on a 1–5 scale, with 1 being very unpleasant and 5 being highly pleasurable. A sample Daily Activity Record form is shown in Appendix B.

Counselors then look at the completed activity record with their clients. Most clients find they experience pleasure in their lives, providing evidence that their self-defeating thoughts are inaccurate.

Typical Course of Treatment

Those with mild to moderate depression usually complete cognitive therapy within twelve to twenty sessions. The first six to eight sessions are used to identify and correct automatic thoughts. The final six to twelve sessions are used to revise core beliefs and as maintenance sessions.

Even with this short-term therapy, clients can expect to have ups and downs. One week they may have complete relief from depression and the next might be much worse. Warning clients about ups and downs keeps them from reasoning, *Things are as bad as ever; it's no use.* Some clients have sudden insights about their beliefs and show immediate improvement, whereas others make steady, gradual improvement.

Cognitive therapy for depression sometimes takes longer than twenty sessions. Those with a history of recurrent depression may have genetic biological factors working against them and will probably benefit from medication in addition to longer-term cognitive counseling. Others require more than twenty sessions because they have an additional disorder superimposed on their depression. For example, a person might have both depression and panic attacks. Both issues need to be treated, requiring more time than either would alone. Some have personality disorders (longstanding problems in relating to others that interfere with relationships and normal adjustment) in addition to depression. Although cognitive therapy has been used with some success for treating personality disorders, it is long-term treatment with no guarantees of success.

SPECIAL ISSUES FOR CHRISTIAN COUNSELORS

Although depression brings similar symptoms to Christians and agnostics, Christian clients often face unique pressures because of their beliefs, the beliefs of other Christians, and church traditions.

Death and Grief

" 'Death has been swallowed up in victory.' 'Where, O death, is your victory? Where, O death, is your sting?' " (1 Cor. 15:54b–55). Paul's words, intended originally to describe Jesus Christ's ultimate victory over death when the dead are resurrected and given immortal bodies, are often distorted to imply death is no problem for Christians. So Christians in grief often feel guilty and unspiritual for their sadness, reasoning, *Good Christians don't feel this way.* In addition to distorting the Bible (for example, Jesus grieved when John the Baptist was executed), this denial of grief contributes to the fallacy that Christians should always be happy.

Although social support helps a great deal in times of grief, many grieving people find Christian friends frustrating. They tire of hearing Christian platitudes and simplistic applications of Bible verses. They are frustrated by the words and expressions of concerned others that imply, *Shouldn't you be better by now?* So as they look for a Christian counselor, they look for one who will not apply Bible verses as Band-Aids and one who will give them time and permission to feel bad.

Christians often need permission to grieve their losses. Regardless of religious faith, loss results in grief, and grief results in sadness, even depression. When the grief process is not allowed or is prematurely shut off, greater problems often emerge years later.

I assign grief periods to my Christian clients. Assigning them the job of actively grieving ten or fifteen minutes per day gives them permission to identify and accept their feelings. If they deny their feelings, they cannot deal with them; but once they openly acknowledge their feelings, they can learn to cope with their losses and restore what is left of their lives.

Since grief is a long-term process, often requiring months or years to complete, it is unwise to expect a twelve-week cognitive therapy program to be satisfactory. A better option is to meet weekly or semiweekly until the initial crisis phase is past, and then less frequently, twice monthly or less, for a prolonged period of time. Some clients find it helpful to meet once monthly for many years after losing a loved one.

Guilt

When we violate God's law, we do right to feel sorry. When Israel's King David committed adultery and murder, he felt deep remorse:

Wash away all my iniquity and cleanse me from my sin. For I know my transgressions, and my sin is always before me. Against you, you only, have I sinned and done what is evil in your sight, so that you are proved right when you speak and justified when you judge. (Ps. 51:2–4)

But David's sorrow led him to marvel at God's grace rather than excessive self-deprecation. David didn't say, "I'm such a dirty, filthy person that no one could ever love me." He concluded: "Cleanse me with hyssop, and I will be clean; wash me, and I will be whiter than snow" (Ps. 51:7).

Sorrow is a gift from God, enabling us to see when we sin and motivating us to do better next time. But when sorrow festers and turns into self-hatred, the process of correction goes awry.[14] Those basting in self-hatred have difficulty experiencing God's grace and feeling his love. In their doubt and confusion, they become more vulnerable to sin again.

This is further complicated because many Christians are depressed about being depressed. That is, they believe depression symbolizes a moral or spiritual problem. Coming to a counselor, they reason, demonstrates spiritual weakness. They self-talk, *If I were living right before God, I would not be depressed.* Of course, this reasoning is faulty since many biological and psychosocial factors contribute to depression. Nonetheless, many Christian clients use their depression as evidence that they are worthless sinners, unlovable and despicable.

Depressed Christians need help untangling healthy sorrow for sin from self-condemnation. Some believe they deserve to be depressed and miserable since they have sinned. But depression and misery make them more, not less, vulnerable to future sin. Those who are most resistant to sin combine appropriate sorrow for wrongdoing with a healthy appreciation for God's forgiveness and unconditional love. Here are some examples of ways self-deprecating thoughts can be revised:

Automatic Thought: *I'm no good at all.*
Revision: *I'm not perfect, but God loves me anyway.*

Automatic Thought: *I'm a terrible, awful, dirty person.*
Revision: *I struggle with temptation and sin. I feel sorry when I sin and am amazed that God's love is bigger than any sin.*

Automatic Thought: *God could never love me.*
Revision: *God does love me because his love is so amazing.*

God's redemption and grace are seen throughout the Bible as a solution to human depravity. Depressed Christians need to feel God's love rather than God's condemnation. "Therefore, there is now no condemnation for those who are in Christ Jesus, because through Christ Jesus the law of the Spirit of life set me free from the law of sin and death" (Rom. 8:1–2).

Loneliness

When Glen's eighteen-year-old daughter was killed in a car accident, he became depressed. His work performance faltered, he withdrew from his friends, and he stopped going to church. By cutting off those close to him, he added loneliness to his depression. Because social withdrawal is a symptom of depression, many, like Glen, deal with loneliness and depression at the same time.[15]

According to Richard Parsons and Robert Wicks, loneliness may be particularly painful for Christians because our Christian community contributes to denial.[16] When Christians feel lonely, they sometimes deny their feelings by noting they are surrounded by other caring Christians. But deep inside they feel alone and isolated from those with whom they sing and pray. Others deny loneliness by living life in the future—focusing on eternal life as a way to mask present pain.

Because Christians deny loneliness, Parsons and Wicks believe Christian clients have poor awareness of their automatic thoughts. Rather than assuming the clients can recall automatic thoughts during the counseling session, they routinely assign thought/feeling logs, asking their lonely clients to record the thoughts they are having during times of loneliness. This allows them to capture the automatic thoughts as they occur. They then work with clients to change dysfunctional automatic thoughts.

Parsons and Wicks suggest that two forms of automatic thoughts are prevalent among lonely religious individuals. First, they feel being alone is awful—a major catastrophe. They tell themselves, *I must never be alone,* or *Being alone is unbearable.* Second, they belive they are undeserving of friendship: *I'm such a bad person, I do not deserve meaningful relationships*. Both these cognitive distortions can be challenged with the techniques described in earlier chapters. As clients challenge these thoughts, they become more willing to take risks and form relationships with others.

Hopelessness and Suicide

Christians are called to hope: "Be joyful in hope, patient in affliction, faithful in prayer" (Rom. 12:12). But depressed Christians often feel hopeless, as if they have no reason to live. Although hopelessness is a common symptom of depression, it may be worse for Christians because they reason, *I'm supposed to have hope, yet I am hopeless. I must be a disobedient Christian and an awful person*. Rather than seeing hope as a privilege of Christian faith, they see it as an imperative they are failing to meet. So they feel more hopeless, depressed, and defeated.

Hopelessness is a better predictor of suicidal intent than depression, so it must be taken seriously.[17] When clients want to escape life and have a plan for killing themselves, they must be considered at risk for suicide. Counselors need to prevent suicide by considering hospitalization, having family members dispense anti-depressant medications (overdoses are very toxic), and getting a written suicide contract (an agreement that the client will call the counselor before attempting suicide).

Depression and hopelessness need not be seen as signs of weakness or lack of spirituality. Moses, Elijah, David, Paul, and other godly Bible characters experienced despair, even hopelessness. Perhaps God provides us with these examples to prepare us for our own times of discouragement. Hopelessness, like pain, causes us to look deeper into our faith, our world, and ourselves to find meaning.

CHAPTER ELEVEN
ANXIETY

THE HIGH-SCHOOL SENIOR SITTING IN an unknown classroom, number-two pencil in hand, waiting to open the Scholastic Aptitute Test booklet, knows about anxiety. The same student feels a different kind of anxiety standing on the free-throw line with five seconds remaining in a tie-score basketball game, and still another when eating dinner at an expensive restaurant with an unfamiliar date. And a few years later, when SATs, basketball games, and dates have passed, the same person anxiously sits on a crowded commuter freeway most mornings. Anxiety follows us throughout our lives.

While no one seeks depression, many of us appear to enjoy some level of anxiety. People watch suspense movies because they enjoy the tense excitement. Others climb cliffs, ski challenging slopes, hang glide, or jump from airplanes. Still others, called couch potatoes by those who prefer higher doses of anxiety, vicariously stress themselves by watching sports on television. We seek anxiety, but we want to turn it off with the television remote or when we reach the bottom of the ski slope or the end of the suspense movie. Unfortunately, some cannot turn off anxiety so easily.

When Rhonda sees a spider, she feels anxious. She nervously smashes it with a thick paper towel, discards the corpse outside, and begins to feel better. When Jane sees a spider, she feels terror. Her heart begins to pound, her breathing rate increases, she becomes restless and agitated, and she fears she will die from a poisonous spider's bite. Several hours later, after a friend has come to kill the spider, she begins to calm down. Both Rhonda and Jane feel anxiety, but only Rhonda has control over her feelings. Jane's anxiety interferes with her daily functioning—it is an anxiety disorder.

Greg trims trees each year on his Christmas-tree farm. He feels anxious about the sharp blade of his machete coming so close to his leg, but goes on trimming until his work is done. Wayne also trims trees each year, but his anxiety is different. Every few days, he falls suddenly to his stomach, breaks into a sudden sweat, and is sure Vietcong soldiers are just over the hill. His flashbacks to the Vietnam war interfere with his work and his emotional well-being. Greg experiences mild anxiety, but Wayne has an anxiety disorder.

Wayne and Jane both demonstrate the symptoms of anxiety disorder. First, they both have mood symptoms—apprehension, tension, panic. Second, they have cognitive symptoms. Both believe their well-being is threatened. Aaron Beck, Gary Emery, and Ruth Greenberg see danger or threat as the central cognitive theme in anxiety reactions.[1] Third, they have physical symptoms. Their hearts race, they breathe rapidly, and they move restlessly and nervously. With prolonged anxiety, they will eventually feel fatigue, weakness, and headaches.

Like depression, anxiety disorders are common: about 15 percent of the population will experience an anxiety disorder at least once during their lives,[2] and 2 to 5 percent currently have anxiety disorders.[3] Unlike depressed clients, those with anxiety disorders often experience more than one disorder at the same time. They are brought on by a variety of factors, including genetic predisposition,[4] childhood traumas, physical disease, and unproductive thinking patterns.[5]

There are many types of anxiety disorders, and cognitive therapy has been used to treat most. What follows is not a comprehensive list of anxiety disorders, but an overview of the ways cognitive therapy can be used to treat common anxiety disorders.

GENERALIZED ANXIETY DISORDER

Generalized anxiety disorder (GAD) produces free-floating feelings of anxiety that are not associated with particular objects or situations. Clients who feel constant and inescapable aanxiety for at least one month can be diagnosed as experienceing GAD. Because no one object causes the stress, those with GAD are hypervigilant, looking continually for sources of threat and danger. They feel tense, frightened, weak, unsteady, and unable to relax. They have difficulty concentrating, fear losing control or being rejected, and feel confused.[6]

Causes of GAD

Aaron Beck, Gary Emery, and Ruth Greenberg identify three psychological factors that bring on generalized anxiety disorder. First, a person facing increased demands is vulnerable to GAD. A parent has a new child and desires to be an excellent parent while pursuing a promising career. The increased pressure may bring on generalized anxiety. Second, some face increased danger or threat in their life situations. The business executive whose company is bought out may feel the threat of unemployment, causing more anxiety. Third, stressful events that detract from self-confidence may bring on GAD. After failing a major examination, a medical student may develop symptoms of generalized anxiety.[7]

Those with chronic anxiety have what Beck, Emery, and Greenberg call a "hypersensitive alarm system."[8] They anticipate the future with dread. They "catastrophize," assuming awful things are bound to happen. Some of the beliefs they hold are:

1. Any strange situation should be regarded as dangerous.
2. A situation or a person is unsafe until proven to be safe.
3. It is always best to assume the worst.
4. My security and safety depend on anticipating and preparing myself at all times for any possible danger.
5. I cannot entrust my safety to someone else. I have to ensure my own security.
6. In unfamiliar situations, I must be wary and keep my mouth shut.

7. My survival depends on my always being competent and strong.
8. Strangers despise weakness.
9. They will attack at a sign of weakness.
10. If I am attacked, it will show that I appeared weak and socially inept.[9]

Cognitive Therapy Techniques

Cognitive therapy techniques help those with GAD to challenge their catastrophizing, logically analyze their unreasonable thoughts, and come to more reasonable conclusions. Counselors follow the same scheme presented earlier in this book: identify and change automatic thoughts, then identify and change core beliefs. Some techniques are particularly well suited for working through these steps with anxiety-prone clients.

Technique 1: Reality Testing. Those with GAD often come to illogical and unlikely conclusions as they anticipate the future. Cognitive counselors can help clients test their conclusions with logic and common sense by asking the question, "What evidence do you have for that belief?"

Frances believed her husband Rick was about to leave her. She lost sleep and shed many tears over her worry. I asked what evidence she had for her fear, and she had none. Her belief had no basis in truth. Rick repeatedly expressed his commitment and love to her. As she balanced her anxiety-provoking thought with logic and common sense, she felt better and saw her marriage more accurately.

Technique 2: "What if . . . ?" Ironically, despite the monumental amount of time anxious clients spend thinking about future problems, they often do not complete their thoughts. They merely assume, "It would be awful if_____," or "_____ would be a catastrophe." Counselors can help clients finish their thinking by asking, "What if . . . ?" as demonstrated in the following dialogue:

CLIENT: I'm afraid I won't have enough time tonight to get everything done.

COUNSELOR: Everything?

CLIENT: I have to get laundry in the washer, then make dinner. After I clean the kitchen I need to make cookies for school lunches. Then I have a PTA meeting at eight o'clock.

COUNSELOR: Sounds busy.

CLIENT: Yeah. It seems like this every night.

COUNSELOR: I was just wondering, *what if* you didn't have enough time to get everything done.

CLIENT: Oh, I will. I have to. I can stay up late when I get home if I don't get it done before my meeting.

COUNSELOR: You're saying, "I have to go to my meeting, I have to cook dinner for my family, I have to do the laundry, and I have to make cookies for school lunches." Let's just take one of those things and think about it. *What if* you didn't get the cookies done?

CLIENT: The kids would hate me. And my husband would, too. He likes cookies.

COUNSELOR: What evidence do you have that others would hate you if they didn't have cookies in their lunches?

CLIENT: They wouldn't hate me, but they would be upset. They always get cookies in their lunches.

COUNSELOR: Okay. Well *what if* your kids got upset.

CLIENT: That would be bad.

COUNSELOR: How bad would it be?

CLIENT: They would live through it.

By asking, "What if . . . ?" the counselor forces the client to think beyond her previous reasoning, *I have to make cookies because I have to.* Next, the counselor could look at other arbitrary demands: laundry, going to the PTA meeting, and fixing dinner.

Technique 3: Evaluate Dichotomous and Perfectionistic Thinking. Those with GAD are prone to dichotomous thinking—for example, *If things aren't perfect, they are awful,* or *If I don't have complete control over the future, then I am completely out of control.* These thoughts can be challenged by having clients rate their experiences on a 0–10 scale, as with the continuum technique described in chapter 8.

Those who believe, *If things aren't perfect, they are awful,* can be asked to rate their lives on a perfection scale. Start by defining the ends of the scale. A 10 is reserved for the perfect life—the one who gives and receives love, has self-confidence, financial resources, meaningful relationships, a clear sense of meaning and direction, and a growing closeness to God. The other end of the scale (0) represents an awful life. One might imagine a lonely, homeless person sleeping on a cold sidewalk in the middle of winter. Most clients admit their lives are in the middle of the scale; this admission forces them out of their dichotomous beliefs.

Scaling has similar benefits for those with perfectionistic tendencies. Linda believed her house must always be perfect. An out-of-place newspaper or a few dirty dishes in the kitchen sink symbolized housekeeping failure to her. She saw her reasoning error once we created a 0–10 scale, with 0 being the messiest house she had ever seen and 10 being the neatest. Even with newspapers scattered, she admitted her house was above average.

Technique 4: Problem-Solving.   Those who build their own houses become experts at breaking down big problems into their smaller parts. Building a house is overwhelming, but the task becomes manageable if it is viewed as a series of smaller tasks: excavating, pouring the foundation, framing, and so on. Dieters face a similar obstacle. They feel overwhelmed with a goal of losing sixty pounds, so they break it down to smaller goals and try to lose one or two pounds per week.

Similar principles apply to anxiety management. In our fast-paced age, many feel anxious about the tasks and time pressures they face, and sometimes the anxiety handcuffs them and keeps them from moving toward their goals. Problem-solving by breaking big goals down into little goals helps relieve anxiety.

Writing a list is often a good beginning point. Because generalized anxiety is free-floating and unfocused, those with GAD often need help defining their fears or worries. They feel overwhelmed with all the pressures of their lives, but they have not stopped to identify the specific stressors. If they don't identify their problems, they cannot work proactively toward resolving them.

Wanda comes for counseling because she feels her life is "out of control." The counselor helps Wanda list her stressors: She is trying to lose weight, her job requires her to work fifty-hour weeks, she worries that her teen-age son may rebel, and she fears her husband may die suddenly of a heart attack, as his father did. Making a list helps Wanda, because her list is shorter than she thought it might be. Next, her counselor helps her focus on one problem at a time. She is considering a weight-loss program but has not yet arranged to begin. Yes, she probably could call for an initial appointment this week. She could work fewer hours if she were transferred to another department, but she would have to bid for another job. Yes, she could discuss the possibilities with her supervisor.

In the face of anxiety and rigid thinking, some clients overlook acceptable solutions, focusing instead on the plethora of unacceptable solutions. Counselors help clients break down big problems into manageable problems and then help them cope with the smaller problems. In the process, they coach clients on time management, assertiveness, decision-making, morality, financial matters, and many other issues.

Effectiveness of Cognitive Therapy

Several published studies support the effectiveness of cognitive therapy in treating GAD, though one study showed little difference between cognitive therapy and nondirective counseling.[10] Other researchers treated half of their GAD clients with nondirective therapy and the other half with cognitive therapy. All clients concurrently received training in progressive muscular relaxation. Although both groups showed reduced anxiety after treatment, the cognitive therapy group showed the greatest improvement on several outcome questionnaires.[11] Additional studies compared the effectiveness of cognitive therapy to medication (Diazepam) or no treatment. In one study, those receiving cognitive therapy responded the best and required fewer follow-up visits than those in other groups.[12] In another study, those receiving medications showed the best initial improvement, but the improvement declined as treatment progressed. Those receiving cognitive therapy were doing much better than those receiving medication by the end of the treatment period.[13]

PANIC ATTACKS

Panic attack is to generalized anxiety what winning the lottery is to a regular paycheck. Rather than steady, chronic levels of anxiety, those with panic attacks experience acute, intense anxiety that lasts for only a few minutes. Panic attacks come and go without warning, bringing terror to their victims. Physical symptoms include shortness of breath, dizziness, heart palpitations, chest pains, tingling in fingers or toes, trembling, or sweating. Thoughts race as panic-attack victims tell themselves, *I'm going to die,* or *I'm going crazy,* or *I'm having a heart attack.* Beck, Emery, and Greenberg give the following narrative of a young woman as she experiences panic:

> My breathing starts getting very shallow. I feel I'm going to stop breathing. The air feels like it gets thinner. I feel the air is not coming up through my nose. I take short rapid breaths. *Then I see an*

image of myself gasping for air and remember what happened in the hospital. I think that I will start gasping. I get very dizzy and disoriented. I cannot sit or stand still. I start pacing. Then I start shaking and sweating. I feel I'm losing my mind and I will flip out and hurt myself or someone else. My heart starts beating fast and I start getting pains in my chest. My chest tightens up. I become very frightened. I get afraid that these feelings will not go away. Then I get really upset. I feel no one will be able to help me. I get very frightened I will die. I want to run to some place safe but I don't know where.[14]

Causes of Panic Attacks

Panic attacks are often precipitated by a change in physical condition. A person may walk into a cool room on a hot day, stand up suddenly and feel lightheaded, laugh intensely to the point of not being able to breathe normally, or breathe rapidly while chopping wood. Often the physical changes are accompanied by rapid breathing that rids the lungs of carbon dioxide, resulting in lower levels of carbon dioxide in the blood. This, in turn, elevates the blood pH and produces physical symptoms of panic.

These physical changes are followed by catastrophizing thoughts: *Something awful is happening,* or *I'm going to stop breathing,* or *I'm losing control,* or *I'm having another panic attack.* These thoughts contribute to more anxiety, producing more physical symptoms, more extreme thoughts—and the cycle escalates. Cognitive therapists attempt to interrupt the cycle by teaching clients to use calming, rational thoughts when confronted with the first symptoms of panic.

Cognitive Therapy Techniques

Drs. Ronald Rapee and David Barlow have developed and researched a cognitive treatment for panic attacks at the Center for Stress and Anxiety Disorders at the State University of New York at Albany. Their treatment program includes three components: breathing retraining, cognitive restructuring, and interoceptive exposure.[15] First, teach clients to breathe slowly and smoothly to compensate for the hyperventilation of panic disorder. Breathing training is important because recent studies have shown those vulnerable panic attacks breathe more rapidly than others and that panic attacks decrease in frequency and severity as they learn to breathe properly.[16] Clients learn to count as they inhale and say to themselves, *relax,* as they exhale. *One, relax, two, relax, three, relax,* and so on.

The second treatment component, cognitive restructuring, requires clients to challenge their thoughts that they are "going crazy" or dying. This requires counselors to give clients accurate information about panic attacks and their symptoms. Clients learn to challenge their automatic thoughts and use more adaptive self-talk. For example, instead of thinking, *I'm having a heart attack and I'm going to die,* they might conclude, *I'm short of breath from climbing the stairs, but I can stay calm and breathe deeply.* Third, "interoceptive exposure" involves deliberately creating the symptoms the client fears. There are several ways to induce panic symptoms in the counseling office: breathing rapidly into a paper bag, holding one's breath, and spinning in place. After clients feel panic symptoms, they are instructed to breathe slowly and smoothly and use productive self-talk to cope with the panic attack. By having an attack in the safety of a counselor's office, clients gain confidence in their ability to control their symptoms.[17]

The same basic components have been promoted by others developing cognitive treatments for panic attacks. All cognitive treatment programs educate clients about panic disorder, teach new breathing and relaxation skills, emphasize accurate and reasonable self-talk in the midst of panic attacks, and provide practice by putting clients in anxiety-provoking situations.

Although Rapee and Barlow create symptoms of panic in the counseling office,[18] there are other ways to provide clients with panic-provoking situations. Patti Lou Watkins, Ellie Sturgis, and George Clum successfully treated a client by having her imagine a panic attack and then use self-talk to cope with the attack, a technique they call *guided imaginal coping.*[19] Katherine Shear, Gordon Ball, and Stephen Josephson advocate developing anxiety hierarchies with clients, and then assigning homework which exposes clients to the things they fear.[20] Early in the treatment process, homework is focused on troubling internal sensations, such as heart palpitations or rapid breathing. Clients might be assigned an exercise period, creating the internal sensations they fear. After they learn to deal with uncomfortable internal sensations without panic, they progress to the next level on the hierarchy: sites of previous panic. So a client who previously had a panic attack in a Chinese restaurant might be assigned the task of eating again at the same restaurant. After mastering previous panic situations, the client moves to the highest level on the hierarchy: situations where he or she feels trapped. Homework assignments might include riding in a crowded elevator, driving alone at night, or going to the dentist. As clients successfully handle more challenging homework assignments, they become confident in their ability to avoid panic with accurate self-talk, slow breathing, and relaxation.

Effectiveness of Cognitive Therapy

Until recently, panic attack has been treated by psychodynamic therapy or with medication. Both are long-term treatments and medication often has negative side effects. Cognitive therapy is a promising alternative because it is short-term and appears to be effective.

Rapee and Barlow report complete cessation of panic attacks in 85 percent of their clients receiving cognitive therapy compared with 36 percent of those on a waiting list.[21] Shear, Ball, and Josephson report that "panic is highly responsive to our treatment program," but do not give outcome data to support their claim.[22] Other researchers have found similar effectiveness, with cognitive treatment virtually eliminating panic attacks in most or all of the clients.[23] The guided imaginal coping technique described by Watkins, Sturgis, and Clum also proved effective, though their report was a case study of a single client. By the end of the fourth session, the client showed complete cessation of panic attacks.[24]

PHOBIAS

John Madden was a successful coach for the Oakland Raiders football team for ten years, compiling a record of 103 wins, 32 losses, and 7 ties. But the anxiety he felt as a coach led to "burnout," so Madden got out of coaching and began his career as a sports commentator (and a frequent actor in advertisements). Part of Madden's anxiety was due to claustrophobia—a fear of closed places. He dislikes crowds and elevators because they make him feel "hemmed in."[25]

Those with phobias have persistent, irrational fears, such as Madden's fear of closed spaces. They realize their fears are irrational, but they have little control over their feelings. Madden knows that millions of people ride elevators every day without harm, but he still feels fearful in them.

Phobias are more intense than the normal fears we all experience. Most people feel mild anxiety as a plane takes off or lands, but those with phobias feel intense fear. Most of us are startled to see a mouse scampering across the floor, but those with phobias are terrified.

Generalized anxiety is free-floating nervousness and panic attacks can occur in a variety of situations; but phobias are focused on specific events or situations. Symptoms of phobic reactions include racing heart, dizziness, nausea, dry mouth, and profuse sweating. Those with phobias begin avoiding the situations that cause them fear, inhibiting a normal lifestyle in order to prevent coming in contact with the dreaded situation.

There are many kinds of phobias, but they can be grouped into three divisions: agoraphobia, social phobias, and simple phobias. Agoraphobia is literally the fear of open places, but almost always is associated with numerous other fears which cluster around the theme of losing control. An agoraphobic may remain housebound for weeks at a time because of what might happen outside—losing control of the car, having a panic attack in public, being caught in a crowd, and so on. Those with social phobias also avoid people, but do so to avoid criticism and embarrassment. Social phobics fear eating or speaking in public, talking on the phone, or not being dressed appropriately. Most of us feel nervous about these things from time to time, but those with social phobias avoid the situations because of their anxiety. Simple phobias are all other phobias, including the fear of heights, blood, darkness, crowds, animals, and so on.

Causes of Phobias

Genetic factors appear to put some people at more risk for phobic disorders than others.[26] In addition to genetic factors, phobias are probably caused by negative associations. The small child attacked by a dog will associate dogs with danger and pain. After being stuck in a jammed elevator, a person will associate elevators with discomfort. When an anxious child is compelled by friends to watch a horror movie, it is not surprising when a fear of the dark results.

Agoraphobia and panic attacks often go together. Some have suggested that having a panic attack in public is the beginning of agoraphobia. After the panic attack, the person reasons, *I can't go outside again because I might have another panic attack*. Of course, the fear of a panic attack makes it more likely one will occur next time the person leaves the house.

From a cognitive perspective, phobias are caused by faulty rules. These rules cause those with phobias to interpret ambiguous situations as threatening. The rules are learned in childhood and not adapted for adulthood.[27] Children learn, "Strangers are dangerous," or "High places are dangerous." Those failing to adapt those rules to an adult world may end up with a social phobia (fear of strangers) or a simple phobia (fear of heights). Inflexible thoughts from the past cause people to interpret present events in a threatening way,[28] and to overestimate the likelihood of future danger.[29] Even when the phobic person realizes the rules are unreasonable, the rules still guide behavior and emotions until they are replaced with more adequate rules.

Cognitive Therapy Techniques

In general, cognitive therapy for phobias involves the principles discussed throughout this book: understanding and challenging automatic thoughts, generating rational responses to automatic thoughts, finding and revising underlying core beliefs, and preventing relapse with maintenance sessions. A few techniques are especially appropriate for phobic clients.

Technique 1: Reattribution Training. Those who feel anxiety attribute their feelings to the event they fear. So if John Madden were to enter a plane, he would attribute his anxiety to the airplane. Or if an agoraphobic woman felt anxious when leaving the house, she would attribute her anxiety to being outdoors. These attributions are circular: *I'm nervous because I'm entering an airplane, and airplanes make me nervous.* Or, *I'm nervous because I'm leaving my house, and leaving my house always makes me nervous.* Cognitive therapists help clients learn new ways of understanding their anxiety. Instead of saying to themselves, *I feel nervous because I am leaving my house,* they can reattribute their feelings to, *I'm nervous because of the things I'm telling myself.*

Technique 2: Paradoxical Intention. Much of phobic anxiety is in anticipation of a feared event. The snake phobic reasons, *I can't mow the lawn because I might see a snake, become terrified, and faint.* Thus, the anxiety occurs even when the feared event does not. Some counselors have used paradoxical intention to break the pattern of anticipatory anxiety.

A counselor might ask this snake phobic client to become as nervous as possible: "Tremble and shake as much as you can. Try to make your heart race and try to feel dizzy from the anxiety. Go ahead and faint if you see a snake. In fact, try to be the best fainter anywhere." By using these instructions, the client breaks the pattern of anticipatory anxiety and often feels calmer.

Technique 3: Imagery. Most phobics use images as they think about feared events. Some picture being stuck in a crowded elevator, unable to escape. Others see themselves bitten by a poisonous snake or being rejected by a large audience. Counselors can help clients revise images to be more realistic. The distorted images are based on unreasonable fears, and probing questions can help point out the distortions. The counselor and client can then work together to revise the image appropriately.

COUNSELOR: Tell me what you picture happening as you start to mow the lawn.

CLIENT: There's a snake in a bush—a rattlesnake—and as I push the mower by it lashes out and bites me on the leg. I rush in the house, get a knife, cut a slice out of my leg, and bleed to death.

COUNSELOR: As you think about it now, how reasonable does that image sound?

CLIENT: Not very.

COUNSELOR: Okay. How might you revise the picture to make it more reasonable?

CLIENT: Well, it probably wouldn't be a rattlesnake, but it would still scare me.

COUNSELOR: I see. So you're mowing the lawn, a snake jumps out of the bushes, but it's not poisonous. Then what?

CLIENT: Then I feel scared, go inside for awhile, pray for a long time, and let my husband finish mowing the lawn!

COUNSELOR: Okay. Are there other possible endings to your image after you are startled by the snake?

CLIENT: Well, with some more help, I suppose I might see the snake, feel scared, and keep on mowing the lawn.

COUNSELOR: That image is quite different than what you started with a few minutes ago.

CLIENT: Yes.

Next time the client anticipates mowing the lawn, she can challenge her automatic image with the revised, more realistic version. Beck, Emery, and Greenberg describe a number of other ways to disrupt fear-producing images.[30]

Technique 4: Combine Cognitive and Behavioral Techniques. Although this is a book about cognitive therapy, the most effective treatments for phobias often combine cognitive techniques with behavioral techniques, such as graduated exposure and relaxation training. *Graduated exposure* provides clients opportunities to cope with their phobia by doing the things they fear. At first, mild exposure is assigned. Then, as clients gain confidence, they can handle bigger challenges. For example, Holly, who is afraid of heights, might be asked to look for thirty seconds at a tall building. Holly's next assignment might be to enter the tall building, look around the lobby, and then leave. Next, she could try riding the elevator to the fifth floor, then returning to the lobby. Eventually, she could ride to the top floor and look out the window.

Relaxation training is another effective behavioral technique used to treat phobias. By progressively tensing and relaxing muscles, clients train their bodies to remain calm. Often the relaxation is paired with mental images of the anxiety-provoking event.

Effectiveness of Cognitive Therapy

Several studies support the effectiveness of cognitive therapy combined with behavioral techniques in treating social phobias.[31] Cognitive therapy also appears to help agoraphobic clients: Larry Michelson, Matig Mavissakalian, and Karen Marchione found paradoxical intention alone was about as effective as relaxation training or graduated exposure alone.[32] Marchione, Michelson, Michael Greenwald, and Constance Dancu found cognitive therapy combined with graduated exposure was more effective than graduated exposure alone in treating agoraphobia.[33] Combining cognitive and behavioral strategies seems to be the most effective way to treat agoraphobia.[34]

In addition to generalized anxiety, panic attacks, and phobias, cognitive therapy has been successfully applied to other anxiety symptoms and disorders. These applications of cognitive principles are wide-ranging, including treatment of childhood anxiety,[35] athletic performance anxiety,[36] test anxiety,[37] and anxiety among coronary patients.[38] Cognitive therapy is also useful in dealing with stress-related anxiety and anger problems, as discussed in chapter 12.

SPECIAL ISSUES FOR CHRISTIAN COUNSELORS

The apostle Paul instructed his readers:

Do not be anxious about anything, but in everything, by prayer and petition, with thanksgiving, present your requests to God. And the peace of God, which transcends all understanding, will guard your hearts and your minds in Christ Jesus. (Phil. 4:6, 7)

Unfortunately, this wonderful promise of God's peace can be twisted to amplify anxiety in some Christians.

Two Ways to Interpret Anxiety

Angela has a generalized anxiety disorder. She feels free-floating anxiety most of the time and has for several years. If she weren't a Christian, she might see her anxiety as a problem and seek help from a qualified counselor. But as a Christian, her self-talk is complicated by her doctrine: *I'm anxious, and I'm not supposed to be anxious. Good Christians don't feel this way. I must be a bad Christian. I should rely more on the Lord.* Angela is anxious about being anxious. Paul's words to the Philippians, which were intended to relieve anxiety, have increased Angela's anxiety.

Christian counselors need to give clients permission to have anxious feelings rather than treating anxiety as a sin, which only heightens anxiety. Consider the following two interpretations of Paul's words:

> Option 1: Paul meant anxiety is a sin.
> Resulting Self-Talk: *I am anxious, and am therefore a disobedient Christian, unable to rely on God's provision.*
> Resulting Emotions: Heightened anxiety.
>
> Option 2: Paul meant anxiety is unnecessary, because God watches us and cares for us.
> Resulting Self-Talk: *My anxiety is not necessary because God will take care of me.*
> Resulting Emotions: Reduced anxiety.

Option 2, which gives clients permission to honestly accept their feelings and helps them feel better, is consistent with Jesus' teaching in Matthew 6:25–34. Jesus told his listeners that God provides for the birds of the air and the lilies of the field—and that God will provide for them. He concludes, "Therefore do not worry about tomorrow, for tomorrow will worry about itself. Each day has enough trouble of its own" (Matt. 6:34).

Christians do not overcome anxiety by adding a *should not* to their already long list of *shoulds*. But as they accept God's grace and provision and learn to talk to themselves in productive ways, they voluntarily release their fears and feel God's peace.

Demands for Holiness

Another issue relevant to Christian counselors is the biblical demand to be holy: "But just as he who called you is holy, so be holy in all you do; for it is written: 'Be holy, because I am holy'" (1 Peter 1:15, 16). These words increase anxiety for those who believe they must be perfect to be loved.

Donald didn't like church. Each Sunday after going, he felt dirty, inadequate, anxious, and unloved. The guiltier he felt, the worse he behaved. He eventually stopped going when he decided he wasn't good enough to earn God's love. Several years later, his anxiety worsened, and he came for counseling. Donald's incomplete faith was a major contributor to his anxiety. Convinced God could never love him, he felt dread for the future and interpreted the present as God's judgment. One of Donald's beliefs was, *God only loves perfect people.* This belief needed revising before Donald's anxiety and guilt could be reduced and managed.

The Bible demands obedience and faithfulness, but another theme of Scripture is redemption and grace. Christian counselors can help clients balance biblical demands for obedience with the forgiving grace of God. Helping clients reach this balance requires psychological and theological sensitivity.

One unfortunate method used by some Christian counselors is the minimization of sin. When clients justify sin by reasoning, *Nobody's perfect,* or *That's just the way I am,* or *God will forgive me so it's no big deal,* they underestimate the consequences of sin. Sin drove Christ to the cross. Throughout Scripture, God never concludes about sin, "Don't worry about it." Sin is a big deal.

A better alternative is to emphasize that God loves us despite our sin. Redemption is based solely on God's love and not on human performance: "But when the kindness and love of God our Savior appeared, he saved us, not because of righteous things we had done, but because of his mercy" (Titus 3:4, 5a). God hates sin but loves us enough to save us from the eternal consequences of sin. Holiness is our goal, but God's love remains with us when we sin and when we obey.

We are all pilgrims, learning to live more consistently and to know God more fully. Rather than placing unrealistic perfection demands on ourselves or our clients, we need to see spiritual growth as a process initiated and maintained by God's grace, ". . . being confident of this, that he who began a good work in [us] will carry it on to completion until the day of Christ Jesus" (Phil. 1:6).

CHAPTER TWELVE

STRESS AND ANGER

NANCY HELPLESSLY WATCHES HER THREE children be shot by one-eyed aliens with machine guns before waking to realize the machine-gun fire is really her alarm clock, her children are sleeping soundly in their bedrooms, and another day has started. She continues to awaken while she showers, dresses quickly, wakes the children, and begins school lunches for the kids. After driving two children to school on one side of town and the other to daycare on the other side of town, she begins her thirty-minute commute to work. The freeway is crowded again—isn't it always? She finds the last parking spot in her usual lot, arrives ten minutes late for work, and begins calling customers with overdue accounts. Two breaks and a lunch hour later, Nancy drives the other direction on the crowded freeway, picks up kids from after-school care and daycare, then goes home to cook dinner, do laundry, and clean house. She goes to bed exhausted at 10 P.M., dreading the machine-gun alarm scheduled to wake her up again at 5:30 A.M.

Nancy's life is stressful, partly because she is a single parent. But regardless of their family constellations, many people are familiar with the repeated stress of daily living: the crowded freeway that seems to get worse each year, getting bumped from a flight because of airline overbooking, an adolescent child living in rebellion, too much to do in too few hours. And stress often is accompanied by anger, as seen in our expressions: pounding the steering wheel on the crowded freeway, glaring at the innocent airline reservation agent, or yelling at the wayward adolescent. Stress and anger are a vicious combination, putting people at risk for ulcers, hypertension, stroke, heart disease, or kidney failure.

UNDERSTANDING STRESS

Getting married, going to Disneyland, celebrating Christmas, and being promoted at work all cause stress. Positive experiences cause *eustress*. Being divorced or widowed, looking at the bills after the Disneyland vacation or Christmas, and being fired from work also cause stress—*distress*. Although eustress and distress cause similar physiological responses, distress usually does more damage.

Types of Stressors

Several kinds of stressors lead to distress. *Frustration* occurs when one's goal is blocked. As Nancy drives home from work, she has a goal of picking up the kids on time, before the daycare center closes. A traffic jam frustrates her because it blocks her goal.

Conflict occurs when we have two or more goals pulling us in opposite directions, and calling for a decision. Choosing which college to attend or which car to buy is an example of an *approach-approach conflict,* when a person must choose between two or more good choices. An *avoidance-avoidance conflict* occurs when a person must choose the lesser of two evils. The teen-ager who doesn't want to fight the school bully but also doesn't want to be called "chicken" faces this kind of conflict. An *approach-avoidance conflict* occurs when a goal is a mixed blessing: it brings both pleasure and pain. An ex-drinker wants to attend a party but realizes the temptation could be overwhelming. A young woman wants to marry the man she loves but fears giving up her freedom.

Pressure, another stressor, occurs when situations or other people push us to achieve or perform in specific ways. Nancy feels pressure when her boss expects her to make fifty collection calls per day. Teen-agers often feel pressure from parents to get certain grades or behave in certain ways.

Stress Is to Be Managed, Not Eliminated

Frustration, conflict, and pressure are unavoidable sources of stress. Stress itself is unavoidable. A stressless life is difficult to imagine, because anything becomes stressful with enough repetition. Sitting home and reading or watching television sounds like a nice break to most of us, but if we spent every day in such leisure, it would become stressful. We would eventually complain, "Do I have to read another book today?" or "Do I have to watch more game shows on television this morning?" Going golfing every day might sound relaxing, but eventually it would become stressful. So *eliminating* stress is an unrealistic goal for counseling. *Counselors teach others to manage stress, realizing it is impossible to eliminate stress.*

Clients often come with unrealistic self-talk about stress. They tell themselves, *I am stressed and being stressed is bad.* Helping them realize stress is necessary, and even good, is the first task counselors often face. Many people thrive in the midst of stress, but not those who believe stress must be avoided. The lives of Abraham, Joseph, Moses, David, Jesus, Paul, and many other Christian leaders throughout history have been filled with stress. Had they eliminated that stress, they would also have compromised their ministries.

Hassles and Catastrophes

People often equate stress with catastrophes or monumental life changes. In 1967, two stress researchers developed the Social Readjustment Rating Scale which has been commonly used to measure the amount of stress a person experiences. Recently being widowed rates 100 points on the scale, recently being divorced rates 73, having trouble with in-laws is worth 29 points, celebrating Christmas is worth 12, and so on. By totaling points from the past year's events, one gets an estimate of total stress experienced. Those with more than 200 points are at greater risk than others to develop health problems in the coming year.[1]

Scales such as the Social Readjustment Rating Scale have been only modestly successful in predicting stress-related illness, because most stressors are daily irritations rather than life-changing events.[2]

Psychologist Richard Lazarus and his colleagues believe life's hassles, not cataclysmic events, are the biggest contributors to stress.[3] The most common hassles for a sample of 100 adults were:

1. Concern about weight
2. Health of family member
3. Rising prices of common goods
4. Home maintenance
5. Too many things to do
6. Misplacing or losing things
7. Yard work or outside home maintenance
8. Property, investment, or taxes
9. Crime
10. Physical appearance.

Additionally, the way we interpret life's hassles is as important as how many we have. One person may lie awake at night worrying about an unmowed lawn, and another may not worry about the yard even when irritated neighbors begin to complain. Although neither extreme is ideal, the nonchalant approach prevents stress-related problems.

UNDERSTANDING ANGER

Most people feel angry several times each week, mostly toward friends and loved ones,[4] but most people do not have serious anger problems. Anger, like any other emotion, can be handled assertively and productively. Nonetheless, questions about anger arise: Should I hold in my anger? Should I vent it? How can I express my anger appropriately?

Some hold anger in and others express it freely. Neither extreme is ideal. Those who deny anger or refuse to express it often become resentful and may experience health problems as a result. For example, those who hold their anger in tend to have higher blood pressure than others.[5] Popular psychology and self-help authors often conclude that venting anger is healthier than holding it in, overlooking the problems faced by those who vent anger inappropriately. Venting anger often increases hostility, reinforces bad habits, and increases health risk.[6] Those with a so-called Type-A personality vent anger frequently. They are hard-driving, competitive, impatient, and easily angered. The Type-A personality demonstrates how stress, anger, and health are intertwined in human personality. Those not managing stress well are more prone to anger, those who are angry are more prone to the negative effects of stress, and those who are highly stressed and angry are more prone to a variety of health problems, especially coronary heart disease.

Assuming anger must either be held in or expressed without restraint reflects dichotomous thinking. Those seeking to control anger often do both: They hold in anger until resentment builds, then they explode, often justifying their overreaction by saying, "It's not healthy to hold anger in." But there are more than two options for most human problems, including anger management. Those who handle anger well neither hold it in nor vent it explosively—they learn to manage anger with appropriate self-talk and express their feelings calmly and assertively.

COGNITIVE THERAPY TECHNIQUES FOR STRESS AND ANGER

Clients with stress-and anger-related problems often describe problems with their marriage, health, job, or finances during the first interview. They have not considered how their thinking influences their feelings, so they come convinced their circumstances require them to feel angry or overwhelmed. Effective counselors will listen sensitively to these complaints while realizing the situations often cannot be changed. Within the first session or two, clients need to take more ownership over their feelings so they begin to see themselves as active participants rather than passive victims.

Stress and anger do not just happen to us. Stressful or anger-provoking events occur, then we interpret the events cognitively and experience emotions. Those who believe they must be perfect, who blame themselves for misfortunes, and who interpret small events as catastrophes are more prone than others to anger and anxiety.[7] *Events combine with one's cognitive appraisal of the circumstances to determine the effects of stress or anger.*

Give clients hypothetical examples to demonstrate this principle. For example, a person receiving chemotherapy for treatable cancer might handle that significant stressor as well as another who is concerned about being ten pounds overweight. The events—cancer versus ten pounds—differ in seriousness, but the cancer patient copes as well as the dieter because of healthy thinking. Once clients accept partial responsibility for their stress- and anger-related feelings, the following techniques become useful:

189

Cognitive Relaxation

Psychologists at Colorado State University have developed *cognitive relaxation training,* combining relaxation training with coping self-talk to treat anger control problems.[8] In the first two sessions, clients learn relaxation and deep breathing skills. They also practice relaxing at home and keep track of their times of anger. In the third session, clients learn how self-talk affects their anger responses. In sessions four through eight, counselors teach clients to apply new skills to anger situations by having clients imagine an anger-provoking scene and then use self-talk to lower the anger.

Harriett is frustrated with her work. She was passed up for a promotion which was given to a man she believes is inept. Even casual encounters with this man, now her boss, evoke anger. The day before her first session, Harriett's boss complimented her appearance. Harriett smiled politely, but said to herself, *He's a sexist idiot! Women aren't just here to look nice!* In cognitive relaxation training, Harriett first learns breathing and relaxation skills, then pictures images of interactions with her boss before using self-talk to calm herself. For example, she imagines him asking her to get coffee. Her automatic thoughts are, *Who does he think I am? He has no respect for my competence.* Then Harriett's counselor instructs her to use coping self-talk: *I can simply say no, I don't need to let this get to me. I can stay calm and relaxed.* As she learns to cope with imagined anger-provoking situations in the counseling office, she becomes better prepared to cope with similar situations in life.

Cognitive relaxation training is not a complete regimen of cognitive therapy because it does not address core beliefs. Nonetheless, results from several research studies suggest it is an effective component of cognitive therapy for anger control.[9]

Stress Inoculation

Those involved in school athletics often recall their favorite coach's voice as they face life's challenges. While playing basketball with colleagues during the noon hour, I remember my junior-high basketball coach saying, "Use the crossover step." When warming up before the game, I remember my high-school football coach's advice, "Practice doesn't make perfect—perfect practice makes perfect." These voices from my past still shape the way I think while enjoying athletics.

Self-instruction training assumes we can be our own coaches, instructing ourselves through life's stressful events. *Stress-inoculation training* is one of the most popular and useful ways of teaching clients to coach themselves through stressful and anger-provoking events.[10]

Stress-inoculation training involves three phases. During the first phase, *conceptualization* (called the educational phase in earlier writings), clients learn to understand the nature and effects of stress. The conceptualization phase may last one session or many sessions, depending on the client's symptoms and emotional resources. Goals for the first phase are:

1. Establish a good counselor-client relationship.
2. Understand the client's stress problem, focusing on specific situations, thoughts, and feelings.
3. Discover the client's expectations for treatment.
4. Teach the client how thoughts and emotions interact and how they relate to stress events.
5. Provide the client with a new way of looking at stress by emphasizing that stress can be managed with physical relaxation, appropriate self-talk, and gradual exposure to stressful events.[11]

During phase two, *skills acquisition and rehearsal* (formerly called rehearsal), clients learn and refine coping skills to deal with stress. They learn deep muscle relaxation, new ways of talking to themselves (self-instruction), and effective problem-solving strategies. Relaxation and self-talk have been discussed in previous chapters; an effective model for problem-solving follows the steps outlined in Figure 12–1.[12] Some clients may understand the principles of good problem-solving but have difficulty applying those principles to stressful situations in their lives. They may need help breaking down large goals or decisions into smaller ones; or they may need a calming, supportive counselor to keep them from making impulsive decisions.

Skills acquisition and rehearsal is when clients learn to coach themselves effectively. Instead of telling themselves they cannot cope with a stressful situation, they learn calming, coping self-talk. Listed below are some examples of ineffective and effective self-instructions.

Ineffective self-instructions (bad coaching):
I can't stand this.
This is too much. I can never keep up.
He (she) is impossible!
I can't take anymore!
She (he) is making my life miserable.

191

Effective self-instructions (good coaching):
This is difficult, but I am coping okay.
I wish things were different, but I can make the best of it.
I can remain calm even when others aren't.
Although I'm angry, I don't need to lose control.
I can control my feelings. Others don't have to make me miserable.

Wasik's Model of Problem-Solving

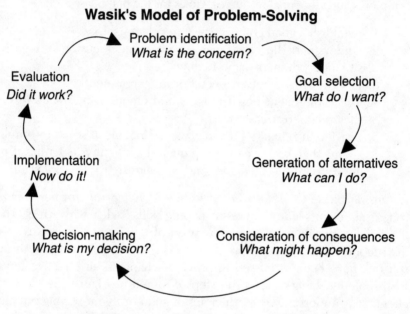

Problem identification
What is the concern?

Goal selection
What do I want?

Generation of alternatives
What can I do?

Consideration of consequences
What might happen?

Decision-making
What is my decision?

Implementation
Now do it!

Evaluation
Did it work?

Fig. 12–1

(Based on B. Wasik, "Teaching Parents Effective Problem-Solving: A Handbook for Professionals," unpublished manuscript, cited by D. Meichenbaum in *Stress-Inoculation Training*, page 67.)

In the third phase, *application and follow-through* (formerly called application), clients are gradually exposed to the events causing them anger or stress. Some of the exposure can be through imagery, as with cognitive relaxation (discussed previously). For example, a stressed administrative assistant could practice calming self-talk while visualizing the phone lines all ringing at the same time. Other exposure can come through role-play. If a client routinely feels angry when dealing with a boss, the counselor could play the role of the boss reprimanding the client for a mistake. The client, who presumably has developed trust in the counselor, could practice coping self-talk while doing the role-play. Sometimes the application phase involves *in vivo* (real life) exposure to stressors. The business executive who finds traveling stressful will eventually need to try out her new coping methods by taking another trip. The school teacher who struggles with anger while on lunch duty will eventually need to transfer his calming self-talk from the counseling office to the lunchroom.

Stress-inoculation has been successfully used for those with anger problems,[13] anxiety reactions,[14] medical problems,[15] and general stress reactions.[16] Some researchers have combined the elements of stress-inoculation training under a different name, and still found the technique effective. For example, Martin Whiteman, David Fanshel, and John Grundy found greater anger alleviation among those trained in cognitive restructuring, relaxation, and problem-solving than among those trained in any one of the three. [17]

Assertiveness

Those with anger-control problems often resist assertiveness training. "I'm already way too assertive," they say, reflecting a misunderstanding of assertiveness. Assertiveness training helps people express feelings appropriately, preventing angry overreactions.

Christians sometimes object to assertiveness training for different reasons. "Christians aren't supposed to fight for their rights," they say. This objection reduces assertiveness to selfishness, which may be true of some popular psychology writings on the topic, but is not true of the assertiveness taught by most counselors. Jesus was assertive without being selfish; he spoke his thoughts and feelings directly, without disguising or avoiding them.

Because people have misgivings—and misunderstanding—about assertiveness, I present my clients with a written discussion of assertiveness, as shown in Appendix B. The handout reminds clients that assertive expressions are straightforward and direct, but they are socially appropriate and are given after considering the feelings and welfare of others.

Then I give specific examples of assertiveness to distinguish assertiveness from aggressiveness or passivity. If a man's wife comes home with an unattractive new dress and asks, "How do you like it?" he has several options. An assertive response is, "I prefer you in other styles." This is direct and honest. Less direct responses are harsh or hide the truth. A passive response is, "It's beautiful, dear." An aggressive response

————————————————

is, "You look awful in that dress; I can't believe you spent money on that." Some responses are both passive and aggressive, such as refusing to respond to the question or saying, "Let me think about it." Many similar examples can be drawn from clients' work or home situations. Here are a few more examples:

Situation: You ordered a medium-rare steak, but it is served well-done.

Passive Response: "It's okay. Well-done is fine."

Aggressive Response: "I can't believe this. I ordered a medium-rare steak and you brought me a well-done one. What do you think I am, stupid? Bring me another one!"

Passive-Aggressive Response: "My steak is overdone, but that's fine— I'll eat it anyway. I won't be coming back to this restaurant though."

Assertive Response: "My steak is overdone. May I please have one medium-rare?"

Situation: You are asked to serve on a church committee but don't feel you have time.

Passive Response: "Yeah. I guess I could do that."

Aggressive Response: "You people are always asking for more. I simply don't have any more to give."

Passive-Aggressive Response: "Okay." (Then never show up for committee meetings.)

Assertive Response: "No, I'd prefer not to. Thank you for thinking of me."

Situation: You are asked to sign a petition in favor of a position you do not support.

Passive Response: "I guess I could sign it."

Aggressive Response: "You're an idiot to support this viewpoint. It's dead wrong!"

Passive-Aggressive Response: "Let me think about it. I'll probably come back later today and sign it."

Assertive Response: "I prefer not to sign it because I hold a different opinion."

After defining assertiveness and giving specific examples, go through each of the categories on the Assertiveness handout in Appendix B, having clients discuss their assertiveness skills in each. Then assign them one category of assertiveness to work on after each session. For example, a counselor might assign a sub-assertive client the task of looking some-one in the eye during a conversation in the coming week. At the next session, the counselor and client could discuss how the conversation went, how the other person responded, and so on.

Those who learn to assert their feelings in appropriate ways are less apt to express feelings in explosive, inappropriate ways. Nonetheless, assertiveness training is best seen as an adjunct to cognitive counseling rather than a stand-alone treatment. Those who learn to express feelings appropriately *and* use calming self-talk to cope with stressful situations are best able to manage anger and stress.

Treating Type-A Behavior

Those with Type-A personality experience high levels of stress and anger. They want to get more and more done in less and less time and feel angry when others get in their way. They drive fast, play video games with intensity, are always victorious when playing games with their children, and work zealously. Push, push, push . . . (until the first heart attack).

Can a Type-A personality be changed? This question was tested among heart-attack survivors in San Francisco. Half were given standard medical advice while the other half received ongoing counseling. Those receiving counseling were encouraged to exercise moderately, enjoy life more, admit mistakes, and pursue their religious faith. Over a three-year period, the second group experienced only half as many heart attacks as the first.[18] Although it is unclear what aspect of the counseling helped the second group live healthier, it seems likely that many in the second group changed their core beliefs in the process of counseling. Instead of earning love by unusual performance or perfection, they learned to take life slowly, appreciate God's unconditional love, and admit imperfections.

Psychologist Christopher Thurman found group cognitive therapy could reduce Type-A behavior among university faculty. Those receiving training in anger management and rational thinking reported fewer Type-A tendencies after treatment than those in a control group, and the differences remained a year after treatment.[19]

Changing personality style is more difficult and time-consuming than just providing clients with new ways of coping with stress. Those approaching the world with hard-driving perfectionism may respond to cognitive relaxation or stress-inoculation training, but they also need transformed views of themselves and the world. They need to exchange old core beliefs that demand perfection and control for more flexible beliefs. The strategies described in this chapter need to be combined with techniques from earlier chapters to change the core beliefs of those with chronic anger or stress-related problems.

SPECIAL ISSUES FOR CHRISTIAN COUNSELORS

The treatment issues and goals that follow are relevant to all clients, not just Christians; but our evangelical traditions and subculture sometimes complicate normal stress and anger reactions.

Denial of Anger

A psalmist writes, "Refrain from anger and turn from wrath; do not fret—it leads only to evil" (Ps. 37:8). And Jesus taught, "Anyone who is angry with his brother will be subject to judgment" (Matt. 5:22). Not surprisingly, Christians hesitate to admit anger, often feeling their anger is sinful. But there are at least three problems with Christians denying anger.

First, viewing anger as sin misrepresents Scripture. Rather than categorically condemning anger, Scripture teaches us to control our anger. Jesus was angry, yet was without sin. (See Mark 3:5, for example.) Paul instructed, " 'In your anger do not sin': Do not let the sun go down while you are still angry" (Eph. 4:26). And when Jesus said those who are angry are subject to judgment, he was using hyperbole, as he did throughout the Sermon on the Mount. His point was that outward behavior starts in the mind. The one who has uncontrolled anger or lust is likely to act impulsively—we need to control our feelings in order to control our behaviors. Paul's requirement that church overseers not be quick-tempered (see Titus 1:7) is good advice for all of us. "A gentle answer turns away wrath, but a harsh word stirs up anger" (Prov. 15:1). Eliminating anger is an unreasonable goal; Scripture teaches us to *manage* our anger.

A second problem is that denying anger does not rid one of anger, but only covers it up. Ignoring the anger actually makes it grow stronger.[20] Christians who believe they should never be angry set themselves up for intermittent explosions of anger. As a Christian psychologist, I frequently hear of committed Christians with serious anger-control problems. No one would suspect them because they appear calm and collected in public, but their private lives are seasoned with tirades and fits of anger.

Third, denying anger means we cannot use it constructively. Anger kept Rosa Parks from giving up her seat in the Caucasian section of a crowded bus, and she became a powerful symbol for the civil rights movement. Anger motivated Jesus to clear the temple of the moneychangers who were desecrating it. Anger motivated a few people to speak out against drunk driving, resulting in greater social awareness and preventative legislation. If we deny anger, we cannot use it for social and personal good.

Recognizing these three problems with Christians denying their anger, we could set goals for managing those feelings.

Goal 1: Be Aware of Anger. For these reasons and others, a goal of counseling is to help clients be aware of felt anger. Try assigning an anger log, having clients record times each week when they feel angry. This implicitly gives permission for anger and makes clients aware how often they feel this emotion.

Many people euphemize (or deny) anger by using milder terms: irritated, annoyed, frustrated, bothered, bugged. These all refer to anger, though they differ in intensity. Some of my clients call all these feelings anger; I ask them to rate the anger on a 1–10 scale to communicate intensity. (One is very mild anger and ten is the most angry they have ever been.) Eventually this exercise helps them become skilled at admitting their anger and labeling it accurately.

I also use the word "angry" when reflecting clients' feelings. For example:

CLIENT: She told me I was selfish. I can't believe that! I work my tail off for her and the kids, and she calls me selfish.

COUNSELOR: You felt angry about that comment.

CLIENT: I guess I did.

COUNSELOR: And it sounds like you're angry now as you think about it.

Here the counselor helps the client admit feelings of anger by using appropriate reflection. The client's self-talk may change from an external, uncontrollable focus (*She's such a jerk*) to an internal controllable one (*I'm feeling angry*).

Goal 2: Assertively Express Feelings. Being aware of feelings is not enough; often they need to be assertively expressed. Consider the following situation as Glenda and John, a hypothetical couple, come home from work.

John arrives home first, tired after a long day's work. He finds the newspaper on the front porch, sits down and reads the sports page.

197

Glenda arrives next, notices John hasn't started dinner and feels angry. She says to John, "Hello, how was your day?" She says to herself, *He is so insensitive! I don't know how much longer I can stand him.*

John notices Glenda is quiet and feels instantly angry. He says nothing to her, but to himself he says, *What did I do wrong now? Nothing is good enough for her.*

The evening gets worse.

If Glenda had expressed her anger when she first experienced it by saying, "John, I feel angry that you haven't started dinner yet," John might have responded, "Yeah, sorry dear, I was so tired. I'll help you now, though." Then the evening might have gone better.

As with John and Glenda, unexpressed anger gets rehearsed over and over in one's mind. With each rehearsal, the feelings intensify and resentments build. Expressing anger short-circuits this destructive pattern.

Delusions of Productivity

Every now and then my slothful nature grabs hold of my thoughts on Sunday mornings and I think, *Wouldn't it be nice to sleep in today?* The thoughts continue, *The rest of the world gets two-day weekends, but not Christians.* For many Christians, Sundays are among the busiest days of the week. Teaching Sunday school, attending morning service, singing in the choir, potluck dinners after church, evening service, and committee meetings fill Sundays so full they hardly seem like a day of rest.

Busy Sundays reinforce a false belief many Christians have: that every moment of life should be productive. So they feel guilty while watching television, reading a book for fun, or going fishing. They believe whatever time is left after work, family, devotions, housework, cooking, home and car maintenance, and community service should be given to the church. Work, work, work . . .

Goal 3: Look for Core Beliefs. Some jokingly say they would be fine if they could have four more hours in each day. But what we ultimately need is not to have more time, but to feel loved. Counselors can never find more time for their clients (in fact, they take time away from their clients by setting counseling appointments, charging fees, and assigning homework), but they can help them challenge core beliefs in order to meet more significant needs. Despite core beliefs to the contrary, the kind of love people want cannot be earned with success or accomplishment. God's love is the best example, and it is given because of God's nature, not because of our accomplishments.

Tom believes he must earn love through unusual accomplishment. So he works eleven-hour days, says yes to every church activity he can, and keeps his yard immaculate. But he still doesn't feel loved—just pressured. Brenda believes others only love her if they agree with her and do what she asks. Sometimes she disagrees with her husband or an employee, and reasons, *They don't agree with me so they don't love me.* She becomes angry and acts irresponsibly. Tom and Brenda have stress and anger problems, both caused by deep feelings of unlovability. They need help changing core beliefs, not just more time.

Goal 4: Practice Relaxation. When helping those with anger and stress problems, emphasize the need for relaxation. Several kinds of relaxation are helpful. First, *physical relaxation* helps combat the effects of high-stress living. Teaching clients muscle relaxation and deep-breathing helps them cope with stress and anger. The adage to count to ten when one is angry isn't bad advice—it gives the person a few seconds to physically relax before responding.

Second, *relaxed expectations* are useful for those who believe they must be productive at all times. Relaxing in front of a sit-com is sometimes wiser than cleaning dinner dishes, and reading a funny novel is better than trimming shrubs.

Third, *relaxed interpretations* of unpleasant events help people cope with stress and anger. Clyde finds his lawnmower won't start. He eventually kicks the mower, curses at the dog, and storms back into the house, yelling at everyone in his way. Teaching Clyde to scale his experience on a 1–10 scale would help him cope better. If a 10 is the worst thing he could imagine (for example, being paralyzed for life or watching his family murdered), his broken lawnmower won't seem so bad. Clyde's experience is unpleasant, but probably not more than a 3 on a 1–10 scale of awfulness. A more relaxed interpretation of the aging mower would reduce Clyde's anger and frustration.

An Overlooked Solution

Many helpful stress management books have appeared on bookstore shelves in recent years, but most overlook the best advice possible: live obediently. This does not mean those who live godly lives are free of stress. But those who live selfishly and disobediently build their lives on tenuous foundations that crumble in the midst of life's stress.

In our psychologized stress-management era, we need to critically examine the philosophical assumptions of our day. We assume the symptoms of stress can be removed without addressing the underlying issues of dehumanization and the widespread acceptance of diverse values. It may be more accurate to assume certain social values produce more stress than others. Just as God's natural law of gravity predicts that the apple will fall from the tree, God's natural law also predicts those who make immoral choices will experience stressful consequences. Christian counselors see this principle repeatedly. Those choosing adultery choose pain for themselves and others. Those who rewrite the golden rule to, "Do unto others before you get done to," end up with broken relationships and emptiness. Those who judge others mercilessly end up embarrassed and lonely.

Though many create stress with self-destructive choices, stress is not always a result of disobedient living. Many people who feel stress are faithful Christians who face unavoidable circumstances. Christian obedience does not eliminate stress, but it does give hope for the stress we face. Faith provides meaning for present suffering and hope for the future. Jesus' words remind us of this promise:

Come to me, all you who are weary and burdened, and I will give you rest. Take my yoke upon you and learn from me, for I am gentle and humble in heart, and you will find rest for your souls. For my yoke is easy and my burden is light. (Matt. 11:28–30)

CHAPTER THIRTEEN
OTHER APPLICATIONS

IN THE LAST MINUTES OF A tense basketball game, Mindy gets pushed by an opponent. She angrily pushes back and screams, "Back off!" Unfortunately, the referee only sees Mindy's push and she gets slapped with a technical foul. Her team loses by one point.

Robert sits tensely in the dentist's chair, his hands clenched into white-knuckled fists. By the end of his appointment, he feels exhausted.

Frank and his boss frequently argue about small matters. When Frank suggests the breaks be changed from 10:30 A.M. to 10:00 his boss lets loose a verbal tirade. Frank goes home and kicks his dog.

Mindy, Robert, Frank, and Frank's boss could all benefit from learning to think more flexibly and calmly. The cognitive therapy techniques described in this book were initially developed to treat depression and have since been used for anxiety, stress, and anger problems; but the potential for applying cognitive therapy techniques is much broader. Cognitive therapy principles may someday be taught to school children as an effort to prevent emotional problems. Sports psychologists will become more popular as athletes experience benefits from thinking accurately and relaxing during competition. Businesses will find cognitive techniques useful in training clerks who deal with angry customers or in training managers to work together effectively.

It would be impossible to cover all the expanding applications of cognitive therapy in one chapter, but two of the most commonly encountered will be considered: treating eating disorders and couples therapy.

EATING DISORDERS

Not many years ago, most counselors had never encountered clients with eating disorders—many counselors had not even heard of bulimia until the 1980s. But society has changed, and so has the prevalence of eating disorders. An informal study in 1983 indicated as many as 25 percent of college women had binged and purged at least once.

It's not surprising. Notice the mannequins at any shopping mall: Their legs and arms are the diameter of thick crayons. Or what about real fashion models? Most women are not able to look as slim as mannequins or fashion models, for whom anorexia sometimes seems a requirement. Although weighing more than a model may be good since being underweight is a health risk, beauty and glamour are so highly valued in our society that women keep trying to lose more weight. They learn to believe, *I must look and be perfect to be loved,* so they literally starve themselves to find that love. Cognitive therapists teach those with eating disorders to stop defining self-worth by comparing themselves to others and to reduce unrealistic perfection demands.[1]

Understanding Eating Disorders

Anorexia nervosa is diagnosed when the person (usually female) weighs 15 percent or more below the ideal, has a distorted view of her body and a fear of being fat, and has missed at least three consecutive menstrual cycles. Although she believes she is fat, she is actually starving. *Bulimia nervosa* is diagnosed when a person recurrently eats large quantities and then purges the food by vomiting, using laxatives, compulsively exercising, or compulsively dieting.

Susan, a twenty-five-year-old assembly line worker, had thinking patterns common to many of those with eating disorders. When her high school boyfriend broke up with her eight years earlier, she became convinced she was fat. Although she lost weight—from 125 pounds to 105, she still thought she was fat. She went days at a time eating only green salads, carrot sticks, and celery. She avoided foods on her danger list: breads, sweets, and meats. But as anyone would, she became famished about twice a week, and cheated by eating something on her prohibited list. After one bite she reasoned, *I've already blown it so I might as well enjoy myself.* A double-cheese pizza and a carton of ice cream later, she felt guilty and bloated. Vomiting was her solution. After vomiting, she felt more guilt and convinced herself she would never binge again, never eat sugar again, never have anything but salad, carrot sticks, and celery again.

Susan's unrealistic expectations (eating carrot sticks and celery for days) set her up for failure by making food so appealing. Her recovery required her to abandon her unrealistic demands and accept herself as a person with a normal appetite. She eventually ripped up her list of prohibited foods and enjoyed moderation and variety in her eating.

Special Considerations

Cognitive therapy for eating disorders requires two special considerations. First, the counselor must be sure to assess medical risk. Those with eating disorders may have electrolyte imbalances, dehydration, or other medical complications. Insist on a thorough medical evaluation as counseling begins.

Second, it is crucial to remember that, although a trusting counselor-client relationship is always important, it is particularly significant in working with eating-disordered clients. Many anorexics and bulimics come for help against their wills and will resist any approach they perceive to be artificial or mechanical. They first need to establish trust in their counselor. Because the therapeutic alliance takes time to develop, cognitive therapy for eating disorders often takes longer than for depression, anxiety, or anger.

Allow trust to develop before giving suggestions. Those with eating disorders want to diet, and counselors want to discourage their dieting, creating a potential power struggle. Counselors who insist on no dieting too early in the treatment are perceived as insensitive or pushy. *My counselor doesn't even care if I get fat,* reasons the anorexic. *If I didn't diet, I would be a blimp in a month,* thinks the bulimic. Although these fears are partially valid, trust must be established before the necessity of weight gain can be productively discussed. Many bulimics end up gaining weight, sometimes above ideal body weight, as part of their recovery. But if the counselor were to say during the first session, "You will probably gain a lot of weight during our treatment," the client would not come back. After several weeks or months of counseling, the client will recognize the need to eat without dieting and will be more open to reasonable weight gains.

As emphasized throughout this book, counselors need to *collaborate* with clients to sensitively set treatment goals and reasonable timelines. This is especially important for counseling those with eating disorders since establishing trust is so important. Collaboration is more important than efficiency: the counselor is wise to not prescribe tasks the client is unable to handle. Techniques of cognitive therapy need to be introduced gradually and more slowly than with other forms of cognitive therapy.

As counselors, we need to monitor our own self-talk. We may reason, *A good counselor would be finished treating this person by now,* implying counseling is something we do to people instead of something we do with people. Every human transaction is different; it seems pointless to compare one with another to determine our worth as counselors.

Techniques

David Garner suggests several techniques which are appropriate for those with eating disorders.[2] In the following discussion, I have subtracted from Garner's list techniques discussed in earlier chapters and added some techniques I find useful.

Articulating Beliefs. Just having clients say their beliefs helps them challenge their faulty, rigid ways of thinking. One client believed, *Others are worthwhile regardless of their weight, but my worth depends on my weight.* As she stated her belief, she realized how silly it sounded.

Decentering. Those with eating disorders often evaluate others with different standards than they use for themselves. Have clients look at others of a similar weight and height and report their impressions. Although they feel "too fat," others of similar build may appear slender or emaciated. This helps clients evaluate themselves as another might, decentering them from their egocentric perceptions.

Combining Cognitive and Behavioral Strategies. It is not enough for clients to think differently about food; they need to behave differently with food. Specific food related assignments are appropriate. These can be framed as collaborative experiments, as discussed in previous chapters. For example, Susan believed she could never eat sugar because sugar always triggered a binge. After she trusted me sufficiently, we worked out an experiment where she ate one piece of candy without overeating afterwards. After she successfully had just one piece, we experimented with two pieces, then three, and so on. She continued to succeed and eventually changed her belief that she could never eat sugar.

Reattribution. Few of us go a full week without hearing a disparaging comment about an obese person. Those with eating disorders interpret these comments as personal attacks: *This person thinks I'm fat and thinks being fat is awful.* By challenging these thoughts and providing alternatives, counselors can help clients think more accurately—for example, *People are often insensitive about those who are overweight, but it doesn't mean I am overweight.* Instead of attributing weight-related comments to being overweight, they learn to attribute them to the insensitivity of the speaker.

Challenge Unrealistic Social Views. Those with eating disorders begin counseling as critics of themselves and end counseling as critics of social values. It is appropriate to feel angry about a culture that equates personal worth with physical attractiveness and physical attractiveness with weight. Appropriate anger helps those with anger recognize and challenge their faulty thoughts.

Before Counseling
I am worthless because I am fat.
No one wants to be with a fat person.

After Counseling
My worth cannot be measured by my body size.
Even if I were fat (and I'm not), my closest friends would still care for me.
People have no right to judge me by my appearance!

Scripting. Clients learn to compromise unreasonable perfection demands by writing scripts of their self-talk. I borrow Freud's metaphor of id, ego, and superego and teach clients to recognize each of these voices as they make decisions. The id insists on pleasure, the superego on perfection, and the ego compromises. After going through several examples in a counseling session, clients write out their thoughts at home. For example:

Situation: Came home late (about 7:30 P.M.) and felt hungry.

Id: *Eat everything. I should eat all the ice cream, the rest of the corn chips, make some spaghetti, and eat a package of crackers.*

Superego: *Be perfect. Don't eat anything at all or you'll never lose that weight. If you must, eat a few carrots.*

Ego: *I'll compromise. I'll have a handful of chips, four or five crackers, a small bowl of ice cream, and some spaghetti.*

Writing out their thoughts in three-part scripts helps clients recognize compromise solutions. Although this sounds simple, it may take many weeks for clients to learn to compromise between id and superego demands.

Assign Imperfection. By doing tasks that require them to relax unrealistic perfection demands, clients learn to separate their personal value from their performance. Joan, a woman with chronic bulimia, believed her house had to be constantly immaculate. She reasoned, *If friends stopped by and saw a dirty house, they would think I am a bad person.* She felt anxious when I asked if she could deliberately leave a dirty dish in the sink overnight. But she came back the next week reporting success. The assignments became more challenging, and eventually she left a dirty sock in the middle of the living-room floor. As she successfully completed these and other assignments, she realized others did not love her for her tidiness and she began to change the core beliefs that maintained her eating disorder.

Similar assignments can be prescribed for eating behavior. Those who weigh each portion before eating and carefully avoid certain foods are smothering themselves with their own perfection demands. Instruct clients to find a safe food, one which is not high in fat, and to overeat. Have clients eat as much popcorn, pasta, or rice as they can. With some coaching, they realize they can eat freely and not be rejected by others.

Of course, these techniques are best used in concert with the overall road map of cognitive therapy. Revising core beliefs is the essential element of effective cognitive therapy.

Effectiveness

Several studies support the effectiveness of cognitive therapy in treating bulimia. A team of Stanford University researchers found 56 percent of their bulimic participants completely abstained from binging and purging after fourteen sessions of individual cognitive therapy and 59 percent were abstinent six months after treatment.[3] The same researchers have also found *group* cognitive therapy effective for treating bulimia.[4] Researchers at the University of Edinburgh found individual cognitive therapy, behavior therapy, and group psychotherapy all reduced the behavioral symptoms of bulimia, but those receiving cognitive therapy showed the greatest reduction of depression and enhancement of self-esteem.[5] Similarly, when English researchers compared cognitive therapy with focused dynamic psychotherapy for treating bulimia, they found cognitive therapy produced better results.[6] And cognitive therapy appears to relax the perfection demands associated with bulimia more effectively than antidepressant medication.[7]

Unfortunately, cognitive treatments for anorexia nervosa have received less research attention than treatments for bulimia. It is difficult to arrange long-term research with those who are medically unstable. Many anorexics are in and out of the hospital for medical reasons during treatment, so they cannot be included in a controlled outpatient research study. Because of their impoverished self-esteem and low body weight, assessing medical and suicidal risk and making appropriate referrals is especially important when counseling with anorexic clients.

CONCERNS FOR CHRISTIAN COUNSELORS

Those with eating disorders often feel unworthy of God's favor. As they try to earn other's approval, they try to earn God's love. Eventually, they feel frustrated, unsuccessful, and unworthy—convinced they can never be perfect enough for God. Alert counselors can help clients feel closer to God by emphasizing three things.

First, Emphasize God's Mercy. "But God demonstrates his own love for us in this: While we were still sinners, Christ died for us," (Rom. 5:8). Most Christians with eating disorders already know about God's justice and hatred for sin, but they don't fully understand God's mercy. They feel they need to earn their way to God's favor. These beliefs need to be challenged with Scripture and the opinions of respected Christians. As clients understand God's mercy, they begin to revise old beliefs:

Original Belief: *God will only love me if I'm perfect.*
Data Supporting God's Mercy:
Scripture (Rom. 5:8, and 8:38, 39; Eph. 2:8, 9; Phil. 1:6; Titus 3:5)
Discussions with Christian leaders (pastors, elders, Christian teachers)
Discussions with Christian friends

Revised Belief: *God loves me, though I'm not perfect.*

Second, Emphasize that Feelings Are Neither Right nor Wrong. Sometimes those who feel distant from God feel God will judge them for their feelings. One woman avoided church because she sometimes felt angry and other times felt attracted toward men. Convinced these were wrong feelings, she was sure God wanted nothing to do with her. When she accepted her feelings as amoral—neither right nor wrong—she was able to understand herself better and eventually return to church.

Third, Emphasize the Need for Diversity and Uniqueness in the Body of Christ. Those with eating disorders often come from backgrounds of sexual or physical abuse, or homes where the identity of the family was valued more than fostering the unique gifts of family members. As children they heard messages such as, "Don't embarrass the family by acting that way," or "We must be our best selves in public," or "This will just be our secret." As a result, they learned to blend in unnoticeably with others. They don't want to disrupt things or draw attention to themselves, so they hide their true feelings, act agreeably, and try to conform to the expectations of others. Indeed, they often evaluate their personal worth by how well they meet others' expectations. But the message of Scripture is different: We need diversity within the body of Christ. (See Romans 12:4–8; 1 Corinthians 12:4–10.) With enough rehearsal and repetition, clients overcome their self-image barriers and believe their uniqueness is a gift to offer others rather than a curse to hide.

COUPLES COUNSELING

With the publication of his book, *Love Is Never Enough,* in 1988, psychiatrist Aaron Beck extended principles of cognitive therapy to couples counseling. Although it has not yet received much attention in research journals, cognitive therapy for couples is a promising horizon for counselors.

What Goes Wrong?

Couples counseling begins with the question, "What went wrong?" Aaron Beck and Christine Padesky suggest four problems lead to relationship stress.[8]

Problem 1: Miscommunication. Any communication process is susceptible to static because words are imperfect and because we use words imperfectly. The problem of misusing words is humorously seen in Richard Lederer's book, *Anguished English*. Lederer, an English teacher, has compiled many misuses of words from students and parents. One parent wrote, "My son is under the doctor's care and should not take PE today. Please execute him."[9] Another wrote, "Please excuse Jimmy for being. It was his father's fault."[10] And one student's essay to a history question read, "Sir Francis Drake circumcised the world with a 100-foot clipper."[11] Although relationships are plagued with similar misuses of words and misunderstandings, the words are often injurious rather than humorous.

Imagine George is in the kitchen cooking dinner while Tonya is studying for a final exam. They have the following interaction:

TONYA (to herself): *I sure would like another fifteen minutes before dinner to study without interruption.*

TONYA (to George): "When will dinner be ready?"

GEORGE (to himself): *She is so impatient! She should appreciate my cooking dinner, but instead she just pushes me to do it faster.*

GEORGE (irritably to Tonya): "I'm working as fast as I can."

TONYA (to herself): *He's angry about cooking. He shouldn't volunteer if he's going to be angry about it.*

TONYA (to George): "You don't have to get upset. You don't even have to cook—I'll do it myself."

GEORGE (to himself): *I knew she thought I was too slow. She doesn't give me enough credit for the things I do. She never appreciates me.*

GEORGE (to Tonya): "You're such a grump."

TONYA (to herself): *He's so selfish. He can't even cook dinner without complaining.*

TONYA (to George): "You're the grump!"

On and on it goes . . .

George and Tonya misunderstood each other because their words did not adequately reflect their thoughts and wishes. Many communications are flawed by misunderstanding.

Problem 2: Misinterpretation. George and Tonya miscommunicated, and they misinterpreted each other. They each assumed they could read the other's mind. In fact, they both did a poor job of mind reading but they assumed they did a good job. George assumed Tonya's initial question, "When will dinner be ready?" reflected hunger and impatience. Actually, Tonya was hoping to have time to study before dinner. Tonya incorrectly assumed George was angry about cooking. Mind reading is a common error couples need to overcome for productive communication.

Problem 3: Misperception. After enough miscommunication and misinterpretation, those in distressed relationships begin seeing their partners as monsters. They use labels when thinking about their partners: selfish, insensitive, workaholic, pushy, controlling, rigid, irresponsible, or impulsive. Misperception can be seen in the previous example where George labeled Tonya a "grump" and Tonya labeled George "selfish."

Labeling causes selective perception. Once George believes Tonya is a grump, he will notice the times she is grouchy and ignore the times she is cheerful. And he will selectively recall past incidents, remembering times she was grouchy and forgetting the good times. Eventually his misperceptions will create a desire to punish Tonya for being a grump, and Tonya will be more convinced than ever that George is selfish. She will eventually punish him and the vicious cycle of attacks and counterattacks begins.

Problem 4: Mismatch of Expectations and Reality. The fourth cognitive factor in relationship distress starts before the relationship does. Long before George and Tonya married, they developed expectations for love and marriage. George learned to expect couples shouldn't have to talk about their problems in a good relationship. Tonya's expectations were different. She believed couples in a good relationship *can* talk about their problems. Not surprisingly, reality was different than either expected.

Individuals come into relationships with *shoulds*—ideas about how the relationship is supposed to work. When reality is different than their expectations, people feel disappointed and betrayed. Cognitive therapists help those in troubled relationships challenge their preconceived expectations as well as their current beliefs and assumptions.

Techniques

Counselors need to carefully create an atmosphere of nonjudgment and collaboration. If one partner feels blamed for the relationship problems, he or she will probably not fully participate in the treatment. As with other forms of cognitive therapy, collaboration between the counselor and clients is an essential component of treatment. The need for collaboration can be seen in the following techniques.

Technique 1: Test Automatic Thoughts and Expectations. Automatic thoughts occur quickly in the midst of an argument and they seem compelling. George and Tonya had several in just a few seconds:

She should appreciate my cooking dinner. (arbitrary should)
He shouldn't volunteer if he's going to be angry about it. (arbitrary should)
She doesn't give me enough credit for the things I do. (mind reading)
She never appreciates me. (overgeneralization)
He's so selfish. (labeling)

All of the distorted automatic thoughts discussed in chapters 5 and 6 can be found in troubled relationships. Counselors can stop clients when they use distorted beliefs and gently confront the automatic thoughts. For example:

HUSBAND: I'm frustrated with her weight. She doesn't seem to care how she looks.

COUNSELOR: I understood the first part of what you said. You are frustrated with your wife being overweight. But I was wondering about the second part. You said she doesn't care how she looks. What evidence do you have for that?

HUSBAND: If she cared, she wouldn't be overweight.

COUNSELOR: Are there other ways to think about this?

HUSBAND: I suppose. She could care and just not know how to lose weight effectively.

In this example, the counselor collaborates with the frustrated husband to challenge his mind reading, *She doesn't care how she looks*, and his automatic thought gives way to a more reasonable belief.

Dichotomous thinking (forcing experiences into one of two extreme categories) is common in the midst of relationship crises. People sometimes resort to the primitive conclusion, *If my marriage isn't perfect, it is awful*. To confront this, have clients rate their marriage on a 1–10 scale, where 1 is the worst marriage they can imagine (abuse, unfaithfulness, and so on) and 10 is the best. Then ask where they would like their marriage to be. Most desire a 9 or a 10. Then ask what kind of marriage they could tolerate for the rest of their lives. Most could tolerate a 5 or a 6. This forces clients out of dichotomous assumptions as they realize their current relationship is flawed but not too far below what they could tolerate for the rest of their lives.

Most automatic thoughts reflect faulty underlying rules about relationships. Consider several unrealistic (though common) rules:

- Criticism is always destructive.
- Happy couples never disagree.
- Anger is wrong.
- My partner should know what I want without my having to ask.
- My partner should always protect me.
- My partner should always sacrifice his or her needs and desires to help meet mine.
- My partner should do 50 percent of all household tasks.
- My partner should be responsible at all times.
- Our relationship should always be fair.
- Our sex life should always be wonderful.
- My partner should be as kind to me as I am to him or her.

Most people will recognize these rules to be unreasonable once they verbalize their beliefs.

Technique 2. Get Hot Cognitions in Joint Sessions. The snake phobic does not bring snakes to counseling, but those in distressed relationships often bring their partners. This provides a unique opportunity (as well as a unique challenge) to capture distorted thoughts as they occur. Cognitive counselors use joint sessions to focus on thinking patterns, even if this requires interrupting the conversation. This is illustrated in the following interaction:

WIFE: I don't know what happens to our money. Bill works hard—I know he does. But it goes so fast. Most times I can't even pay all the bills. Then he asks for lunch money and I can't give it to him.

HUSBAND: All I know is that I'm tired of working sixty hours a week and having nothing to show from it. I just want to know where it all goes.

WIFE: (sobs)

COUNSELOR: Let's take a moment here to focus on thoughts. Carol, you just experienced some painful feelings. What thoughts were going through your head?

WIFE: I was thinking I was sorry. I wish I could do a better job. I know he works hard. I don't mean to fail.

COUNSELOR: And Bill, what was going through your mind as Carol was crying?

HUSBAND: I was wishing she would stop crying and just do something about it.

COUNSELOR: So both your thoughts went something like this: "This is Carol's responsibility and she is failing."

Next, the counselor would look for alternative ways of thinking. Just because Carol pays the bills, does it follow that she fails when they are short of money?

Having both partners in for conjoint sessions gives the counselor opportunity to find *hot cognitions*—thoughts at the moment they occur. Collaborating with clients to understand and articulate their thoughts is an important part of couples counseling.

Technique 3. Empathy Training. There is no record of a man being shot by his wife while washing the dishes. Empathy training is an important part of most couples counseling, and cognitive counseling provides excellent opportunities for understanding one's partner. Consider another approach the counselor could have taken to the previous interaction:

WIFE: I don't know what happens to our money. Bill works hard— I know he does. But it goes so fast. Most times I can't even pay all the bills. Then he asks for lunch money and I can't give it to him.

HUSBAND: All I know is that I'm tired of working sixty hours a week and having nothing to show from it. I just want to know where it all goes.

WIFE: (sobs)

COUNSELOR: Let's take a moment here to focus on thoughts. Bill, what do you suppose was going through Carol's mind just then?

HUSBAND: I don't know. She was probably mad about what I said.

COUNSELOR: How did he do, Carol?

WIFE: Not very well. I was just thinking what a failure I am with the finances.

This gives Bill a chance to see he is a poor mind reader and to better empathize with Carol. The counselor could do the same for Carol, asking her what thoughts Bill was having.

Another way to build empathy is *reverse role-playing*. Have the clients reverse roles and replay an interaction. Bill becomes Carol and Carol becomes Bill. After the role-play, have each discuss how they thought and felt throughout the exercise and what they learned about their partner.

Technique 4. Draw from Other Marital Therapies. Cognitive couples therapy does not conflict with other models of treatment. Most counselors find it wise to combine cognitive techniques with other counseling techniques such as communication training, anger management, assertiveness, problem-solving, and negotiation.

Concerns for Christian Counselors

Couples in contemporary society face the challenge of role division. Who does the cooking? Who works outside the home? Who changes diapers? Who mows the lawn? Christian couples are facing these questions while trying to understand what the Bible says about roles.

Many couples, Christian and not, come for help because their inflexible roles have led to problems. So we hear, "No wife of mine will ever work outside the home," or "My husband is responsible for my spiritual growth," or "Cooking is the woman's job." But only Christian couples support their inflexible role assignments with Bible verses or opinions of Christian authors or speakers.

How do Christian counselors help those with inflexible role assignments? Direct confrontation is usually unwise. The following examples demonstrate the defensiveness created by direct confrontation. The first example might occur among those who are Christian or not; the second is specific to Christians.

Example 1

HUSBAND: I came home and was really tired, so I sat down and read the paper. It seemed okay to me. Then Mary came home and started dinner. I heard the cupboard doors slamming and pans crashing. I knew she was mad.

WIFE: I was mad because you didn't even say hello. I don't expect you to cook when you get home before I do, but it would be nice for you to be friendly.

COUNSELOR: Why is it always Mary's job to cook? I think you need to share that responsibility when you both work.

HUSBAND: I don't know how to cook and it's not my job. I take care of the cars and yard; Mary cooks and takes care of the house.

WIFE: I don't expect him to cook.

Example 2

HUSBAND: She wants to go out and leave me with the kids all the time.

WIFE: No, I don't. I just would like to spend an evening with a friend of mine every now and then and not feel guilty for leaving the kids with you.

COUNSELOR: It seems to me that Mary's social life should be her decision.

HUSBAND: That's not what my Bible says. I'm responsible for making sure she makes good decisions. If she leaves every night to be with friends, that's not good for our kids.

Rather than confronting rigid role definitions, counselors are wise to collaborate with clients, first to find the clients' values and then to find alternative perspectives. The following example demonstrates this technique. The counselor first looks for the clients' values and then gently probes for alternative ways of thinking.

HUSBAND: She wants to go out and leave me with the kids all the time.

WIFE: No, I don't. I just would like to spend an evening with a friend of mine every now and then and not feel guilty for leaving the kids with you.

COUNSELOR: As you see marriage, how do the two of you decide whether or not Mary goes out and leaves the kids with Jack?

HUSBAND: Well, we go with what's best for the family.

COUNSELOR: I see. Sometimes that must be difficult to determine.

WIFE: Yeah. I think it would be good for our kids to spend a couple evenings a month with Jack. They almost never see him.

HUSBAND: They see me a lot.

COUNSELOR: Different couples have different values about who makes decisions. Tell me about how it works in your family.

WIFE: Well, if we disagree, I try to submit to Jack's authority.

HUSBAND: We agree on a lot of things. But if we don't, I guess it's my job to make a final decision.

COUNSELOR: I see. So Jack is the leader on the tough decisions and Mary is the follower. Jack, you said it's your job to make final decisions.

HUSBAND: Well, you know, from the Bible.

COUNSELOR: I was wondering if there are other ways to look at what the Bible has to say about this.

From here, the counselor and clients can go on to set up an experiment—perhaps interviewing a pastor from another denomination or reading books with differing perspectives on roles. Couples who come for counseling thinking there is only one Christian perspective on roles may leave thinking much more flexibly.

Varying beliefs about divorce create another difficulty for Christian couples counselors. Christian counselors and clients often believe divorce is wrong. These beliefs are strongly rooted in Christian tradition and Scripture. Jesus taught:

> It has been said, "Anyone who divorces his wife must give her a certificate of divorce." But I tell you that anyone who divorces his wife, except for marital unfaithfulness, causes her to become an adulteress, and anyone who marries the divorced woman commits adultery. (Matt. 5:31, 32)

This prohibition of divorce puts counselors in a difficult spot. What do we do when one spouse has been unfaithful? What about spouse or child abuse? What if one partner is so dominating and unwilling to change that the other is depressed and suicidal?

Although it is beyond the scope of this book to answer these questions (diverse opinions are available from informed theologians), it is important to consider ways counselors talk to themselves when clients choose divorce. Counselors without Christian values can say to themselves, *They came for help and discovered the best decision is to divorce. I've done my job.* Meanwhile, Christian counselors struggle with thoughts of inadequacy or failure as they say to themselves, *If I were a better counselor, I could have saved this marriage.*

Two reminders are helpful. First, remember clients make their own choices. Counselors do not tell their clients what to do, but instead give them freedom to make choices—right or wrong. Counselors need not take responsibility for clients' poor choices.

Second, many couples have to choose between several bad options. Divorce is a bad option because it violates marriage vows and Christian expectations, separation is a bad option because of the financial and emotional stress it causes, and keeping their current relationship is a bad option because people are being hurt. The only good option, improving the relationship, depends on the skill of the counselor, but also on the personality and commitment of both partners. When one or both lack the necessary skills or motivation to change, only bad outcomes are possible, regardless of the counselor's ability. Counselors who personalize these bad outcomes by blaming themselves carry an unnecessary burden.

A FINAL PARABLE

Imagine being born and raised in prison. The dark colors, damp cells, and smelly courtyard become a way of life. You never feel the sand between your toes while walking beside the ocean or enjoy the colors of a summer sunset. The seasons pass unnoticed, and life blurs with routine. Then one day you discover you have been pardoned, released from prison. You feel happy, but find your problems are not yet solved. Although you are pardoned, no one has shown you how to leave. Endless walls of cement block and steel bars create a maze of confusion and uncertainty. The door is nowhere to be found. After many days of being "freed," you are still a prisoner. Then someone finally shows you the door, and you pass from an old way of life to a better one.

In this parable, the prison is one of self-doubt. As we grow in this prison we feel unloved and unworthy, wondering if there is a better world somewhere. Then Christ pardons us, frees us from prison, and tells us, "I love you unconditionally." Many feel happy and immediately escape to the world of bright colors and sunlight. Others can't seem to pass through the door to leave their prison of self-doubt and faulty core beliefs.

As Christian counselors, we don't do the pardoning or the freeing. We just help others pass through the door to the love, joy, and peace God provides.

CLIENT INFORMATION FORM

Name:	_____	Birthdate:	_____
Address:	_____	Today's date:	_____
City, State:	_____ Zip: _____	Phone:	_____
Job:	_____	Phone:	_____
Insurance:	_____	Group #:	_____
Address:	_____	ID#:	_____

Your signature below authorizes release of medical information necessary to process insurance claims and authorizes payment directly to the psychologist for services provided.

_____
Signature

Briefly describe your reason for seeking help:

Who suggested that you contact me?

When were you last examined by a physician?

List any major health problems for which you currently receive treatment:

List any medications you now are taking:

Have you ever received psychiatric or psychological help or counseling before? Please explain:

Please list the members of your family and all others in your home, *including yourself*:

Name	Age/Birthdate	Relationship	Occupation

HOMEWORK FORMS

Daily Mood Record

Record your activities and your moods during each activity.

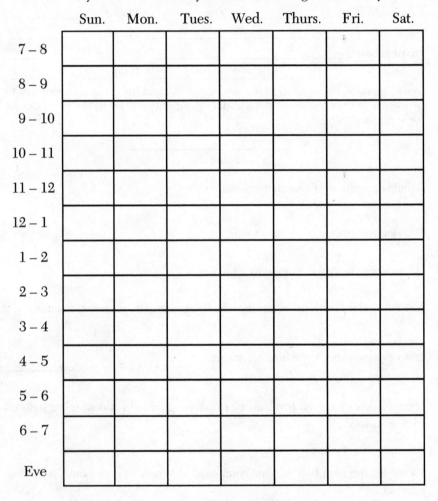

	Sun.	Mon.	Tues.	Wed.	Thurs.	Fri.	Sat.
7 – 8							
8 – 9							
9 – 10							
10 – 11							
11 – 12							
12 – 1							
1 – 2							
2 – 3							
3 – 4							
4 – 5							
5 – 6							
6 – 7							
Eve							

Mood Rating Scale: 1 = Feeling fine
5 = Somewhat depressed (anxious, etc.)
10 = Very depressed (anxious, etc.)

Emotion Report

Target Emotion (anger, anxiety, depression, other)

The situation was:

My feelings were:

My thoughts were:

What I learned is:

Identifying Feelings

List the emotions you experience. Examples are listed below. Try to identify at least twenty-five different feelings in the next week.

_____ _____ _____
_____ _____ _____
_____ _____ _____
_____ _____ _____
_____ _____ _____
_____ _____ _____
_____ _____ _____
_____ _____ _____
_____ _____ _____
_____ _____ _____
_____ _____ _____
_____ _____ _____
_____ _____ _____

EXAMPLES

Accepting	*Adoring*	*Afraid*	*Amazed*
Angry	*Annoyed*	*Anticipating*	*Anxious*
Apprehensive	*Aroused*	*Ashamed*	*Blue*
Bored	*Calm*	*Cheerful*	*Confident*
Content	*Delighted*	*Depressed*	*Disappointed*
Distracted	*Disgusted*	*Ecstatic*	*Elated*
Embarrassed	*Energetic*	*Enraged*	*Enthused*
Euphoric	*Excited*	*Exuberant*	*Frustrated*
Grieved	*Guilty*	*Happy*	*Hateful*
Hopeless	*Hostile*	*Humiliated*	*Hungry*
Hurt	*Intense*	*Jealous*	*Joyful*
Loving	*Moody*	*Nervous*	*Peaceful*
Sad	*Sick*	*Surprised*	*Terrified*
Tranquil	*Troubled*	*Watchful*	*Zestful*

Feelings and Alternatives

Our feelings influence our behaviors and vice versa. On this sheet, list your problem feelings and what behaviors you could consider as alternatives. For example, if you feel tired you could take a warm bath, listen to music, or take a nap.

Feeling	**Alternatives**
	Talk with her
Angry with boss	Take a walk
	Pray for patience

Daily Record of Dysfunctional Thoughts

Situation	Feelings	Automatic Thoughts	Rational Responses

Should Statements Record

During the coming week, record your arbitrary should statements. In each case, record an alternative way of thinking about the same experience without using a should statement.

Should Statement	Alternative
_____	_____
_____	_____
_____	_____
_____	_____
_____	_____
_____	_____
_____	_____
_____	_____
_____	_____
_____	_____
_____	_____
_____	_____
_____	_____

Catastrophizing Record

During the coming week, record the times that you awfulize or catastrophize. In each case, rate how bad the event actually is according to your awfulness scale. A 100 on the scale is the worst thing that could possibly happen to you and a 0 is something that is neither bad nor good.

Catastrophe	Rating (0–100)

Cognitive Distortions

Distortion	Explanation	Example
All-or-none thinking	Tendency to see things in absolute, black-and-white categories.	Either I am perfectly competent in everything I do or else I'm a failure.
Overgeneralization	Assuming bad events will happen over and over or that things are always a certain way.	The dogs will always choose my lawn for relief.
Mental filter	Focusing on the negative parts of life and filtering out the positive.	My job's awful because I don't get paid enough (overlooking good work conditions, hours).
Disqualifying the positive	Discounting success or compliments.	I got the promotion because I'm lucky.
Jumping to conclusions	**Mind reading**	Everybody is noticing that my socks don't match my shirt.
	Fortune telling	I'm going to fail this exam.
Magnification and minimization	Magnifying errors and minimizing successes.	I'm terrible with the kids since I just yelled at them.
Emotional reasoning	Basing thoughts on feelings.	I feel like a loser, therefore I am a loser.
Should statements	Setting arbitrary requirements without considering consequences.	I should be friendly with everyone I meet.
Labeling and mislabeling	Categorizing people based on limited exposure.	The person in that yellow car is really selfish!
Personalization	Accepting the blame for some negative event involving others.	My family would be well-adjusted if it weren't for me.

Cognitive distortions identified by David Burns in *Feeling Good* (New American Library: New York, 1980).

Snapshots

Record your most significant memories from childhood.

Event	Specific memories (sights, sounds, smells)	Feelings	Thoughts

Progress Report

Imagine God writing a progress report about you. Fill in this form as you think God might.

Progress report

Name of human: _____

This person's strengths are:

This person needs improvement in the following areas:

Appropiate goals for the next six months are:

Rehearsal

Write revisions to your core beliefs in the spaces below. Be creative and practical. After writing your new self-statements, cut out the cards to carry with you.

Daily Mood Record

Record your activities and your moods during each activity.

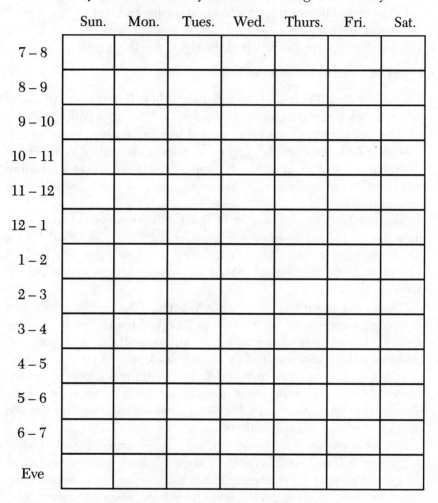

	Sun.	Mon.	Tues.	Wed.	Thurs.	Fri.	Sat.
7 – 8							
8 – 9							
9 – 10							
10 – 11							
11 – 12							
12 – 1							
1 – 2							
2 – 3							
3 – 4							
4 – 5							
5 – 6							
6 – 7							
Eve							

Pleasure Rating Scale: 1 = **Very unpleasurable**
2
3 = **Neutral**
4
5 = **Very pleasurable**

Assertiveness

What Is Assertiveness?

1. The straightforward expression of thoughts and feelings.
2. Socially appropriate.
3. Involves the consideration of the rights and feelings of others. [*]

Types of Assertive Responses:

Assertive Talk. Do not let the actions of others ferment into resentful attitudes. Ask for accountability. Examples: "I'd like more coffee, please," or "This radio doesn't work properly and I would like my money back."

Feeling Talk. Express likes and dislikes spontaneously. Do not bottle up emotions. Answer questions honestly. Examples: "What a beautiful new dress!" "I'm really tired." "Since you asked, I much prefer you in another type of outfit."

Greeting Talk. Be outgoing and friendly with those you would like to know better. Do not avoid people because of shyness. Smile brightly at people. Be pleased to see them. Examples: "Hi, how are you?" "Hello, I haven't seen you in months." "What are you doing with yourself these days?"

Disagreeing Passively and Actively. When you disagree with someone do not feign agreement for the sake of "keeping the peace" by smiling, nodding, or paying close attention. Instead, change the topic. Look away. Disagree actively and emotionally when you are sure of your ground.

Asking Why. When you are asked to do something that does not sound reasonable by a person in power or authority, ask why you should do it. Have it understood that you will live up to voluntary commitments and be open to reasonable suggestions.

Talking about Oneself. When you have done something worthwhile or interesting, let others know about. Let people know how you feel about things. Relate your experiences. Do not monopolize conversations, but do not be afraid to bring them around to yourself when it is appropriate.

Agreeing with Compliments. Do not depreciate yourself or become flustered when someone compliments you with sincerity. At the very least, offer an equally sincere, "Thank you." Or reward the complimenter by saying, "That's an awfully nice thing to say." In other words, reward

---

[*] Definition from D. C. Rimm and J. C. Master, *Behavior Therapy*, 2nd ed. (New York: Academic Press, 1979), 63.

rather than punish others for complimenting you. When appropriate, extend compliments. For example, if someone says, "What a beautiful sweater!" respond, "Isn't is a lovely color? I had a hard time finding it."

Avoiding Trying to Justify Opinions. Be reasonable in discussions, but when someone goes out of his or her way to dominate a social interaction by taking issue with any comments you offer, say something like, "It sounds like we may just disagree on that issue," or "We all have different perspectives on these things."

Looking People in the Eye. Do not avoid the gaze of others. When you argue, express an opinion, or greet a person, look him or her directly in the eye.

Saying No. When a request is unreasonable, say "No," and persist in your no. Offer other suggestions or a brief explanation, but don't explain to the point of defensiveness. Examples: "No, I'm going to relax right now," or "I'm sorry, but I must say no."

BIBLIOGRAPHY

Achmon, J., M. Granek, M. Golomb, and J. Hart. 1989. Behavioral treatment of essential hypertension: A comparison between cognitive therapy and biofeedback of heart rate. *Psychosomatic Medicine* 51:152–64.

Agras, W. S., J. A. Schneider, B. Arnow, S. D. Raeburn, and C. F. Telch. 1989. Cognitive-behavioral and response-prevention treatments for bulimia nervosa. *Journal of Consulting and Clinical Psychology* 57:215–21.

Averill, J. R. 1983. Studies on anger and aggression: Implications for theories of emotion. *American Psychologist* 38:1145–60.

Barlow, D. H., M. G. Craske, J. A. Cerny, and J. S. Klosko. 1989. Behavior treatment of panic disorder. *Behavior Therapy* 20:261–82.

Beck, A. T. *Love Is Never Enough.* 1988. New York: Harper and Row.

———. *Cognitive Therapy and the Emotional Disorders.* 1976. New York: International Universities Press.

———. 1988. Cognitive approaches to panic disorder: Theory and therapy. In S. Rachman and J. D. Maser, eds., *Panic: Psychological Perspectives.* Hillsdale, N.J.: Lawrence Erlbaum Associates.

Beck, A. T., M. Kovacs, and A. Weissman. 1975. Hopelessness and suicidal behavior: An overview. *Journal of the American Medical Association* 234:1146–49.

Beck, A. T., A. J. Rush, B. F. Shaw, and G. Emery. 1979. *Cognitive Therapy of Depression*. New York: Guilford.

Beck, A. T., G. Emery, with R. L. Greenberg. 1985. *Anxiety Disorders and Phobias: A Cognitive Perspective*. New York: Basic Books.

Beck, A. T., S. D. Hollon, J. E. Young, R. C. Bedrosian, and D. Budenz. 1985. Treatment of depression with cognitive therapy and amitriptyline. *Archives of General Psychiatry* 42:142–48.

Beck, A. T., and C. A. Padesky. Love is never enough. An advanced clinical workshop for mental health professionals. Los Angeles, 12 November 1988.

Bellah, R. N., R. Madsen, W. M. Sullivan, A. Swidler, and S. M. Tipton. 1985. *Habits of the Heart*. New York: Harper and Row.

Bergin, A. E. 1983. Religiosity and mental health: A critical reevaluation and meta-analysis. *Professional Psychology* 14:170–184.

Bergin, A. E., and M. J. Lambert. 1978. The evaluation of therapeutic outcomes. In S. L. Garfield and A. E. Bergin, eds., *Handbook of Psychotherapy and Behavior Change: An Empirical Analysis*, 2nd ed. New York: Wiley.

Bergin, A. E., R. D. Stinchfield, T. A. Gaskin, K. S. Masters, and C. E. Sullivan. 1988. Religious life-styles and mental health: An exploratory study. *Journal of Counseling Psychology* 35:91–98.

Beutler, L. E., F. Scogin, P. Kirkish, D. Schretlen, A. Corbishley, D. Hamblin, K. Meredith, R. Potter, C. R. Bamford, and A. I. Levenson. 1987. Group cognitive therapy and alprazolam in the treatment of depression in older adults. *Journal of Consulting and Clinical Psychology* 55:550–56.

Biran, M. 1988. Cognitive and exposure treatment for agoraphobia: Reexamination of the outcome research. *Journal of Cognitive Psychotherapy: An International Quarterly* 2:165–78.

Blackburn, I. M., S. Bishop, M. I. Glenn, L. J. Whalley, and J. E. Christie. 1981. The efficacy of cognitive therapy in depression: A treatment trial using cognitive therapy and pharmacotherapy, each alone and in combination. *British Journal of Psychiatry* 139:181–189.

Blowers, C., J. Cobb, and A. Mathews. 1987. Generalized anxiety: A controlled treatment study. *Behaviour Research and Therapy* 25:493–502.

Bobgan, M., and D. Bobgan. 1977. *The Psychological Way/The Spiritual Way*. Minneapolis: Bethany House.

———. 1987. *Psychoheresy*. Santa Barbara, Calif.: Eastgate.

Borkovec, T. D., A. M. Mathews, A. Chambers, S. Ebrahimi, R. Lytle, and R. Nelson. 1987. The effects of relaxation training with cognitive or nondirective therapy and the role of relaxation-induced anxiety in the treatment of generalized anxiety. *Journal of Consulting and Clinical Psychology* 55:883–88.

Bruun, C. V. 1985. A combined treatment approach: Cognitive therapy and spiritual dimensions. *Journal of Psychology and Christianity* 42:9–11.

Burns, D. 1980. *Feeling Good*. New York: New American Library.

Butler, G. 1989. Issues in the application of cognitive and behavioral strategies to the treatment of social phobia. *Clinical Psychology Review* 9:91–106.

Carson, R. C., J. N. Butcher, and J. C. Coleman. 1988. *Abnormal Psychology and Modern Life*, 8th ed. Glenview, Ill.: Scott, Foresman and Company.

Carter, J. D., and B. Narramore. 1979. *The Integration of Psychology and Theology: An Introduction*. Grand Rapids, Mich.: Zondervan.

Clark, D. M., P. M. Salkovskis, and A. J. Chalkley. 1985. Respiratory control as a treatment for panic attacks. *Journal of Behavior Therapy and Experimental Psychiatry* 16:23–30.

Clinebell, H. 1984. *Basic Types of Pastoral Care and Counseling: Resources for the Ministry of Healing and Growth*. Nashville: Abingdon.

Collet, L., J. Cottraux, and R. Ladouceur. 1987. Cognitive therapy of depression and counterdemand effects: A pilot study. *Psychological Reports* 60:555–60.

Collins, G. R. 1981. *Psychology and Theology: Prospects for Integration*. Nashville: Abingdon.

Cook, M. L., and C. Peterson. 1986. Depressive irrationality. *Cognitive Therapy and Research* 10:293–98.

Crabb, L. J., Jr. 1977. *Effective Biblical Counseling*. Grand Rapids, Mich.: Zondervan.

Craigie, F. C., Jr., and S.-Y. Tan. 1989. Changing resistant assumptions in Christian cognitive-behavioral therapy. *Journal of Psychology and Theology* 17:93–100.

Deffenbacker, J. L. 1988. Cognitive-relaxation and social skills treatments of anger: A year later. *Journal of Counseling Psychology* 35:234–36.

Deffenbacher, J. L., D. A. Story, A. D. Brandon, J. A. Hogg, and S. L. Hazaleus. 1988. Cognitive and cognitive-relaxation treatments of anger. *Cognitive Therapy and Research* 12:167–84.

Deffenbacher, J. L., D. A. Story, R. S. Stark, J. A. Hogg, and A. D. Brandon. 1987. Cognitive-relaxation and social skills interventions in the treatment of general anger. *Journal of Counseling Psychology* 34:171–76.

Dendata, K. M., and D. Diener. 1986. Effectiveness of cognitive/relaxation therapy and study-skills training in reducing self-reported anxiety and improving the academic performance of test-anxious students. *Journal of Counseling Psychology* 33:131–35.

Depue, R. A., and S. M. Monroe. 1986. Conceptualization and measurement of human disorder in life stress research: The problem of chronic disturbance. *Psychological Bulletin* 99:36–51.

DeRubeis, R. J., and A. T. Beck. 1988. Cognitive therapy. In K.S. Dobson, ed., *Handbook of Cognitive-Behavioral Therapies.* New York: Guilford.

Dobson, K. S., and B. F. Shaw. 1986. Cognitive assessment with major depressive disorders. *Cognitive Research and Therapy* 10:13–29.

Egan, G. *The Skilled Helper.* 1975. Monterey, Calif.: Brooks/Cole.

Ekman, P., R. W. Leveson, and W. V. Friensen. 1983. Autonomic nervous system activity distinguishes among emotions. *Science* 221:1208–10.

Elkin, I. 1986. Outcome findings and therapist performance. Paper presented at the American Psychological Association convention.

Ellis, A. 1960. There is no place for the concept of sin in psychotherapy. *Journal of Counseling Psychology* 7:188–92.

———. 1962. *Reason and Emotion in Psychotherapy.* Secaucus, N.J.: Citadel Press.

———. 1971. *The Case Against Religion: A Psychotherapist's View.* New York: Institute for Rational Living.

———. 1980. Psychotherapy and atheistic values: A response to A. E. Bergin's "psychotherapy and religious values." *Journal of Consulting and Clinical Psychology* 48:635–39.

———. 1984. Rational-emotive therapy (RET) and pastoral counseling: A reply to Wessler. *The Personnel and Guidance Journal* 62:266–67.

———. 1987. A sadly neglected cognitive element in depression. *Cognitive Therapy and Research* 11:121–46.

Ellis, A., and R. Grieger. 1977. *Handbook of Rational-Emotive Therapy.* New York: Springer-Verlag.

Emrick, C. D. 1975. A review of psychologically oriented treatment of alcholism. *Journal of Studies on Alcohol* 36:88–108.

Eysenck, H. J. 1952. The effects of psychotherapy: An evaluation. *Journal of Consulting Psychology* 16:319–24.

Fairburn, C. G., J. Kirk, M. O'Connor, and P. J. Cooper. 1986. A comparison of two psychological treatments for bulimia nervosa. *Behavior Research and Therapy* 24:629–643.

Farnsworth, K. E. 1985. *Wholehearted Integration: Harmonizing Psychology and Christianity through Word and Deed*. Grand Rapids, Mich.: Baker Book House.

Feindler, E. L., and R. B. Ecton. 1986. *Adolescent Anger Control: Cognitive-Behavioral Techniques*. New York: Pergamon Press.

Fennel, M. J. V., and J. D. Teasdale. 1987. Cognitive therapy for depression: Individual differences and the process of change. *Cognitive Therapy and Research* 11:253–71.

Frank, J. D. 1971. Therapeutic factors in psychotherapy. *American Journal of Psychotherapy* 25:350–61.

———. 1982. The present status of outcome research. In M. R. Goldfried, ed., *Converging Themes in Psychotherapy*. New York: Springer.

Freeman, C., F. Sinclair, J. Turnbull, and A. Annandale. 1985. Psychotherapy for bulimia: A controlled study. *Journal of Psychiatric Research* 19:473–78.

Friedman, M., and D. Ulmer. *Treating Type A Behavior—and Your Heart*. 1984. New York: Knopf.

Garner, D. M. 1986. Cognitive-behavioral therapy for eating disorders. *The Clinical Psychologist* 39:36–39.

Graff, R. W., G. I. Whitehead, III, and M. LeCompte. 1986. Group treatment with divorced women using cognitive-behavioral and supportive insight methods. *Journal of Counseling Psychology* 33:276–81.

Graham, S. R. 1980. Desire, belief and grace: A psychotherapeutic paradigm. *Psychotherapy: Theory, Research and Practice* 17:370–71.

Hamilton, S. A., and W. J. Fremouw. 1985. Cognitive-behavioral training for college basketball free-throw performance. *Cognitive Therapy and Research* 9:479–83.

Hazaleus, S. L., and J. L. Deffenbacher. 1986. Relaxation and cognitive treatments of anger. *Journal of Consulting and Clinical Psychology* 54:222–26.

Heimberg, R. G. 1989. Cognitive and behavioral treatments for social phobia: A critical analysis. *Clinical Psychology Review* 9:107–28.

Herman, C. P., and D. Mack. 1975. Restrained and unrestrained eating. *Journal of Personality* 43:647–60.

Hewitt, P. L., and D. G. Dyck. 1986. Perfectionism, stress, and vulnerability to depression. *Cognitive Therapy and Research* 10:137–42.

Higgins, E. 1980. Logos. In Nancy Thomas, ed., *On the Edge of a Truth* Newberg, Ore.: Barclay Press. Used by permission.

Hogg, J. A., and J. L. Deffenbacher. 1988. A comparison of cognitive and interpersonal-process group therapies in the treatment of depression among college students. *Journal of Counseling Psychology* 35:304–10.

Holcomb, W. R. 1986. Stress inoculation therapy with anxiety and stress disorders of acute psychiatric inpatients. *Journal of Clinical Psychology* 42:864–72.

Holmes, D. S. 1991. *Abnormal Psychology*. New York: HarperCollins Publishers.

Holmes, T. H., and R. H. Rahe. 1967. The social readjustment rating scale. *Journal of Psychosomatic Research* 11:213–18.

Horowitz, L. M., R. S. French, and C. A. Anderson. 1982. The prototype of a lonely person. In L. A. Peplau and D. Perlman, eds., *Loneliness: A Sourcebook of Current Theory, Research and Therapy*. New York: Wiley Interscience.

Hunt, D., and T. A. McMahan. 1985. *The Seduction of Christianity: Spiritual Discernment in the Last Days*. Eugene, Ore.: Harvest House.

Jacobson, N. S. 1989. The therapist-client relationship in cognitive behavior therapy: Implications for treating depression. *Journal of Cognitive Psychotherapy* 3:85–96.

Kendall, P. C., B. L. Howard, and J. Epps. 1988. The anxious child: Cognitive-behavioral strategies. *Behavior Modification* 12:281–310.

Kilpatrick, W. K. 1983. *Psychological Seduction: The Failure of Modern Psychology*. New York: Thomas Nelson.

Klosko, J. S., and D. H. Barlow. 1987. Cognitive-behavioral treatment of panic attacks. *Journal of Integrative and Eclectic Psychotherapy* 6:462–69.

Kovacs, M., A. D. Rush, A. T. Beck, and S. D. Hollon. 1981. Depressed outpatients treated with cognitive therapy or pharmacotherapy: A one-year follow up. *Archives of General Psychiatry* 38:33–39.

Laird, J. D. 1974. Self-attribution of emotion: The effects of expressive behavior on the quality of emotional experience. *Journal of Personality and Social Psychology* 29:475–86.

————. 1984. The real role of facial response in the experience of emotion: A reply to Tougangeau and Ellsworth, and others. *Journal of Personality and Social Psychology* 47:909–17.

Lazarus, R. Little hassles can be hazardous to health. *Psychology Today*, July 1981, 58–62.

————. 1982. Thoughts on the relations between emotion and cognitive. *American Psychologist* 37:1019–24.

————. 1984. On the primacy of cognition. *American Psychologist* 39:124–29.

Lederer, R. 1987. *Anguished English*. New York: Dell Publishing.

Leerhsen, C. John Madden on a Roll. *Newsweek*, 9 January 1984, 66–67.

Lewis, C. S. 1952. *Mere Christianity*. New York: Macmillan.

Lindsay, W. R., C. V. Gamsu, E. McLaughlin, E. M. Hood, and C. A. Epsie. 1987. A controlled trial of treatments for generalized anxiety. *British Journal of Clinical Psychology* 26:3–15.

Luborsky, L., L. Singer, and L. Luborsky. 1975. Comparative studies of psychotherapies. *Archives of General Psychiatry* 32:995–1008.

Luka, L. P., W. S. Agras, J. A. Schneider. 1986. Thirty month follow-up of cognitive-behavioral group therapy for bulimia. *The British Journal of Psychiatry* 148:614–15.

Marchione, K. E., L. Michelson, M. Greenwald, and C. Dancu. 1987. Cognitive behavior treatment of agoraphobia. *Behaviour Research and Therapy* 25:319–28.

Marks, I. M., and M. Lader. 1973. Anxiety states anxiety neurosis: A review. *Journal of Nervous and Mental Disease* 156:3–18.

Marshall, T. K., and A. S. Mazie. 1987. A cognitive approach to treating depression. *Social Casework* 68:540–45.

Martin, R. P. 1978. *The Epistle of Paul to the Philippians*. Grand Rapids, Mich.: Eerdmans.

Marzillier, J. 1987. A sadly neglected cognitive element in depression: A reply to Ellis. *Cognitive Therapy and Research* 11:147–52.

McLean, P. D., and A. R. Hakstian. 1979. Clinical depression: Comparative efficacy of outpatient treatments. *Journal of Consulting and Clinical Psychology* 47:818–36.

McMinn, M. R. 1988. *Your Hidden Half: Blending Your Public and Private Self*. Grand Rapids, Mich.: Baker Books.

————. 1990. *Dealing with Desires You Can't Control*. Colorado Springs, Colo.: NavPress.

————. 1991. Religious Values, Sexist Language, and Perceptions of a Therapist. *Journal of Psychology and Christianity* 10:132–36.

McMinn, M. R., and C. J. Lebold. 1989. Collaborative efforts in cognitive therapy with religious clients. *Journal of Psychology and Theology* 17:101–09.

McMullin, R. E. 1986. *Handbook of Cognitive Therapy Techniques*. New York: Norton.

McNally, R. J. and E. B. Foa. 1987. Cognition and agoraphobia: Bias in the interpretation of threat. *Cognitive Therapy and Research* 11:567–81.

McNamara, K., and J. J. Horan. 1986. Experimental construct validity in the evaluation of cognitive and behavioral treatments for depression. *Journal of Counseling Psychology* 33:23–30.

Meador, A. E., and T. H. Ollendick. 1984. Cognitive behavior therapy with children: An evaluation of its efficacy and clinical utility. *Child and Family Behavior Therapy* 63:25–44.

Meichenbaum, D. 1977. *Cognitive-Behavior Modification: An Integrative Approach*. New York: Plenum.

————. 1985. *Stress Inoculation Training*. New York: Pergamon Press.

————. Cognitive-behavioral approach with adults, adolescents, and children. A workshop sponsored by the Oregon Psychological Association, Portland, December, 1987.

Meichenbaum, D., and R. Novaco. 1985. Stress inoculation: A preventative approach. *Issues in Mental Health Nursing* 7:419–35.

Meichenbaum, D., and D. Turk. 1987. *Facilitating Treatment Adherence: A Practitioner's Guidebook*. New York: Plenum Press.

Michelson, L., M. Mavissakalian, and K. Machione. 1985. Cognitive and behavioral treatments of agoraphobia: Clinical, behavioral, and psychophysical outcomes. *Journal of Consulting and Clinical Psychology* 53:913–25.

Miller, I. W., W. H. Norman, G. I. Keitner, S. B. Bishop, and M. G. Dow. 1989. Cognitive-behavioral treatment of depressed inpatients. *Behavior Therapy* 20:25–47.

Murphy, G. E., A. D. Simons, R. D. Wetzel, and P. J. Lustman. 1984. Cognitive therapy and phramacotherapy, singly and together in the treatment of depression. *Archives of General Psychiatry* 41:33–41.

Murphy, S. M., and R. L. Woolfolk. 1987. The effects of cognitive interventions on competitive anxiety and performance on a fine motor skill accuracy task. *International Journal of Sport Psychology* 18:152–66.

Myers, D. 1989. *Psychology*, 2nd ed., New York: Worth Publishers.

Narramore, S. B. 1984. *No Condemnation*. Grand Rapids, Mich.: Zondervan.

Novaco, R. 1978. Anger and coping with stress: Cognitive-behavioral interventions. In J. P. Foreyt and D.P. Rathjen, eds., *Cognitive Behavior Therapy*. New York: Plenum.

Parsons, R. D., and R. J. Wicks. 1986. Cognitive pastoral psychotherapy with religious persons experiencing loneliness. *The Psychotherapy Patient* 2:47–59.

Pecheur, D. R., and K. J. Edwards. 1984. A comparison of secular and religious versions of cognitive therapy with depressed Christian college students. *Journal of Psychology and Theology* 12:45–54.

Persons, J. B., and D. D. Burns. 1985. Mechanisms of action of cognitive therapy: The relative contributions of technical and interpersonal interventions. *Cognitive Therapy and Research* 9:539–51.

Power, K. G., D. W. A. Jerrom, R. J. Simpson, M. J. Mitchell, and V. Swanson. 1989. A controlled comparison of cognitive-behaviour therapy, diazepam, and placebo in the management of generalized anxiety. *Behavioural Psychotherapy* 17:1–14.

Propst, L. B. 1980. The comparative efficacy of religious and nonreligious imagery for the treatment of mild depression in religious individuals. *Cognitive Therapy and Research* 4:167–78.

————. 1988. *Psychotherapy in a Religious Framework*. New York: Human Sciences Press.

Quackenbos, S., G. Privette, and B. Klentz. 1985. Psychotherapy: sacred or secular? *Journal of Counseling and Development* 63:290–93.

Rapee, R. M., and D. H. Barlow. 1988. Panic disorder: Cognitive-behavioral treatment. *Psychiatric Annals* 18:473–77.

Reynolds, W. M., and K. I. Coats. 1986. A comparison of cognitive-behavioral therapy and relaxation training for the treatment of depression in adolescents. *Journal of Consulting and Clinical Psychology* 54:653–60.

Rimm, D. C., and J. C. Master. 1979. *Behavior Therapy*, 2nd ed., New York: Academic Press.

Rogers, C. R. 1957. The necessary and sufficient conditions of therapeutic personality change. *Journal of Consulting Psychology* 21:95–103.

Rosenthal, R., and L. Jacobsen. 1968. *Pygmalion in the Classroom: Teacher Expectation and Pupils' Intellectual Development*. New York: Holt, Rinehart, and Winston.

Rossi, A. S. 1985. Change in the client and in the client's God. *Psychotherapy Patient* 1:55–62.

Rossiter, E. M., W. S. Agras, M. Losch, and C. F. Telch. 1988. Dietary restraint of bulimic subjects following cognitive-behavioral or pharmacological treatment. *Behavior Research and Therapy* 26:495–98.

Rush, A. J., A. T. Beck, M. Kovacs, and S. Hollon. 1977. Comparative efficacy of cognitive therapy and pharmacotherapy in the treatment of depressed outpatients. *Cognitive Therapy and Research* 1:17–37.

Salkovskis, P. M., and H. M. C. Warwick. 1986. Morbid preoccupations, health anxiety and reassurance: A cognitive-behavioral approach to hypochondriasis. *Behavior Research and Therapy* 24:597–602.

Salkovskis, P. M., D. R. O. Jones, and D. M. Clark. 1986. Respiratory control in the treatment of panic attacks: Replication and extension with concurrent measurement of behaviour and pCO_2. *British Journal of Psychiatry* 148:526–32.

Schneider, J. A., and W. S. Agras. 1985. A cognitive behavioural group treatment of bulimia. *British Journal of Psychiatry* 146:66–69.

Schneider, J. A., A. O'Leary, and W. S. Agras. 1987. The role of perceived self-efficacy in recovery from bulimia: A preliminary examination. *Behavior Research and Therapy* 25:429–32.

Seamands, D. A. 1981. *Healing for Damaged Emotions*. Wheaton, Ill.: Victor Books.

Seligman, M. E. P., and D. L. Rosenhan. 1984. *Abnormal Psychology*. New York: Norton.

Shaw, B. 1977. Comparison of cognitive therapy and behavior therapy in the treatment of depression. *Journal of Consulting and Clinical Psychology* 45:543–51.

Shear, M. K., G. Ball, and S. Josephson. 1987. An empirically developed cognitive-behavioral treatment of panic. *Journal of Integrative and Eclectic Psychotherapy* 6:421–33.

Shrauger, J. S., and R. E. Silverman. 1971. The relationship of religious background and participation to locus of control. *Journal for the Scientific Study of Religion* 10:11–16.

Silvestri, P. J. 1979. Locus of control and God-dependence. *Psychological Reports* 45:89–90.

Simons, A. D., P. J. Lustman, R. D. Wetzel, and G. E. Murphy. 1985. Predicting response to cognitive therapy of depression: The role of learned resourcefulness. *Cognitive Therapy and Research* 9:79–89.

Simons, A. D., G. E. Murphy, J. L. Levine, and R. D. Wetzel. 1986. Cognitive therapy and pharmacotherapy for depression. *Archives of General Psychiatry* 43:43–48.

Smith, M. L., and G. V. Glass. 1977. Meta-analysis of psychotherapy outcome studies. *American Psychologist* 32:752–60.

Smith, M. L., G. V. Glass, and R. L. Miller. 1980. *The Benefits of Psychotherapy*. Baltimore: Johns Hopkins Press.

Strickland, B. R., and S. Shaffer. 1971. I-E, I-E, and F. *Journal for the Scientific Study of Religion* 10:366–69.

Strupp, H. H. 1963. The outcome problem in psychotherapy revisited. *Psychotherapy: Theory, Research, and Practice* 1:1–13.

Swanson, H. L. 1985. Effects of cognitive-behavioral training on emotionally disturbed children's academic performance. *Cognitive Therapy and Research* 9:201–16.

Tan, S-Y. 1987. Cognitive-behavior therapy: A biblical approach and critique. *Journal of Psychology and Theology* 15:103–12.

Taylor, F., and W. Marshall. 1977. Experimental analysis of a cognitive-behavioral therapy for depression. *Cognitive Therapy and Research* 1:59–72.

Teasdale, J. D., M. J. V. Fennell, G. A. Hibbert, and P. L. Amies. 1984. Cognitive therapy for major depressive disorder in primary care. *British Journal of Psychiatry* 144:400–06.

Thomas, J. R, R. A. Petry, and J. R. Goldman. 1987. Comparison of cognitive and behavioral self-control treatments of depression. *Psychological Reports* 60:975–82.

Thurman, C. W. 1985a. Effectiveness of cognitive-behavioral treatments in reducing Type A behavior among university faculty. *Journal of Counseling Psychology* 32:74–83.

———. 1985b. Effectiveness of cognitive-behavioral treatments in reducing Type A behavior among university faculty—one year later. *Journal of Counseling Psychology* 32:445–48.

Torgersen, S. 1983. Genetic factors in anxiety disorders. *Archives of General Psychiatry* 40:1085–89.

Valliant, P. M., and B. Leith. 1986. Impact of relaxation-training and cognitive-therapy on coronary patients post surgery. *Psychological Reports* 59:1271–78.

Walls, G. 1980. Values and psychotherapy: A comment on "psychotherapy and religious values." *Journal of Consulting and Clinical Psychology* 48:640–41.

Wasik, B. 1984. Teaching parents effective problem-solving: A handbook for professionals. Unpublished manuscript. University of North Carolina, Chapel Hill.

Watkins, P. L., E. T. Sturgis, and G. A. Clum. 1988. Guided imaginal coping: An integrative treatment for panic disorder. *Journal of Behavior Therapy and Experimental Psychiatry* 19:147–55.

Weissman, M. M., J. K. Myers, and P. S. Harding, 1978. Psychiatric disorders in a U.S. urban community. *American Journal of Psychiatry* 135:459–62.

Wessler, R. L. 1984. A bridge too far: Incompatibilities of rational-emotive therapy and pastoral counseling. *The Personnel and Guidance Journal* 62:264–66.

Whiteman, M., D. Fanshel, and J. F. Grundy. November-December, 1987. Cognitive-behavioral interventions aimed at anger of parents at risk of child abuse. *Social Work*, 469–74.

Williams, J. M. G. 1984. Cognitive-behaviour therapy for depression: Problems and perspectives. *British Journal of Psychiatry* 145:254–62.

Wolpe, J. 1961. The systematic desensitization treatment of neuroses. *Journal of Nervous and Mental Disease* 132:189–203.

———. 1973. *The Practice of Behavior Therapy*, 2nd ed., New York: Pergamon Press.

Worthington, E. L. 1986. Religious counseling: A review of published empirical research. *Journal of Counseling and Development* 64:421–31.

Zajonc, R. B. 1980. Feeling and thinking: Preferences need no inferences. *American Psychologist* 35:151–75.

———. 1984. On the primacy of affect. *American Psychologist* 39:117–23.

Zis, A. P., and F. K. Goodwin. 1982. The amine hypothesis. In E. S. Paykel, ed., *Handbook of Affective Disorders*. New York: Guilford Press.

Zwemer, W. A. , and J. L. Deffenbacher. 1984. Irrational beliefs, anger, and anxiety. *Journal of Counseling Psychology* 31:391–93.

NOTES

Chapter 1 Choosing a Road Map

1. Carl R. Rogers, "The Necessary and Sufficient Conditions of Therapeutic Personality Change," *Journal of Consulting Psychology* 21 (1957), 95–103.

2. H. J. Eysenck, "The Effects of Psychotherapy: An Evaluation," *Journal of Consulting Psychology* 16 (1952), 319–24.

3. See, for example A. E. Bergin, "The Evaluation of Therapeutic Outcomes," in A. E. Bergin and S. L. Garfield, eds., *Handbook of Psychotherapy and Behavior Change* (New York: Wiley, 1971); A. E. Bergin and M. J. Lambert, "The Evaluation of Therapeutic Outcomes," in S. L. Garfield and A. E. Bergin, eds., *Handbook of Psychotherapy and Behavior Change: An Empirical Analysis*, 2nd ed. (New York: Wiley, 1978); I. Elkin, "Outcome Findings and Therapist Performance," a paper presented at the American Psychological Association convention, 1986; C. D. Emrick, "A Review of Psychologically Oriented Treatment of Alcoholism," *Journal of Studies on Alcohol* 36 (1975), 88–108; L. Luborsky, L. Singer, and L. Luborsky, "Comparative Studies of Psychotherapies," *Archives of General Psychiatry* 32 (1975), 995–1008; and H. H. Strupp, "The Outcome Problem in Psychotherapy Revisited," *Psychotherapy: Theory, Research, and Practice* 1 (1963), 1–13.

4. M. Bobgan and D. Bobgan, *The Psychological Way/The Spiritual way* (Minneapolis: Bethany House, 1977); M. Bobgan and D. Bobgan, *Psychoheresy* (Santa Barbara: Eastgate, 1987); D. Hunt and T. A. McMahan, *The Seduction of Christianity: Spiritual Discernment in the Last Days* (Eugene, Ore.: Harvest House, 1985); and W. K. Kilpatrick, *Psychological Seduction: The Failure of Modern Psychology* (New York: Thomas Nelson, 1983).

5. Mary Lee Smith and G. V. Glass, "Meta-analysis of Psychotherapy Outcome Studies," *American Psychologist* 32 (1977):752–60; Mary Lee Smith, G. V. Glass, and R. L. Miller, *The Benefits of Psychotherapy* (Baltimore: Johns Hopkins Press, 1980).

6. Smith, Glass, and Miller, *The Benefits of Psychotherapy*, 183.

7. Smith and Glass, "Meta-analysis of Psychotherapy Outcome Studies," 760.

8. Jerome Frank, "Therapeutic Factors in Psychotherapy," *American Journal of Psychotherapy* 25 (1971), 350–61.

9. Rogers, "The Necessary and Sufficient Conditions of Therapeutic Personality Change."

10. Frank, "Therapeutic Factors in Psychotherapy."

11. Ibid.

12. Ibid.

13. R. Rosenthal and L. Jacobsen, *Pygmalion in the Classroom: Teacher Expectation and Pupils' Intellectual Development* (New York: Holt, Rinehart, & Winston, 1968).

14. Frank, "Therapeutic Factors in Psychotherapy."

15. Ibid.

16. Ibid.

17. Smith and Glass, "Meta-analysis of Psychotherapy Outcome Studies."

18. Aaron T. Beck, *Cognitive Therapy and the Emotional Disorders* (New York: International Universities Press, 1976).

19. Aaron T. Beck, S. D. Hollon, J. E. Young, R. C. Bedrosian, and D. Budenz, "Treatment of Depression with Cognitive Therapy and Amitriptyline," *Archives of General Psychiatry* 42 (1985), 142–48; I. M. Blackburn, S. Bishop, M. I. Glenn, L. J. Whalley, and J. E. Christie, "The Efficacy of Cognitive Therapy in Depression: A Treatment Trial Using Cognitive Therapy and Pharmacotherapy, Each Alone and in Combination," *British Journal of Psychiatry* 139 (1981), 181–189; K. S. Dobson and B. F. Shaw, "Cognitive Assessment with Major Depressive Disorders," *Cognitive Research and Therapy* 10 (1986), 13–29; K. McNamara, and

J. J. Horan, "Experimental Construct Validity in the Evaluation of Cognitive and Behavioral Treatments for Depression," *Journal of Counseling Psychology* 33 (1986), 23–30; G. E. Murphy, A. D. Simons, R. D. Wetzel, and P. J. Lustman, "Cognitive Therapy and Pharmacotherapy, Singly and Together in the Treatment of Depression," *Archives of General Psychiatry* 41 (1984), 33–41; W. M. Reynolds and K. I. Coats, "A Comparison of Cognitive-Behavioral Therapy and Relaxation Training for the Treatment of Depression in Adolescents," *Journal of Consulting and Clinical Psychology* 54 (1986), 653–60; A. J. Rush, Aaron T. Beck, M. Kovacs, and S. Hollon, "Comparative Efficacy of Cognitive Therapy and Pharmacotherapy in the Treatment of Depressed Outpatients," *Cognitive Therapy and Research* 1 (1977), 17–37; B. Shaw, "Comparison of Cognitive Therapy and Behavior Therapy in the Treatment of Depression," *Journal of Consulting and Clinical Psychology* 45 (1977), 543–51; A. D. Simons, P. J. Lustman, R. D. Wetzel, and G. E. Murphy, "Predicting Response to Cognitive Therapy of Depression: The Role of Learned Resourcefulness," *Cognitive Therapy and Research* 9 (1985), 79–89; A. D. Simons, G. E. Murphy, J. L. Levine, and R. D. Wetzel, "Cognitive Therapy and Pharmacotherapy for Depression," *Archives of General Psychiatry* 43 (1986), 43–48; F. Taylor and W. Marshall, "Experimental Analysis of a Cognitive-Behavioral Therapy for Depression," *Cognitive Therapy and Research* 1 (1977), 59–72; J. D. Teasdale, M. J. V. Fennell, G. A. Hibbert, and P. L. Amies, "Cognitive Therapy for Major Depressive Disorder in Primary Care," *British Journal of Psychiatry* 144 (1984), 400–406.

20. Aaron T. Beck and G. Emery, *Anxiety Disorders and Phobias*, (New York: Basic Books, 1985); K. M. Dendata and D. Diener, "Effectiveness of Cognitive/Relaxation Therapy and Study-Skills Training in Reducing Self-Reported Anxiety and Improving the Academic Performance of Test-Anxious Students," *Journal of Counseling Psychology* 33 (1986), 131–5; and C. W. Thurman, "Effectiveness of Cognitive-Behavioral Treatments in Reducing Type A Behavior among University Faculty," *Journal of Counseling Psychology* 32 (1985), 74–83.

21. P. M. Salkovskis and H. M. C. Warwick, "Morbid Preoccupations, Health Anxiety and Reassurance: A Cognitive-Behavioral Approach to Hypochondriasis," *Behavior Research and Therapy* 24 (1986), 597–602.

22. R. W. Graff, G. I. Whitehead, III, and M. LeCompte, "Group Treatment with Divorced Women Using Cognitive-Behavioral and Supportive Insight Methods," *Journal of Counseling Psychology* 33 (1986), 276–81.

23. A. E. Meador and T. H. Ollendick, "Cognitive Behavior Therapy with Children: An Evaluation of its Efficacy and Clinical Utility," *Child and Family Behavior Therapy* 6 no. 3 (1984), 25–44; and H. L. Swanson, "Effects of Cognitive-Behavioral Training on Emotionally Disturbed Children's Academic Performance," *Cognitive Therapy and Research* 9 (1985), 201–16.

24. Aaron T. Beck, *Love Is Never Enough* (New York: Harper & Row, 1988).

Chapter 2 An Overview of Cognitive Therapy

1. R. P. Martin, *The Epistle of Paul to the Philippians* (Grand Rapids, Mich.: Eerdmans, 1978).

2. Aaron T. Beck, *Cognitive Therapy and the Emotional Disorders* (New York: International Universities Press, 1976).

3. Albert Ellis, *Reason and Emotion in Psychotherapy*, (Secaucus, N.J.: Citadel Press, 1962).

4. David Burns, *Feeling Good* (New York: New American Library, 1980).

5. Robert Zajonc, "Feeling and Thinking: Preferences Need No Inferences," *American Psychologist* 35 (1980), 151–75, and "On the Primacy of Affect," *American Psychologist* 39 (1984), 117–23.

6. P. Ekman, R. W. Leveson, W. V. Friensen, "Autonomic Nervous System Activity Distinguishes among Emotions," *Science* 221 (1983), 1208–10; and J. D. Laird, "Self-Attribution of Emotion: The Effects of Expressive Behavior on the Quality of Emotional Experience," *Journal of Personality and Social Psychology* 29 (1974), 475–86, and "The Real Role of Facial Response in the Experience of Emotion: A Reply to Tougangeau and Ellsworth, and Others," *Journal of Personality and Social Psychology* 47 (1984), 909–17.

7. Richard Lazarus, "Thoughts on the Relations between Emotion and Cognitive," *American Psychologist* 37 (1982), 1019–24; "On the Primacy of Cognition," *American Psychologist* 39 (1984), 124–29.

Chapter 3 Christianity and Cognitive Therapy

1. J. D. Carter and B. Narramore, *The Integration of Psychology and Theology: An Introduction* (Grand Rapids, Mich.: Zondervan, 1979); G. R. Collins, *Psychology and Theology: Prospects for Integration* (Nashville: Abingdon, 1981); L. J. Crabb, Jr., *Effective Biblical Counseling* (Grand Rapids, Mich.: Zondervan, 1977); and K. E. Farnsworth,

Wholehearted Integration: Harmonizing Psychology and Christianity through Word and Deed (Grand Rapids, Mich.: Baker Book House, 1985).

2. H. Clinebell, *Basic Types of Pastoral Care and Counseling: Resources for the Ministry of Healing and Growth* (Nashville: Abingdon, 1984), 26.

3. J. D. Frank, "The Present Status of Outcome Research," in M. R. Goldfried, ed., *Converging Themes in Psychotherapy* (New York: Springer, 1982), 281–90.

4. L. B. Propst, *Psychotherapy in a Religious Framework* (New York: Human Sciences Press, 1988).

5. Albert Ellis, "There Is No Place for the Concept of Sin in Psychotherapy," *Journal of Counseling Psychology* 7 (1960), 188–92.

6. Gary Walls, "Values and Psychotherapy: A Comment on Psychotherapy and Religious Values," *Journal of Consulting and Clinical Psychology* 48 (1980), 640–41.

7. A. E. Bergin, "Religiosity and Mental Health: A Critical Reevaluation and Meta-analysis," *Professional Psychology* 14 (1983), 170–184; A. E. Bergin, R. D. Stinchfield, T. A. Gaskin, K. S. Masters, and C. E. Sullivan, "Religious Life-styles and Mental Health: An Exploratory Study," *Journal of Counseling Psychology* 35 (1988), 91–98.

8. Mark R. McMinn, "Religious Values, Sexist Language, and Perceptions of a Therapist," *Journal of Psychology and Christianity* 10 (1991).

9. S. Quackenbos, G. Privette, and B. Klentz, "Psychotherapy: Sacred or Secular?" *Journal of Counseling and Development* 63 (1985), 290–93.

10. D. Myers, *Psychology* (New York: Worth Publishers, 1989).

11. R. N. Bellah, R. Madsen, W. M. Sullivan, A. Swidler, and S. M. Tipton, *Habits of the Heart* (New York: Harper & Row, 1985), 290.

12. Crabb, *Effective Biblical Counseling*, 20.

13. Beck, *Cognitive Therapy and the Emotional Disorders*.

14. Mark R. McMinn, *Your Hidden Half: Blending Your Public and Private Self* (Grand Rapids, Mich.: Baker Books, 1988).

15. C. P. Herman and D. Mack, "Restrained and Unrestrained Eating," *Journal of Personality* 43 (1975), 647–60.

16. S. R. Graham, "Desire, Belief and Grace: A Psychotherapeutic Paradigm," *Psychotherapy: Theory, Research and Practice* 17 (1980), 370–71.

17. David A. Seamands, *Healing for Damaged Emotions* (Wheaton, Ill.: Victor Books, 1981).

18. Mark R. McMinn and C. J. Lebold, "Collaborative Efforts in Cognitive Therapy with Religious Clients," *Journal of Psychology and Theology* 17 (1989), 101–9; and Siang-Yang Tan, "Cognitive-Behavior Therapy: A Biblical Approach and Critique," *Journal of Psychology and Theology* 15 103–12.

19. Albert Ellis and R. Grieger, *Handbook of Rational Emotive Therapy* (New York: Springer-Verlag, 1977).

20. Beck, *Cognitive Therapy and the Emotional Disorders*, and D. Meichenbaum, *Cognitive-Behavior Modification: An Integrative Approach* (New York: Plenum, 1977).

21. Albert Ellis, *The Case Against Religion: A Psychotherapist's View* (New York: Institute for Rational Living, 1971).

22. J. S. Shrauger and R. E. Silverman, "The Relationship of Religious Background and Participation to Locus of Control," *Journal for the Scientific Study of Religion* 10 (1971), 11–16; P. J. Silvestri, "Locus of Control and God-Dependence," *Psychological Reports* 45 (1979), 89–90; and B. R. Strickland and S. Shaffer, "I-E, I-E, and F," *Journal for the Scientific Study of Religion* 10 (1971), 366–69.

23. E. L. Worthington, "Religious Counseling: A Review of Published Empirical Research," *Journal of Counseling and Development* 64 (1986), 421–31.

24. M. L. Cook and C. Peterson, "Depressive Irrationality," *Cognitive Therapy and Research* 10 (1986), 293–98.

25. A. S. Rossi, "Change in the Client and in the Client's God," *Psychotherapy Patient* 1 (1985), 55–62.

26. Albert Ellis, "A Sadly Neglected Cognitive Element in Depression," *Cognitive Therapy and Research* 11 (1987), 121–46.

27. Albert Ellis, "Psychotherapy and Atheistic Values: A Response to A. E. Bergin's 'Psychotherapy and Religious Values,' " *Journal of Consulting and Clinical Psychology* 48 (1980), 635–39, and "Rational-Emotive Therapy (RET) and Pastoral Counseling: A Reply to Wessler," *The Personnel and Guidance Journal* 62 (1984), 266–67.

28. J. Marzillier, "A Sadly Neglected Cognitive Element in Depression: A Reply to Ellis," *Cognitive Therapy and Research* 11 (1987), 147–52.

29. R. L. Wessler, "A Bridge Too Far: Incompatibilities of Rational-Emotive Therapy and Pastoral Counseling," *The Personnel and Guidance Journal* 62 (1984), 264–66.

30. C. V. Bruun, "A Combined Treatment Approach: Cognitive Therapy and Spiritual Dimensions," *Journal of Psychology and Christianity* 4, no. 2

(1985), 9–11; D. R. Pecheur and K. J. Edwards, "A Comparison of Secular and Religious Versions of Cognitive Therapy with Depressed Christian College Students," *Journal of Psychology and Theology* 12 (1984), 45–54; and L. B. Propst, "The Comparative Efficacy of Religious and Nonreligious Imagery for the Treatment of Mild Depression in Religious Individuals," *Cognitive Therapy and Research* 4 (1980), 167–78.

Chapter 4 The First Interview

1. Ed Higgins, "Logos," in Nancy Thomas, ed., *On the Edge of a Truth* (Newberg, Ore.: Barclay Press, 1980). Used by permission.

2. Aaron T. Beck, A. J. Rush, B. F. Shaw, and G. Emery, *Cognitive Therapy of Depression* (New York: Guilford, 1979).

3. G. Egan, *The Skilled Helper* (Monterey, Calif.: Brooks/Cole, 1975).

4. D. Meichenbaum and D. Turk, *Facilitating Treatment Adherence: A Practitioner's Guidebook* (New York: Plenum Press, 1987).

5. The Beck Depression Inventory is available through The Psychological Corporation, P.O. Box 839954, San Antonio, Texas 78283–3954, telephone: 800-228-0752. The Minnesota Multiphasic Personality Inventory is distributed by National Computer Systems, Inc., P.O. Box 1416, Minneapolis, Minnesota 55440.

Chapter 5 Finding Automatic Thoughts

1. Beck, Rush, Shaw, and Emery, *Cognitive Therapy of Depression*.

2. Aaron Beck, *Cognitive Therapy and the Emotional Disorders*; Burns, *Feeling Good*; and Beck, Rush, Shaw, and Emery, *Cognitive Therapy of Depression*.

Chapter 6 Disputing Automatic Thoughts

1. Burns, *Feeling Good*.

2. Beck, Rush, Shaw, and Emery, *Cognitive Therapy of Depression*; DeRubeis and Beck, "Cognitive Therapy."

3. Burns, *Feeling Good*.

4. See J. Wolpe, "The Systematic Desensitization Treatment of Neuroses," *Journal of Nervous and Mental Disease* 132 (1961), 189–203, and *The Practice of Behavior Therapy*, 2nd ed. (New York: Pergamon Press, 1973).

5. Donald Meichenbaum, *Stress Inoculation Training* (New York: Pergamon Press, 1985), 73.

6. R. E. McMullin, *Handbook of Cognitive Therapy Techniques* (New York: Norton, 1986).

7. Donald Meichenbaum, "Cognitive-Behavioral Approach with Adults, Adolescents, and Children," a workshop sponsored by the Oregon Psychological Association, Portland, Oregon, December, 1987.

8. McMullin, *Handbook of Cognitive Therapy Techniques*.

Chapter 7 Finding Core Beliefs

1. Beck, *Cognitive Therapy and the Emotional Disorders*, and Beck, Rush, Shaw, and Emery, *Cognitive Therapy of Depression*.

2. Meichenbaum, "Cognitive-Behavioral Approach with Adults, Adolescents, and Children."

Chapter 8 Changing Core Beliefs

1. C. S. Lewis, *Mere Christianity* (New York: Macmillan, 1952), 174.

2. L. R. Propst, "The Comparative Efficacy of Religious and Nonreligious Imagery for the Treatment of Mild Depression in Religious Individuals," *Cognitive Therapy and Research* 4 (1980), 167–78.

3. Beck, *Cognitive Therapy and the Emotional Disorders*.

4. McMullin, *Handbook of Cognitive Therapy Techniques*.

5. F. C. Craigie, Jr., and Siang-Yang Tan, "Changing Resistant Assumptions in Christian Cognitive-Behavioral Therapy," *Journal of Psychology and Theology* 17 (1989), 93–100.

Chapter 10 Depression

1. D. S. Holmes, *Abnormal Psychology* (New York: HarperCollins Publishers, Inc., 1991); and M. E. P. Seligman and D. L. Rosenhan, *Abnormal Psychology* (New York: Norton, 1984).

2. R. C. Carson, J. N. Butcher, and J. D. Coleman, *Abnormal Psychology and Modern Life*, 8th ed. (Glenview, Ill.: Scott, Foresman and Company, 1988).

3. Holmes, *Abnormal Psychology*.

4. Beck, *Cognitive Therapy and the Emotional Disorders*.

5. Holmes, *Abnormal Psychology*.

6. A. P. Zis and F. K. Goodwin, "The Amine Hypothesis," in E. S. Paykel, ed., *Handbook of Affective Disorders* (New York: Guilford Press, 1982).

7. Beck, *Cognitive Therapy and the Emotional Disorders*, 255–56.

8. Beck, Rush, Shaw, and Emery, *Cognitive Therapy of Depression*.

9. See J. M. G. Williams, "Cognitive-Behaviour Therapy for Depression: Problems and Perspectives," *British Journal of Psychiatry* 145 (1984), 254–62.

10. M. J. V. Fennel, J. D. Teasdale, "Cognitive Therapy for Depression: Individual Differences and the Process of Change," *Cognitive Therapy and Research* 11 (1987), 253–71.

11. L. E. Beutler, F. Scogin, P. Kirkish, D. Schretlen, A. Corbishley, D. Hamblin, K. Meredith, R. Potter, C. R. Bamford, and A. I. Levenson, "Group Cognitive Therapy and Alprazolam in the Treatment of Depression in Older Adults," *Journal of Consulting and Clinical Psychology* 55 (1987), 550–56; R. W. Graff, G. I. Whitehead, III, and M. LeCompte, "Group Treatment with Divorced Women Using Cognitive-Behavioral and Supportive Insight Methods," *Journal of Counseling Psychology* 33 (1986), 276–81; J. A. Hogg and J. L. Deffenbacher, "A Comparison of Cognitive and Interpersonal-Process Group Therapies in the Treatment of Depression Among College Students," *Journal of Counseling Psychology* 35 (1988), 304–10; and T. K. Marshall, and A. S. Mazie, "A Cognitive Approach to Treating Depression," *Social Casework* 68 (1987), 540–45.

12. J. B. Persons and D. D. Burns, "Mechanisms of Action of Cognitive Therapy: The Relative Contributions of Technical and Interpersonal Interventions," *Cognitive Therapy and Research* 9 (1985), 539–51.

13. N. S. Jacobson, "The Therapist-Client Relationship in Cognitive Behavior Therapy: Implications for Treating Depression," *Journal of Cognitive Psychotherapy* 3 (1989), 85–96; McMinn and Lebold, "Collaborative Efforts in Cognitive Therapy with Religious Clients"; and Persons and Burns, "Mechanisms of Action of Cognitive Therapy: The Relative Contributions of Technical and Interpersonal Interventions."

14. For a helpful discussion of constructive sorrow versus guilt, see S. B. Narramore, *No Condemnation* (Grand Rapids, Mich.: Zondervan, 1984).

15. L. M. Horowitz, R. S. French, and C. A. Anderson, "The Prototype of a Lonely Person," in L. A. Peplau and D. Perlman, eds., *Loneliness: A Sourcebook of Current Theory, Research and Therapy* (New York: Wiley Interscience, 1982), 183–205.

16. R. D. Parsons and R. J. Wicks, "Cognitive Pastoral Psychotherapy with Religious Persons Experiencing Loneliness," *The Psychotherapy Patient* 2 (1986), 47–59.

17. Aaron Beck, M. Kovacs, and A. Weissman, "Hopelessness and Suicidal Behavior: An Overview," *Journal of the American Medical Association* 234 (1975), 1146–49.

Chapter 11 Anxiety

1. Aaron Beck, G. Emery, and R. L. Greenberg, *Anxiety Disorders and Phobias: A Cognitive Perspective* (New York: Basic Books, 1985).

2. Holmes, *Abnormal Psychology.*

3. I. M. Marks and M. Lader, "Anxiety States (Anxiety Neurosis): A Review," *Journal of Nervous and Mental Disease* 156 (1973), 3–18; and M. M. Weissman, J. K. Myers, and P. S. Harding, "Psychiatric Disorders in a U.S. Urban Community," *American Journal of Psychiatry* 135 (1978), 459–62.

4. S. Torgersen, "Genetic Factors in Anxiety Disorders," *Archives of General Psychiatry* 40 (1983), 1085–89.

5. Beck, Emery, and Greenberg, *Anxiety Disorders and Phobias: A Cognitive Perspective.*

6. Ibid.

7. Ibid.

8. Ibid.

9. Ibid., 63.

10. C. Blowers, J. Cobb, and A. Mathews, "Generalized Anxiety: A Controlled Treatment Study," *Behaviour Research and Therapy* 25 (1987), 493–502.

11. T. D. Borkovec, A. M. Mathews, A. Chambers, S. Ebrahimi, R. Lytle, and R. Nelson, "The Effects of Relaxation Training with Cognitive or Nondirective Therapy and the Role of Relaxation-Induced Anxiety in the Treatment of Generalized Anxiety," *Journal of Consulting and Clinical Psychology* 55 (1987), 883–88.

12. K. G. Power, D. W. A. Jerrom, R. J. Simpson, M. J. Mitchell, and V. Swanson, "A Controlled Comparison of Cognitive-Behaviour Therapy, Diazepam, and Placebo in the Management of Generalized Anxiety," *Behavioural Psychotherapy* 17 (1989), 1–14.

13. W. R. Lindsay, C. V. Gamsu, E. McLaughlin, E. M. Hood, and C. A. Epsie, "A Controlled Trial of Treatments for Generalized Anxiety," *British Journal of Clinical Psychology* 26 (1987), 3–15.

14. Beck, Emery, and Greenberg, *Anxiety Disorders and Phobias: A Cognitive Perspective.*

15. Ronald Rapee and David Barlow, "Panic Disorder: Cognitive-Behavioral Treatment," *Psychiatric Annals* 18 (1988), 473–77.

16. P. M. Salkovskis, D. R. O. Jones, and D. M. Clark, "Respiratory Control in the Treatment of Panic Attacks: Replication and Extension

with Concurrent Measurement of Behaviour and pCO$_2$," *British Journal of Psychiatry* 148 (1986), 526–32.

17. R. J. DeRubeis and Aaron Beck, "Cognitive Therapy."

18. Rapee and Barlow, "Panic Disorder: Cognitive-Behavioral Treatment."

19. P. L. Watkins, E. T. Sturgis, and G. A. Clum, "Guided Imaginal Coping: An Integrative Treatment for Panic Disorder," *Journal of Behavior Therapy and Experimental Psychiatry* 19 (1988), 147–55.

20. M. K. Shear, G. Ball, and S. Josephson, "An Empirically Developed Cognitive-Behavioral Treatment of Panic," *Journal of Integrative and Eclectic Psychotherapy* 6 (1987), 421–33.

21. Rapee and Barlow, "Panic Disorder: Cognitive-Behavioral Treatment." See also D. H. Barlow, M. G. Craske, J. A. Cerny, and J. S. Klosko, "Behavior Treatment of Panic Disorder," *Behavior Therapy* 20 (1989), 261–82.

22. Shear, Ball and Josephson, "An Empirically Developed Cognitive-Behavioral Treatment of Panic."

23. Aaron T. Beck, "Cognitive Approaches to Panic Disorder: Theory and Therapy," in S. Rachman and J. D. Maser, eds., *Panic: Psychological Perspectives* (Hillsdale, N. J.: Lawrence Erlbaum Associates, 1988); D. M. Clark, P. M. Salkovskis, and A. J. Chalkley, "Respiratory Control as a Treatment for Panic Attacks," *Journal of Behavior Therapy and Experimental Psychiatry* 16 (1985), 23–30; and Salkovskis, Jones, and Clark, "Respiratory Control in the Treatment of Panic Attacks: Replication and Extension with Concurrent Measurement of Behaviour and pCO$_2$."

24. Watkins, Sturgis, and Clum, "Guided Imaginal Coping: An Integrative Treatment for Panic Disorder."

25. C. Leerhsen, "John Madden on a Roll," *Newsweek*, 9 January 1984, 66–67.

26. Torgersen, "Genetic Factors in Anxiety Disorders."

27. Beck, Emery, and Greenberg, *Anxiety Disorders and Phobias: A Cognitive Perspective*.

28. R. J. McNally, and E. B. Foa, "Cognition and Agoraphobia: Bias in the Interpretation of Threat," *Cognitive Therapy and Research* 11 (1987), 567–81.

29. G. Butler, "Issues in the Application of Cognitive and Behavioral Strategies to the Treatment of Social Phobia," *Clinical Psychology Review* 9 (1989), 91–106.

30. Beck, Emery, and Greenberg, *Anxiety Disorders and Phobias: A Cognitive Perspective.*

31. For a review of these studies, see R. G. Heimberg, "Cognitive and Behavioral Treatments for Social Phobia: A Critical Analysis," *Clinical Psychology Review* 9 (1989), 107–128.

32. L. Michelson, M. Mavissakalian, and K. Machione, "Cognitive and Behavioral Treatments of Agoraphobia: Clinical, Behavioral, and Psychophysical Outcomes," *Journal of Consulting and Clinical Psychology* 53 (1985), 913–25.

33. K. E. Marchione, L. Michelson, M. Greenwald, and C. Dancu, "Cognitive Behavior Treatment of Agoraphobia," *Behaviour Research and Therapy* 25 (1987), 319–28.

34. See M. Biran, "Cognitive and Exposure Treatment for Agoraphobia: Reexamination of the Outcome Research," *Journal of Cognitive Psychotherapy: An International Quarterly* 2 (1988), 165–78.

35. P. C. Kendall, B. L. Howard, and J. Epps, "The Anxious Child: Cognitive-Behavioral Strategies," *Behavior Modification* 12 (1988), 281–310.

36. S. A. Hamilton and W. J. Fremouw, "Cognitive-Behavioral Training for College Basketball Free-Throw Performance," *Cognitive Therapy and Research* 9 (1985), 479–83.

37. Beck, Emery, and Greenberg, *Anxiety Disorders and Phobias: A Cognitive Perspective.*

38. P. M. Valliant and B. Leith, "Impact of Relaxation-Training and Cognitive-Therapy on Coronary Patients Post Surgery," *Psychological Reports* 59 (1986), 1271–78.

Chapter 12 Stress and Anger

1. T. H. Holmes and R. H. Rahe, "The Social Readjustment Rating Scale," *Journal of Psychosomatic Research* 11 (1967), 213–18.

2. R. A. Depue and S. M. Monroe, "Conceptualization and Measurement of Human Disorder in Life Stress Research: The Problem of Chronic Disturbance," *Psychological Bulletin* 99 (1986), 36–51.

3. Richard Lazarus, "Little Hassles Can Be Hazardous to Health," *Psychology Today* (July 1981), 58–62.

4. J. R. Averill, "Studies on Anger and Aggression: Implications for Theories of Emotion," *American Psychologist* 38 (1983), 1145–60.

5. D. G. Myers, *Psychology*, 2nd ed. (New York: Worth Publishers, 1989).

6. Ibid.

7. W. A. Zwemer and J. L. Deffenbacher, "Irrational Beliefs, Anger, and Anxiety," *Journal of Counseling Psychology* 31 (1984), 391–93.

8. See J. L. Deffenbacher, D. A. Story, R. S. Stark, J. A. Hogg, and A. D. Brandon, "Cognitive-Relaxation and Social Skills Interventions in the Treatment of General Anger," *Journal of Counseling Psychology* 34 (1987), 171–176; S. L. Hazaleus and J. L. Deffenbacher, "Relaxation and Cognitive Treatments of Anger," *Journal of Consulting and Clinical Psychology* 54 (1986), 222–26.

9. J. L. Deffenbacker, "Cognitive-Relaxation and Social Skills Treatments of Anger: A Year Later," *Journal of Counseling Psychology* 35 (1988), 234–36; J. L. Deffenbacher, D. A. Story, A. D. Brandon, J. A. Hogg, and S. L. Hazaleus, "Cognitive and Cognitive-Relaxation Treatments of Anger," *Cognitive Therapy and Research* 12 (1988), 167-184; Deffenbacher et al., "Cognitive-Relaxation and Social Skills Interventions in the Treatment of General Anger."

10. Meichenbaum, *Stress Inoculation Training*.

11. Ibid.

12. B. Wasik, "Teaching Parents Affective Problem-Solving: A Handbook for Professionals," unpublished manuscript, University of North Carolina, Chapel Hill, 1984, cited in Meichenbaum, *Stress Inoculation Training*.

13. E. L. Feindler and R. B. Ecton, *Adolescent Anger Control: Cognitive-Behavioral Techniques* (New York: Pergamon Press, 1986); and Donald Meichenbaum and R. Novaco, "Stress Inoculation: A Preventative Approach," *Issues in Mental Health Nursing* 7 (1985), 419–35; and R. Novaco, "Anger and Coping with Stress: Cognitive-Behavioral Interventions," in J. P. Foreyt and D. P. Rathjen, eds., *Cognitive Behavior Therapy* (New York: Plenum, 1978), 135–73.

14. W. R. Holcomb, "Stress Inoculation Therapy with Anxiety and Stress Disorders of Acute Psychiatric Inpatients," *Journal of Clinical Psychology* 42 (1986), 864–72.

15. J. Achmon, M. Granek, M. Golomb, and J. Hart, "Behavioral Treatment of Essential Hypertension: A Comparison between Cognitive Therapy and Biofeedback of Heart Rate," *Psychosomatic Medicine* 51 (1989), 152–64.

16. Meichenbaum, *Stress Inoculation Training*.

17. M. Whiteman, D. Fanshel, and J. F. Grundy, "Cognitive-Behavioral Interventions Aimed at Anger of Parents at Risk of Child Abuse," *Social Work* (November-December, 1987), 469–74.

18. M. Friedman and D. Ulmer, *Treating Type A Behavior—and Your Heart* (New York: Knopf, 1984), cited in Myers, *Psychology*.

19. C. W. Thurman, "Effectiveness of Cognitive-Behavioral Treatments in Reducing Type A Behavior among University Faculty," *Journal of Counseling Psychology* 32 (1985a), 74–83; C. W. Thurman, "Effectiveness of Cognitive-Behavioral Treatments in Reducing Type A Behavior among University Faculty—One Year Later," *Journal of Counseling Psychology* 32 (1985b), 445–48.

20. Mark R. McMinn, *Dealing with Desires You Can't Control* (Colorado Springs, Colo.: NavPress, 1990).

Chapter 13 Other Applications

1. See D. M. Garner, "Cognitive-Behavioral Therapy for Eating Disorders," *The Clinical Psychologist* 39 (1986), 36–39.

2. Ibid.

3. W. S. Agras, J. A. Schneider, B. Arnow, S. D. Raeburn, and C. F. Telch, "Cognitive-Behavioral and Response-Prevention Treatments for Bulimia Nervosa," *Journal of Consulting and Clinical Psychology* 57 (1989), 215–21.

4. L. P. Luka, W. S. Agras, and J. A. Schneider, "Thirty Month Follow-up of Cognitive-Behavioral Group Therapy for Bulimia," *The British Journal of Psychiatry* 148 (1986), 614–15; J. A. Schneider and W. S. Agras, "A Cognitive Behavioural Group Treatment of Bulimia," *British Journal of Psychiatry* 146 (1985), 66–69; and J. A. Schneider, A. O'Leary, and W. A. Agras, "The Role of Perceived Self-Efficacy in Recovery from Bulimia: A Preliminary Examination," *Behavior Research and Therapy* 25 (1987), 429–32.

5. C. Freeman, F. Sinclair, J. Turnbull, and A. Annandale, "Psychotherapy for Bulimia: A Controlled Study," *Journal of Psychiatric Research* 19 (1985), 473–78.

6. C. G. Fairburn, J. Kirk, M. O'Connor, and P. J. Cooper, "A Comparison of Two Psychological Treatments for Bulimia Nervosa," *Behavior Research and Therapy* 24 (1986), 629–43.

7. E. M. Rossiter, W. S. Agras, M. Losch, and C. F. Telch, "Dietary Restraint of Bulimic Subjects Following Cognitive-Behavioral or Pharmacological Treatment," *Behavior Research and Therapy* 26 (1988), 495–98.

8. Aaron T. Beck and C. A. Padesky, "Love Is Never Enough," an advanced clinical workshop for mental health professionals, Los Angeles, 12 November 1988.

9. Richard Lederer, *Anguished English* (New York: Dell Publishing, 1987), 22.

10. Ibid., 25.

11. Ibid., 15.

INDEX

Mark R. McMinn, Ph.D.

Mark R. McMinn is associate professor of psychology at George Fox College in Newberg, Oregon, and a licensed psychologist with Valley Psychological Associates, also in Newberg. He has published many articles in professional journals and Christian magazines and is the author of *Your Hidden Half, Christians in the Crossfire* (co-authored with James D. Foster), and *Dealing with Desires You Can't Control*.

Dr. McMinn received a B.S. in psychology and chemistry from Lewis and Clark College and a Ph.D. in clinical psychology from Vanderbilt University. He completed an internship in medical psychology at the Oregon Health Sciences University before joining the faculty at George Fox College. He is currently a member of the American Psychological Association and a contributing editor to the *Journal of Psychology and Theology*.

He and his wife Lisa live in Newberg. They have three daughters: Danielle, Sarah, and Anna.